ABOUT THIS BOOK

A Report on a Joint Participatory Investigation by Civil Society and the World Bank on the Impact of Structural Adjustment Policies

One factor, more than any other, has crippled national economies, increased poverty and inequality, and made many millions of people hungry. It is a set of policies, called structural adjustment, that has been forced on developing countries for more than 20 years by the World Bank, the International Monetary Fund and Western aid agencies. Country after country has been compelled, regardless of circumstances, to adopt this 'one size fits all' economic strategy that exposes the world's most vulnerable peoples and weakest economies to the full force of the global market place dominated by the most powerful and richest economies and corporations.

Born of a unique five-year collaboration among citizens' groups, developing country governments, and the World Bank, this book represents the most comprehensive, real-life assessment of the actual impacts of the liberalization, deregulation, privatization and austerity policies that constitute structural adjustment programmes. Its authors, the members of the Structural Adjustment Participatory Review International Network (SAPRIN) that engaged the World Bank's president in this ambitious and highly participatory endeavour, present the concrete consequences of these policies.

The stark conclusion emerges: if there is to be any hope for meaningful development in the countries of the South and for the sustained reduction of poverty and inequality, the Western-inspired and imposed doctrines of structural adjustment and neoliberal economics must go.

SAPRIN is a global network established to expand and legitimize the role of civil society in economic policymaking and to strengthen the organized challenge to structural adjustment programmes by citizens around the globe. It is composed of broad-based civil society networks in Argentina, Bangladesh, Ecuador, El Salvador, Ghana, Hungary, Mexico, the Philippines, Uganda and Zimbabwe, which along with non-governmental organizations based in Europe, Canada and the United States comprise SAPRIN's Steering Committee. The network has brought together trade unions, small business and farmers' associations, environmental and indigenous peoples' organizations, women's and community groups, religious and human rights organizations, development and research institutes, NGOs, and associations of youth, pensioners and the disabled. SAPRIN's diverse programme has included extensive citizen mobilization, local workshops and national public fora, participatory field research, economic literacy training, and the development and promotion of alternative economic policy proposals at the country level on four continents. At the global level, SAPRIN's advocacy work *vis-à-vis* the World Bank, United Nations agencies and national governments has focused on the elimination of adjustment conditionality and on the democratization of the economic policymaking process and on opening it to new policy options. The SAPRIN Secretariat is based at The Development GAP in Washington, DC.

STRUCTURAL ADJUSTMENT:
THE SAPRI REPORT

The Policy Roots of Economic Crisis, Poverty and Inequality

by
The Structural Adjustment Participatory Review
International Network (SAPRIN)

A Report on a Joint Participatory Investigation
by Civil Society and the World Bank
of the Impact of Structural Adjustment Policies

Zed Books
LONDON & NEW YORK

TWN
MALAYSIA

Books for Change
INDIA

IBON
PHILIPPINES

Structural Adjustment: The SAPRI Report
was first published in 2004

Malaysia: Third World Network, 121-S Jalan Utama, Penang 10450

Philippines: IBON Foundation, 3rd Floor, SCC Building, 4427
International Old Station, Mesa, Manila

India: Books for Change, 139 Richmond Road, Bangalore 560 025

Rest of the World: Zed Books Ltd
7 Cynthia Street, London N1 9JF, UK and
Room 400, 175 Fifth Avenue, New York, NY 10010, USA.
www.zedbooks.co.uk

Cover design by Andrew Corbett
Designed and set in 10/12 pt Bembo XT
by Long House, Cumbria, UK

Transferred to digital printing 2007

Distributed exclusively in the USA by Palgrave Macmillan, a division of
St Martin's Press, LLC, 175 Fifth Avenue, New York, NY 10010.

ISBN   1 84277 388 7 hb
1 84277 389 5 pb
IBON ISBN   971-0325-09-4

CONTACT DETAILS FOR SAPRIN
Saprin Secretariat
927 Fifteenth Street, NW, 4th Floor
Washington, DC 20005 USA
Tel: 202/898-1566
Fax: 202/898-1612
Email: secretariat@saprin.org
Website: www.saprin.org

Contents

8 The Effects of Public Expenditure Policies on Education and Healthcare under Structural Adjustment 174

Ecuador, Ghana, Hungary, Mexico, the Philippines, Uganda and Zimbabwe

9 Structural Adjustment, Poverty and Inequality 203

Tables, Boxes and Figures

Tables

Figures

Boxes

Acronyms

ADB	Asian Development Bank	IFC	International Finance Corporation
ALOP	Asociación Latinamericana de organizaciones de promocion (Latin America)	IFIs	International Financial Institutions
		ILO	International Labour Organization
ASA	Alliance of Social Associations (Hungary)	IMF	International Monetary Fund
AWEPON	African Women's Economic Policy Network (Uganda)	ISODEC	Integrated Social Development Centre (Ghana)
BIDS	Bangladesh Institute of Development Studies	ITESO	Instituto Technologicó de Estudias Superiores de Occidento
BMI	Multisectoral Investment Bank (El Salvador)	MERP	Millennium Economic Recovery Programme
BRAC	Bangladesh Rural Advancement Committee	NAFTA	North American Free Trade Agreement
CAS	Country Assistance Strategy	NGO	Non-governmental organization
CAMC	Climax-Arimco Mining Corporation (Philippines)	NOVIB	Nederlandse Organisatie voor Internationale Bijstand
CASA	Citizens' Assessments of Structural Adjustment	P	Peso
		PAR	Participatory Action Research
CELA	Centre for Latin American Studies	PERD	Public Enterprise Reform and Divestiture
COMECON	Council for Mutual Economic Assistance (Eastern Bloc)	PRA	Participatory Rural Appraisal
COMESA	Common Market for Eastern and Southern Africa	PRONASOL	National Solidarity Programme
		PROGRESA	Education, Health and Nutrition Programme
DAWN	Development Alternatives for Women in a New Era	PROSHIKA	Training, Education and Action (Bangladesh)
DEC	Development Economics Vice Presidency (World Bank)	PRSP	Poverty Reduction Strategy Paper
ECA	Export credit agency	PUCE	Catholic University of Ecuador
EIA	Environmental impact assessment	RMG	Ready-made garments
EPZ	Export processing zone	SADC	Southern African Development Community
ERP	Economic Recovery Programme		
ESAF	Extended Structural Adjustment Facility	SAL	Structural adjustment loan
ESAP	Economic Structural Adjustment Programme	SAMCAF	Southern Africa Microfinance Capacity Building Facility
FDC	Freedom from Debt Coalition (Philippines)	SAP	Structural adjustment programme
		SAPRI	Structural Adjustment Participatory Review Initiative
FOSAFI	Fund for Financial Restructuring and Strengthening (El Salvador)	SAPRIN	Structural Adjustment Participatory Review International Network
FTAAs	Financial and Technical Assistance Agreements	SDA	Social Dimensions of Adjustment
FUNDE	National Foundation for Development (El Salvador)	SMEs	Small and medium-scale enterprises
		TORs	Terms of reference
GATT	General Agreement on Tariffs and Trade	UNCTAD	United Nations Conference on Trade and Development
GDP	Gross domestic product		
GNP	Gross national product	UNDP	United Nations Development Programme
GTZ	Gesellschaft für Technische Zusammenarbeit (Germany)		
		UNICEF	United Nations Children's Fund
HIPC	Heavily Indebted Poor Country	WRI	World Resources Institute
HMC	Hinatuan Mining Corporation (Philippines)	WTO	World Trade Organization
		ZCTU	Zimbabwe Congress of Trade Unions
IDB	Inter-American Development Bank		
IEDECA	Institute for the Ecology and Development of Andean Communities (Ecuador)	ZIMPREST	Zimbabwe Programme for Economic and Social Transformation

Acknowledgements

This book resulted from a five-year process of civil society mobilization, structured consultation and participatory research in nine countries across four continents. Countless people and organizations have contributed to this major undertaking – including government and World Bank officials in most of the countries – and we could not hope to name them all here. We do, however, wish to acknowledge the principal authors of each policy-related chapter, as well as those who were responsible for the national research and reports and the groups that organized the full participatory process in each country. The book and the success of the initiative owe everything to their efforts and to those who worked with them to record and interpret the knowledge and experiences of civil society regarding the impact of structural adjustment policies on people's lives. The individual country reports from which these chapters were drawn can be found on the SAPRIN website (*www.saprin.org*).

Chapter 2: **Trade Liberalization Policies and Their Impact on the Manufacturing Sector** – *principal author:* Debapriya Bhattacharya (*Bangladesh*). The chapter draws on papers for each country whose primary authors are the following. *Bangladesh*: Mohammed Ali Rashid. *Ecuador:* Simón Ordóñez Cordero (Centre for Latin American Studies, CELA, of the Catholic University of Ecuador, PUCE). *Ghana:* Dr Romanus Dinye (Housing and Planning Research Department, Faculty of Environment and Development Studies, Kwame Nkrumah University of Science and Technology, Kumasi); Clement Nyaba (Ministry of Trade and Industry, Accra). *Hungary:* NGO team – László Fodor, Károly Boór, Csaba Gombár, Éva Voszka; World Bank team – Gábor Obláth. *Mexico:* Manuel Pérez Rocha Loyo. *Philippines:* Marie Lopez. *Zimbabwe:* Moses Tekere (Trade and Development Studies Centre, University of Zimbabwe).

Chapter 3: **Financial Sector Liberalization, Effects on Production and the Small Enterprise Sector** – *principal authors:* Theresa Moyo (*Zimbabwe*) and Juan Fernando Terán (*Ecuador*). The chapter draws on papers for each country whose primary authors are the following. *Bangladesh*: Toufic Ahmad Choudhury; Ananya Raihan. *Ecuador:* Simón Ordóñez Cordero (Centre for Latin American Studies, CELA, of the Catholic University of Ecuador, PUCE). *El Salvador:* Oscar Dada Hutt. *Zimbabwe:* Theresa Moyo (SAMCAF).

Chapter 4: **Employment under Adjustment and the Effects of Labour Market Reform on Working People** – *principal authors:* Luis Ignacio Román Morales (*Mexico*) and Manuel Cantú Rodríguez (*Mexico*). The chapter draws on papers for each country whose primary authors are the following. *Ecuador:* Simón Ordóñez Cordero (Centre for Latin American Studies, CELA, of the Catholic University of Ecuador, PUCE). *El Salvador:* Mario Montecinos. *Mexico:* Manuel Pérez Rocha Loyo. *Zimbabwe:* Blessing Chiripanhura and T. Makwavarara (Zimbabwe Congress of Trade Unions, ZCTU).

Chapter 5: **The Economic and Social Impact of Privatization Programmes** – *principal author:* Károly Lóránt (*Hungary*). The chapter draws on papers for each country whose primary authors are the following. *Bangladesh:* Debapriya Bhattacharya; Rashed A. M. Titumir. *El Salvador:* María Eugenia Ochoa. *Hungary:* NGO team – Károly Lóránt, János Hoós, Sándor Bessenyei, Erzsébet Hanti, Zoltán Kárpáti, Rezsö Gál, Józseg Kozma, Károly Mayer; World Bank – Márton Vági, László Szakadát. *Uganda:* J. Ddumba-Ssentamu and Adam Mugume (Makerere University Institute of Economics).

Chapter 6: **The Impact of Agricultural Sector Adjustment Policies on Small Farmers and Food Security** – *principal authors:* Yao Graham (*Ghana*), Kwasi Anyemedu (*Ghana*) and Kevin Akoyi Makokha (*Uganda*). The chapter draws on papers for each country whose primary authors are the following. *Bangladesh:* Sajjad Zohir (Bangladesh Institute of Development Studies, BIDS); K. A. S. Murshid (BIDS). *Mexico:* Carlos Cortez Ruíz. *Philippines:* Tambuyog Development Centre; Centre for Empowerment and Resource Development; Philippine Network of Rural Development Initiatives; Pablo Medina. *Uganda:* Nyangabyaki Bazaara (Centre for Basic Research). *Zimbabwe:* John Makamure; James Jowa; Hilda Muzuva.

Chapter 7: **The Socioeconomic and Environmental Impact of Mining Sector Reform** – *principal author:* John Mihevc (*Canada*). The chapter draws on papers for each country whose primary authors are the following. *Ghana:* Thomas Akabzaa (Department of Geology, University of Ghana Legon); Alhaji Abdulai Darimani (Third World Network-Africa). *Philippines:* J. J. Josef; Jean Enriquez; Rowil Aguillon; Ian Rivera; Jenny Llaguno.

Chapter 8: **The Effects of Public Expenditure Policies on Education and Healthcare under Structural Adjustment** – *principal authors:* Lidy Nacpil (*Philippines*) and John Mihevc (*Canada*). The chapter draws on papers for each country whose primary authors are the following. *Ecuador:* Enrique Santos (University of Cuenca, Ecuador). *Ghana:* S. K. Avle (Department of Community Health, University of Ghana Medical School, Accra); Francis Ekey (Human Resource Development Division, Ministry of Health); Professor D. K. Agyeman (Department of Sociology, University of Cape Coast); William Boateng (Department of Sociology, University of Cape Coast); Akinyoade Akinyinka (Department of Sociology, University of Cape Coast). *Hungary:* NGO team – Zsuzsa Ferge, Thomas Morva, István Sziklai, Noémi Wells; World Bank team – István György Tóth. *Philippines:* Professor Nymia P. Simbulan; Professor Carol Almeda, Merwin

Salazar. *Uganda:* MSE Consultants Ltd. *Zimbabwe:* Rogers Dhliwayo (University of Zimbabwe).

In addition to the works cited above, many country reports and background papers contributed to this body of work, for which we would like to acknowledge primary authors or editors. **Bangladesh**: *Assessment Using Participatory Techniques* – Atiur Rahman, M. M. Shafuqur Rahman, Abul Quashem, Zulfiqar Ali, Arifur Rahman; *Impact on the Poor* – Rushidan Islam Rahman (Bangladesh Institute of Development Studies, BIDS); *Impact on the Environment* – Kazi Ali Toufique (BIDS); *Impact on Women* – Nasreen Khundker; *Governance and Corruption* – Muzaffer Ahmad; *Country Report* – Debapriya Bhattacharya, Rashed A. M. Titumir (Centre for Policy Dialogue). **Ecuador**: *Country Report* – Alex Zapatta and Iván Cisneros (Institute for the Ecology and Development of Andean Communities, IEDECA); Marcelo Romero (World Bank). **El Salvador**: *Country Report* – Roberto Rubio (National Foundation for Development, FUNDE). **Ghana**: *Country Report* – Akua Britwum, Kwesi Jonah, Ferdinand D. Tay. **Hungary**: *Country Report* – János Hoós, Károly Lóránt, Thomas Morva. **Mexico**: *Theory and Design of SAPs* – Luis Ignacio Román Morales (ITESO); *Implementation of SAPs* – Luis Ignacio Román Morales and Mónica Unda Gutiérrez (ITESO); *Evolution of Economic and Social Indicators* – Jean Yves Chamboux-Leroux (ITESO); *Sample Household Survey* – Tanya Yadira Pérez Hernández and Luis Vallejo Narvaez (ITESO); *Impact on Micro, Small and Medium-Scale Enterprises* – Manuel Pérez Rocha Loyo; *Impact in Rural Areas* – Carlos Cortez Ruíz; *Impact on Children* – Rodolfo Aguirre Reveles; *Participatory Assessment* – Marusia López Cruz; *Constructing Alternatives* – María Isabel Verduzco; *Country Report* – Nina Torres, María Cecilia Oviedo, Susana Cruickshank. **Philippines**: *WB–IMF/ADB at work on the Philippine Privatization Programme* – Violeta Perez-Corral; case studies on water, power and oil by Nerissa Tuñgol-Esguerra, Mae Dolleton and Jolet Fajardo, respectively (Freedom from Debt Coalition, FDC). *Country Report* – Maria Teresa Diokno-Pascual, Clarence Pascual, Lidy B. Nacpil, Frances Lo, Viola G. Torres (FDC). **Uganda**: *Differences in Perceptions of Poverty* – Nansozi K. Muwanga (Department of Political Science and Public Administration, Makerere University); *Country Report* – Kevin Akoyi Makokha. **Zimbabwe**: *Role of the State* – Arnold Sibanda (Institute of Development Studies); *Country Report* – Godfrey Kanyenze (ZCTU), Muriel Mafico (Poverty Reduction Forum).

In each country, a lead organization was responsible for coordinating the full participatory process, the results of which are summarized in this book. This effort would not have been possible without the extensive work and resources invested in this process by the following organizations over more than four years. *Bangladesh:* PROSHIKA (Training, Education and Action); *Ecuador:* IEDECA; *El Salvador:* FUNDE; *Ghana:* ISODEC (Integrated Social Development Centre); *Hungary:* ASA (Alliance of Social Associations); *Mexico:* Equipo Pueblo; *Philippines:* FDC; *Uganda:* Uganda National NGO Forum; *Zimbabwe:* Poverty Reduction Forum, Institute of Development Studies. In addition, three regional centres facilitated coordination of this work: Third World Network–Africa; FUNDE in Latin America; and Focus on the Global South in Asia.

The global SAPRIN Secretariat – Stephanie Weinberg, Doug Hellinger, Steve Hellinger and Kathleen Sugar at The Development Group for Alternative Policies (The Development GAP) in Washington – was responsible for editing this volume, in consultation with the SAPRIN global steering committee.

The global SAPRIN network is grateful for the generous financial contributions from several governments, international agencies, foundations and NGOs, without whose support this extensive effort could not have come to fruition. Special thanks are given to: the governments of Norway, Sweden, the Netherlands and Belgium; the European Commission; the United Nations Development Programme (UNDP); the African Development Foundation (US); the GTZ (Gesellschaft für Technische Zusammenarbeit, Germany); the Charles Stewart Mott Foundation; NOVIB (Nederlandse Organisatie voor Internationale Bijstand, Holland); the Rockefeller Foundation; the American Center for International Labor Solidarity; and USA for Africa. In addition, thanks are owed to the following foundations that provided support for the work of SAPRIN's Secretariat: the Charles Stewart Mott Foundation; the W. K. Kellogg Foundation; the Rockefeller Foundation; the Wallace Global Fund; the Moriah Fund; the Public Welfare Foundation; the General Service Foundation; the CarEth Foundation; the Cohen Foundation; the Funding Exchange; the Stewart R. Mott Charitable Trust; the Three Sigma Fund/Tides Foundation; and the Tortuga Foundation. Finally, thanks are due to the United Nations Children's Fund (UNICEF), the Heinrich Boell Foundation, Oxfam, Save the Children, the government of Denmark and many other agencies and foundations that provided support directly to SAPRIN networks at the country level.

SAPRIN and World Bank Global Steering Committee Members

SAPRIN Global Steering Committee Members (2002)
Gemma Adaba/Peter Bakvis, International Confederation of Free Trade Unions (ICFTU), *International*
Jorge Carpio, Institute for Microenterprise Development (IDEMI), *Argentina*
Joy Chavez/Walden Bello, Focus on the Global South, *Asia*
Ivan Cisneros/Alex Zapatta, Institute for Ecology and Development of Andean Communities (IEDECA), *Ecuador*
Kelly Currah, World Vision, *International*
Yao Graham/Charles Abugre, Third World Network-Africa (TWN)/Integrated Social Development Centre (ISODEC), *Ghana*
Doug Hellinger, The Development GAP, *USA*
John Jones, Centre for Partnership in Development, *Norway*
Godfrey Kanyenze/Muriel Mafico, Zimbabwe Confederation of Trade Unions (ZCTU) / Poverty Reduction Forum, *Zimbabwe*
Mahbubul Karim/Md. Shahabuddin, PROSHIKA: A Center for Human Development, *Bangladesh*
Károly Lóránt, SAPRIN/*Hungary*
Kevin Akoyi Makokha/Warren Nyamugasira, Uganda National NGO Forum, *Uganda*
John Mihevc/Pam Foster, Inter-Church Coalition on Africa & Halifax Initiative, *Canada*
Lidy Nacpil/Maria Teresa Diokno-Pascual, Freedom from Debt Coalition, *The Philippines*
Roberto Rubio, National Foundation for Development (FUNDE), *El Salvador*
Marijke Torfs, Friends of the Earth, *International*
Nina Torres/Susana Cruickshank, Equipo Pueblo, *Mexico*
Barbara Unmuessig/Ted van Hees, WEED/Eurodad, *Europe*
Hellen Wangusa, African Women's Economic Policy Network (AWEPON), *Uganda*

Former SAPRIN Global Steering Committee Members
Peggy Antrobus, DAWN, *International*
Manuel Chiriboga, ALOP, *Latin America*
Steve Commins/Jaisankar Sarma, World Vision, *International*
Carlos Heredia/Victor Quintana, Equipo Pueblo, *Mexico*
Judy Kamanyi, ACFODE, *Uganda*
Kamal Malhotra, Focus on the Global South, *Asia*
Atherton Martin, Conservation Association of *Dominica*
Fatima Mello/Aurelio Vianna, Rede sobre Institucoes Financeiras Multilaterais, *Brazil*
Gita Sen, External Gender Consultative Group, *International*
Veena Siddharth, Oxfam *International*
Aminata Sidibe/Mamadou Sekou Toure, CCA-ONG, *Mali*

Former World Bank SAPRI Steering Committee Members

Caio Koch-Weser	Jacques van der Gaag
Joanne Salop	Branko Milanovic
Lyn Squire	John Clark
Jo Ritzen	Alex Rondos
Lionel Demery	Constance Newman
Emmanuel Jimenez	John Randa

CHAPTER 1

Structural Adjustment and the SAPRI/CASA Experience

In the mid-1970s, Western aid agencies and attendant think tanks were aglow with optimism. As more and more money flowed into their field of endeavour, predictions were made that world poverty would be conquered by the end of the century. The World Bank, under its new president, Robert McNamara, led this charge, expanding its lending five-fold in real terms while also encouraging bilateral donors and private banks to increase their outlays. Today, the field of international development has evolved into a multi-billion-dollar industry, but poverty has broadened and deepened around the globe, and inequality, both within and among nations, has increased at an astounding pace.

A generation ago, as countries in the South borrowed heavily from banks in the North flush with petrodollars they needed to recycle, they were sowing the seeds of severe economic crises. Interest rate charges on external debt skyrocketed and the terms of trade (prices paid and received for goods and services traded) shifted against their exports of primary commodities. The combined effect led to an explosion of debt service charges and of accumulated debt. Non-productive and poorly conceived investments, made with, and often promoted by, private and official lenders, made the repayment challenge even more daunting. And many governments, particularly in Latin America, took on the added responsibility of repaying not only their own debts but also those of private companies, including many loans that they had not guaranteed.

The Origins of Structural Adjustment

The debt crisis and the consequently increased vulnerability of poor nations facilitated the spread of the Thatcher/Reagan economic 'revolution' of the late 1970s and the 1980s. 'Stabilization' measures designed by the International Monetary Fund (IMF) imposed strict fiscal and monetary discipline on indebted countries as a condition for receiving short-term balance of payments credits. These policies were designed to generate savings and foreign exchange with which to bring countries' internal and external accounts into balance and facilitate the repayment of their foreign creditors. When food, fuel and transport costs soared with the removal of government subsidies, and street riots and protests consequently erupted in a number of countries, the World Bank stepped in with funds that were conditioned on longer-term, structural and institutional changes that had less immediate impact than the austerity measures required by the Fund. These structural and, subsequently, sectoral adjustment policies were designed to open markets and reduce the state's role in the economy. They came to include measures of: trade liberalization; investment deregulation; privatization of public utilities, marketing boards and other state enterprises; reform of the agricultural sector, the labour market and pensions; and the liberalization of almost all domestic markets. Along the way, the two principal international financial institutions (IFIs) would cross into each other's territory, sometimes in collaboration, at other times in conflict.

Structural adjustment policies were designed to open markets and reduce the state's role in the economy.

By the second half of the 1980s, one quarter of overall World Bank lending was being extended in the form of non-project, structural adjustment loans at a time when adjustment programmes had not yet been imposed to a significant extent on either Asian or Central European countries. While adjustment programmes were justified at that time as medium-term prescriptions designed to turn around emergency economic situations, they turned out, in fact, to be long-term, one-size-fits-all economic restructuring programmes imposed on countries regardless of their circumstances. Two-year time frames for success turned into five-year, ten-year and, in most cases, two-decade projects without sustained economic development in sight.

The economic theory underlying adjustment programmes came to justify not only measures that would both squeeze savings from national budgets and generate foreign exchange in order to ensure the repayment of foreign creditors, but also those that would create a friendly investment environment for foreign investors. The liberalization of markets, deregulation and privatization – all keyed on the systematic erosion of traditional roles of the state – would, it was argued, attract and retain investment that, in turn, would guarantee growth and development. Structural adjustment became the only economic strategy acceptable to the US Treasury, to the IFIs and, by extension, to other official lenders and donors. When reality contradicted theory, and investment and growth did not consistently ensue – and as foreign investors and some national élites gained handsomely while development prospects dimmed for the vast majority of citizens – these failures of the adjustment 'model' were typically explained away with claims about the long-term nature of the problem or the lack of full compliance of governments in implementing economic reforms.

Structural adjustment became the only economic strategy acceptable to the US Treasury, the IFIs and other official lenders and donors.

In reality, full compliance with the usual myriad of Fund and Bank policy conditions has seldom been feasible, especially in the face of extensive public opposition to the implementation of the policies. Yet, the vast majority of measures required – ranging from the dropping of trade barriers that protected the livelihoods of small farmers and fledgling domestic industries to the rewriting of national labour laws – have typically been adopted as governments have been forced, under threat of being cut off from international financing, to respond to the interests of their official and private creditors over those of their own people. Such policy conditionality has also raised major political issues, including the implications for the sovereignty of states and for the democratic control of policy by national electorates. Although the IFIs are, by statute, prohibited from interfering in the political affairs of their member countries, governments have been pressured to change laws to comply with adjustment conditionality, legislatures have been kept in the dark about loan requirements, and cabinet ministries other than those responsible for strictly financial and economic matters have often been left out of the loop.

Equally problematic and debilitating for these countries and their people has been the impact of the policies themselves. Without democratic control over the key economic decisions that so directly affect their lives, the vast majority of citizens have seen the past generation of policies serve other interests while their own circumstances deteriorate. The worsening plight of urban workers, farmers and small businesspeople, of women, indigenous peoples and the young, of their natural environment and of the productive sectors of the economy as a whole has been one of the major and tragic stories of the past two decades.

By the mid-1990s, before the Seattle, Prague, Washington and other demonstrations in the North against the World Trade Organization (WTO), the World Bank and the IMF, the world had already witnessed almost twenty years of strikes, mobilizations and other forms of popular protest across the countries of the South in reaction to the economic policies of these institutions. The people most affected by those policies were seen by the IFIs as having neither the wisdom nor the right, and certainly not the leverage, to contribute to the economic policy debates in their own countries. Their continued exclusion from the economic decision-making process both at the national and global levels guaranteed that economic policy programmes would not be changed to reflect their growing needs and priorities.

The people most affected by the policies were seen by the IFIs as having neither the wisdom nor the right to contribute to economic policy debates.

To force the architects of adjustment programmes to confront publicly the local economic reality of the South and to give voice to marginalized populations suffering under the weight of those programmes, a broad array of civil society organizations came together across national and sectoral lines to initiate the tripartite initiative that is the subject of this book. While the results of the multi-country investigation launched with governments and the World Bank have contributed to the apparent dissolution of the so-called Washington Consensus behind adjustment policies, the main components of adjustment programmes remain firmly in place as conditions of continued lending by aid agencies.

Some Northern governments, no longer able to justify traditional adjustment programmes to their electorates, claim that IFI-promoted initiatives ostensibly geared towards poverty reduction indicate a change in course, but poverty-generating adjustment policies are, in fact, an integral and required part of these initiatives. Furthermore, civil society consultations supposedly designed to help shape such endeavours are conspicuously void of meaningful discussion of economic policy issues, despite the fact that for two decades changes in economic policy have been emphasized by the IFIs as the road to economic development. In short, the IMF, the World Bank and their most powerful board members still determine national economic frameworks, while the majority of populations, particularly the poor, as well as important economic sectors, continue to suffer the effects of these policies.

At the same time, the rich local knowledge that civil society can contribute to economic policy formulation in the interests of eradicating poverty, reducing inequality and strengthening national economies continues to be ignored in policy determination. This book describes an innovative civil society initiative designed in the mid-1990s to alter this reality. Although new inroads have been made as a result, substantive changes have yet to materialize.

The Genesis of SAPRI

In the context of increasing protests against structural adjustment by civil society in the global South and a growing recognition in official circles of the failure of these policies to deliver on their promise, a number of non-governmental organizations (NGOs), engaged in the original '50 Years Is Enough' campaign, presented the incoming World Bank president, James Wolfensohn, with a new challenge. These and other groups, subsequently organized under the umbrella of the Structural Adjustment Participatory Review International Network (SAPRIN), challenged Wolfensohn to involve his staff in an exercise with civil society organizations in the South in order to bring critically important knowledge, perspectives and analysis into the formulation of Bank economic advice and policy making. Wolfensohn accepted the challenge and requested that a mechanism be proposed by these and other organizations for carrying out such an initiative.

'What I am looking for is a different way of doing business in the future' – James Wolfensohn

In a letter dated 9 April 1996 to the global civil society network organized for this purpose, he noted that 'policy reform has had a mixed track record .... Adjustment has been a much slower, more difficult and more painful process than the Bank recognized at the outset'. He went on to address the proposed initiative:

> What I am looking for – and inviting your help in – is a different way of doing business in the future. My objective is to ensure that economic reform programs make maximum contribution to poverty reduction, that we fully appreciate the impact of reform on disparate population groups, that we promote measures which narrow income differentials, and that we encourage governments to consult and debate with civil society on policy reforms.

Thus was born the Structural Adjustment Participatory Review Initiative (SAPRI), a joint five-year, multi-country participatory investigation into the effects of specific structural adjustment policies on a broad range of economic and social sectors and population groups. Financed by generous contributions from five European governments, the European Union, the United Nations Development Programme (UNDP) and various foundations and NGOs, SAPRI sought to add local knowledge to the economic policy-making process and to legitimize a voice for organized civil society in such decision-making processes at both the national and global levels. The Initiative was a tripartite arrangement involving national governments, World Bank teams and national networks of hundreds of civil society organizations that mobilized around the opportunity to influence the economic course of their respective countries. These networks form the national chapters of the three-tiered SAPRIN structure that was built originally around this engagement with the Bank and that coordinated civil society's participation in SAPRI.

The country exercises followed guidelines negotiated by the SAPRIN global civil society steering committee and its World Bank counterpart. These national assessments of the impact of specific adjustment measures were structured in four stages. The first stage called for extensive and highly inclusive and participatory outreach to, and mobilization of, a broad cross-section of local populations affected by the country's adjustment programme, particularly those who had been most marginalized by the economic decision-making process. The second step in the process involved the convening of national public fora, organized by local civil society steering committees in conjunction with Bank and government officials, to discuss key adjustment measures and issues prioritized by citizens' organizations. The fora were designed to bring local knowledge and analysis related to the impact of adjustment programmes to the doorstep of World Bank country and Washington officials. They were followed in each country by participatory research into the selected issues in order to deepen this analysis. Designed and carried out jointly by World Bank and SAPRIN teams and research consultants, this research constituted the third and longest phase of the programme. The joint results were then reviewed publicly by dozens of civil society organizations and Bank and government representatives at a Second National Forum in each country, at which modifications were suggested for the final national report.

A great deal has been learned from this Initiative, not only with regard to the impact of structural adjustment programmes, but also about the mobilization, organization and participation of civil society in matters related to international economic policy making, as well as about the Bank itself and its much vaunted but highly problematic relationship with civil society. Below, two principal characteristics that made SAPRI unique – the joint, if difficult, nature of the exercise with the Bank and the highly participatory and inclusive nature of the methods employed by civil society independently and with their Bank and government counterparts – are emphasized in a description of the evolution, implementation and method-ologies of the SAPRI experience.

SAPRI sought to add local knowledge to the economic policy-making process and to legitimize a voice for organized civil society.

Forging a Joint Initiative with the World Bank while Maintaining Civil Society Independence

While President Wolfensohn's acceptance of the NGO challenge to carry out a collaborative grassroots assessment of structural adjustment programmes led to the development of a concrete NGO action proposal, that step was but the first in a rather lengthy process of establishing a truly joint initiative.

The proposal, which was the product of a collaboration among some 30 NGOs and NGO coalitions around the world – including Third World Network–Africa, Development Alternatives for Women in a New Era (DAWN), Equipo Pueblo (Mexico), Oxfam–America and The Development GAP as its coordinator in Washington – was sent to Wolfensohn in December 1995. It placed programme emphasis on public and highly inclusive national consultations in 10–12 countries, including emerging-market economies, across four continents, in order to yield representative results. A smaller meeting with Wolfensohn in March 1996, required to cut through bureaucratic delay at the Bank, generated a personal commitment from him to engage his institution seriously in a collaborative endeavour and a mutual acknowledgment that both parties were taking a risk by engaging in the Initiative and hence had to trust each other for it to work. With Wolfensohn's blessing, the NGO proposal became the basis of negotiations that were consummated with an agreement in July 1996.

The Bank's Development Economics Vice-Presidency (DEC), led by the institution's chief economist, took responsibility for the Initiative and insisted on adding a research component to the exercise. It was a proposal that promised to extend the length of the endeavour considerably but was acceptable to the civil society negotiators as long as the field investigations were participatory in nature and studied the political economy of the selection and implementation of the adjustment measures being assessed. The core of the exercise was still to be consultative, however, in order to ensure that affected populations, their knowledge and experience would be at the centre of the process, and that a unique contribution would be made to the knowledge base and decision-making processes related to economic policy programmes. Towards that end, the field research would be bracketed by two public fora, one (as originally proposed by the NGOs) at which citizens' organizations would present their experience with, and analysis of, specific adjustment policies that had directly affected their lives, and the other to assess the research undertaken to deepen the understanding of the issues that these groups had raised.

These and other elements of the programme were hammered out at a two-day joint Bank–SAPRIN steering committee meeting in July 1996.

The SAPRIN negotiating team included representatives from the African Women's Economic Policy Network (AWEPON), Focus on the Global South, FUNDE (El Salvador), ALOP (Latin America), Rede Brasil, Public Services International, Oxfam International, the Halifax Initiative, Friends of the Earth and The Development GAP. The Bank team was drawn from the Policy Research Department of DEC and the Poverty and Social Policy Department, although the Bank's SAPRI committee also included officials from Vice Presidents' and Managing Directors' offices. Agreements were made to proceed jointly with the final selection of SAPRI countries, the establishment of a system of effective civil society access to official adjustment-related documents needed for the national exercises, the development of a global methodological framework to guide country research designs, the completion of a SAPRI budget covering both SAPRIN and Bank projected expenses, SAPRI fundraising from European government sources, and the planning of the first of two Global SAPRI Fora to officially launch the Initiative. A Second Global Forum would subsequently complete the assessment phase of SAPRI by providing a venue for senior Bank management to review the findings drawn from the various participatory field exercises and discuss follow-up measures.

As far as country selection was concerned, it was agreed that Mexico and, ideally, the Philippines would represent the experience of emerging markets, an understanding previously reached with Wolfensohn. Two other Latin American and one other Asian nation would be included, as well as four countries in Africa and one in Central Europe. Taking a variety of criteria into account, including country size, level of development and the presence of an organized civil society sector, the final list included Ecuador, El Salvador, Bangladesh, Ghana, Mali, Uganda, Zimbabwe and Hungary among the ten countries. The Bank asserted its liaison role with member governments within the SAPRI tripartite arrangement, but then failed to obtain the participation of the governments of Mexico, the Philippines and Hungary. Working locally, SAPRIN eventually secured the involvement of Hungary but did not receive the help it needed from the Bank to add larger emerging-market economies to ensure a representative cross-section of countries in SAPRI. For that reason, SAPRIN eventually supported country exercises in Mexico and the Philippines under the rubric of Citizens' Assessments of Structural Adjustment (CASA) and also lent support to less ambitious exercises in Argentina and Brazil, as well as in Central America.

Parallel to the country selection and approval processes, standard operating procedures were established and a joint global research methodology team began its work to create the framework for the country field-investigation processes. The rules of engagement, which were first drafted by SAPRIN and subsequently approved by the Bank, were designed first and foremost to level the playing field and to establish the Bank and civil society as equal partners. While assuring inclusiveness in the participation of civil society in each country, SAPRIN insisted that civil society outreach, mobilization and organization be carried out under the auspices of local groups without interference on the part of the Bank or government. While there would be tripartite steering and technical committees in each country, there would also be local, independent SAPRIN teams and committees with their own decision-making processes. And, while the exercises would be joint in every way, SAPRIN and the Bank would control their own respective financing. In fact, in order to further strengthen the position of the national civil society teams vis-à-vis their stronger Bank and government counterparts, the local SAPRIN committees were given the responsibility for managing the funds for the national fora while, as co-financiers and co-managers of the research teams, they shared with these counterparts a de facto veto over decisions related to the research process and design.

The rules of engagement were designed to level the playing field for the Bank and civil society.

In determining the SAPRI budget, it was clear that, aside from the cost of the research consultants employed jointly by the Bank and SAPRIN, the bulk of the financing would be needed to cover civil society activities, including outreach functions, local-level workshops, travel to fora, and local management. By budgeting, and subsequently maintaining, modest costs for travel and hotel, and by heavily subsidizing personnel costs at all levels of SAPRI operations, SAPRIN was able to reduce its draw on donor resources, with the result that the Bank was allocated approximately one third of the jointly raised funds. Most of the participating local SAPRIN network members, beyond the lead organizations and technical team staff, were not reimbursed for their time, Northern global steering committee members contributed work and time gratis, and the SAPRIN secretariat drew less than half of its funds from the SAPRIN budget, utilizing its own organizational resources for the other 55 per cent. Secretariat tasks included network and steering committee coordination, communications with and the provision of support to SAPRIN's twelve national chapters and three regional centres, materials development, relations with the Bank, programme and financial management, and fundraising.

After separately approaching the Norwegian government for funding, SAPRIN and the Bank submitted a joint SAPRI proposal and received a grant through a World Bank trust fund in the spring of 1997. Similar proposals subsequently generated support from the governments of Sweden and the Netherlands, and SAPRIN, with the help of Belgian trade unions, secured a grant from the Belgian government in early 2000. As negotiated and agreed, SAPRIN's share of these funds was directly earmarked by donors for, and independently managed by, SAPRIN. To ensure this arrangement and subsequent independence of action, the SAPRIN secretariat reworked World Bank standard trust fund agreements to this end and negotiated the final details with the Bank's legal department. When the SAPRI timeline was extended, SAPRIN engaged in a new round of independent fundraising, securing additional resources from the European Union, the UNDP, quasi-governmental institutions in Germany and the United States, and other sources. In all, at the global level SAPRIN raised more than US$4 million for its local, national, regional and global activities over a five-year period, and all levels of the network contributed extensive counterpart resources. These funds and contributions, and the refusal of SAPRIN to take World Bank or local-government funding, provided SAPRIN with a critical source of independence that proved invaluable in its relationship with the Bank.

The first test of this independence came early in the development of the field exercises, when the government of El Salvador withdrew from its official involvement in SAPRI and the Bank followed suit, ignoring procedures established at both the national and global levels to resolve such disputes. Unwilling to abandon its civil society colleagues in El Salvador who had spent many months mobilizing and organizing to ensure full citizen participation in SAPRI, the SAPRIN global steering committee subsequently allocated non-trust-fund resources to the completion of that country exercise. A similar situation evolved in Zimbabwe, although the Bank, and a number of government ministries, remained informally involved in that process. Non-trust-fund resources also allowed SAPRIN to support the CASA exercises in Mexico and the Philippines and hence include large emerging-market countries in the overall investigation, as originally agreed with Wolfensohn.

The final two steps in the preparatory phase of SAPRI also proved problematic, but in the end they yielded two important joint instruments that permitted the national field exercises to proceed effectively, albeit after extensive delays. For the development of a global research methodology, SAPRIN secured the participation of top professionals from three major NGOs that served as the network's regional centres – Focus on the Global South in Thailand, FUNDE in El Salvador and Third World Network in Africa – and the coordinator of the technical team from Oxfam–America. After a solid start with the Bank's research team, the process bogged down, as the Bank's day-to-day work on the development of the research framework was left to a consultant who was unfamiliar with the institution and with the type of participatory, political economy design that had been agreed upon. With the Bank's top participatory researchers excluded from participation in SAPRI and the negotiations thus lacking balance between the two parties, a final design was completed only when a more senior Bank researcher joined the process after a frustrating year of on-again, off-again work.

The global research methodology that emerged, though not as comprehensive as would be needed to give clear guidance to complicated tripartite national research-design processes, did have a number of important and defining characteristics. First, the pair of public national fora that would bracket the field research would give affected populations an opportunity to present their experience under adjustment and take ownership of the results of that research. Second, the research was designed to be highly participatory, as well as gender sensitive, with the subjects helping to define its questions and parameters. Third, qualitative information, including that presented at the fora, would be as valued as quantitative information. Finally, the political economy approach agreed upon would focus analysis on those factors in the economic and political systems (national and global) that had determined the selection and design of adjustment policies and their impact when implemented.

National public fora gave affected populations an opportunity to present their experience under adjustment.

The second important instrument required for effective field exercises was a more open World Bank information disclosure policy with regard to structural adjustment documents. During the negotiations to establish SAPRI procedures, the SAPRIN global steering committee held to the position that the Initiative could not succeed unless all parties were working from the same set of information. That is, it would be unacceptable for the Bank to have various documents that were not available to civil society participants. In March 1996, President Wolfensohn agreed to make the necessary documents available, and this commitment was reiterated by staff in July, but the proposed disclosure arrangement forthcoming from the Bank eight months later was woefully inadequate. Information teams from the Bank and SAPRIN subsequently spent months negotiating an information disclosure policy for the Initiative. Taking into account that the Bank had classified various documents as confidential, SAPRIN compromised to break the impasse by agreeing to have joint information teams established in each country responsible for reviewing all documents relevant to adjustment programmes and for writing a detailed summary to be disseminated widely to civil society. While this compromise was at the heart of the ultimate agreement between the two parties, it took the better part of a year to obtain the approval of the Bank's legal department, senior management and board.

Nevertheless, the SAPRI Information Disclosure Policy Agreement was groundbreaking at the time that it was jointly announced by the Bank and SAPRIN in March 1998. It gave civil society teams access to Policy Framework Papers, Letters of Development Policy, Country Assistance Strategies, President's Reports, Mission Appraisal Reports, Tranche Release Memoranda, Completion Reports and equivalent reports on sectoral operations for all adjustment loans already extended by the Bank (though not for those under negotiation). Detailed information was made available from the Bank and governments on overall national economic frameworks, general and sectoral lending, expected outcomes of macroeconomic and sectoral adjustment policies, what governments agreed to do within adjustment programmes, the conditionality attached to specific tranche releases, the adjustment policies the Bank felt that governments did and did not implement, and views on policy outcomes. This arrangement worked well, and without controversy, in all the countries in which it was utilized, but its lengthy approval process delayed the progress of some of the country exercises by as much as a year.

SAPRI's public launch and Opening Global Forum in Washington in July 1997 captured and projected the significance of the joint Initiative at the time. It featured keynote speeches by Wolfensohn and Argentinian human rights and political leader Graciela Fernandez Meijide, as well as civil society and Bank panels on adjustment policies and their effects on labour and agriculture. Workshops were also held on the methodologies to be utilized and the issues to be explored in the country exercises. While few expected that the introduction of local knowledge about the ways adjustment programmes impacted local populations and sectors would by itself shift the Bank off its adjustment paradigm, SAPRI was helping to establish economic policy as a public issue requiring grassroots knowledge and input. It also embodied the essence of a true tripartite collaboration on a level playing field in which civil society had a legitimate and equal voice. And it set in motion highly participatory and extensive processes of citizen mobilization around global economic decision making and generated broad-based civil society networks and structured capacity to carry on this work in the future.

Civil Society Mobilization and Participation

SAPRIN set out from the beginning to maximize the levels of inclusiveness, participation, decentralization, communication and collective decision making within the SAPRI/CASA Initiative. Two thirds of the original SAPRIN global steering committee members were from the South, and that percentage was maintained or increased as the Initiative evolved. Regional centres were established in Accra at Third World Network– Africa, San Salvador at FUNDE, and in Bangkok at Focus on the Global South. Lead organizations in each of the countries developed their own programmes in conjunction with broad-based national civil society steering committees within the framework of the global guidelines developed by SAPRIN and the Bank. Represented on the global steering committee, these organizations brought their own needs and ideas to bear on the evolution of global programme design, financing priorities, and relationships with government and the Bank. A multi-layered communications system evolved that ensured continual communication among and between the national teams, the regional centres, the global executive committee and the SAPRIN global secretariat.

SAPRI set in motion citizen mobilization around economic decision making and generated broad-based civil society networks.

Of equal importance, participation and inclusiveness were the hallmarks of the national exercises, along with the joint nature of these Bank/civil society exercises in the SAPRI countries. To ensure meaningful participation, clear and firm steps were taken to distance the Bank and governments from the process of local outreach to, and selection of, civil society organizations that would participate in SAPRI. This placed pressure on the local teams to live up to SAPRIN's commitment – to the Bank and government, as well as to local populations – to ensure inclusion of a broad cross-section of organizations in the respective exercises. Other guidelines were established to level the playing field in programme decision making by giving civil society the power to select the major issues to be investigated and to organize the national public fora. Such mechanisms and other vehicles of participation were built into all the stages of the country exercises, as reflected in the large diverse turn-outs and the broad array of citizens' presentations at the national fora, the participatory nature of the field research, and the broad-based feedback received on the interim and final research reports at economic literacy workshops utilized for that purpose, and at the Second National Fora, respectively.

While the problems encountered with the Bank in establishing processes for government approval, methodology design and information disclosure unfortunately delayed progress in some of the national exercises, they were also fortuitous in one way. During the course of 1997, they permitted additional and necessary time for the civil society mobilization and organizing processes to be carried out effectively. And these processes turned out to be among the most interesting, important and successful aspects of the SAPRI/CASA exercises. Adhering to global guidelines designed to ensure inclusiveness, balance and comprehensiveness, they covered the respective countries' major geographical subregions, economic and social sectors, and population groups. Some details on the various national organizing processes follow. For more information, visit SAPRIN's website (*www.saprin.org*).

Bangladesh

Following an agreement by the government of Bangladesh in April 1997 to participate in the tripartite initiative, two civil society outreach meetings were held in Dhaka for the purpose of mobilizing civil society organizations and NGOs to participate in the national SAPRI exercise. A subsequent series of broader meetings led to the formation of a civil society steering committee and to the organizing of five regional meetings, the last of which was held in January 1998. They successfully expanded the civil society network nationwide and provided a forum for the discussion of issues that were of primary importance to people at the grassroots level. This broad-based consultative process continued in 1998 as part of the preparatory process leading up to the Opening National Forum. Over 500 people participated in three additional day-long regional consultative meetings and five sector-based focus group discussions, in which they voiced their concerns about the impact of structural adjustment policies and suggested areas of priority for further research. An additional focus group discussion was held in early 1999 after the October National Forum.

> ### The SAPRI network in Bangladesh grew to include more than 300 organizations.

As a result of this outreach and mobilization, led by the well-established NGO, PROSHIKA (Training, Education and Action), the local SAPRI civil society network in Bangladesh grew to include more than 300 organizations. These included development NGOs, trade unions, and associations of farmers, agricultural workers, small-scale producers, women, teachers, poor people and businessmen. The 15-member civil society steering committee, which worked together with its counterparts from the government and the World Bank in the national steering committee, has included representatives of PROSHIKA, the Bangladesh Rural Advancement Committee (BRAC), the National Association of Small and Cottage Industries of Bangladesh, the Federation of Bangladesh Chambers of

Commerce and Industry, the Coalition of Environmental NGOs, the Bangladesh Road Transport Workers' Federation and other trade unions, women's organizations, agricultural workers' and farmers' associations, as well as members of parliament and the media. A seven-member civil society technical committee was also formed to design and monitor the research process, in coordination with the government and the World Bank.

Ecuador

After overcoming initial problems with civil society organizing and outreach, an extensive process began in Ecuador in late 1997 under the leadership of the Institute for the Ecology and Development of Andean Communities (IEDECA). The intent was to reach out to and involve those sectors and broadly representative organizations normally excluded from national and international processes. Between October 1997 and March 1998, over 450 organizations from 20 of the country's 22 provinces participated in seven regional workshops. These workshops explained the objectives of SAPRI and included round-table discussions with local representatives from different sectors on specific structural adjustment policies in Ecuador and their impacts, as well as smaller group sessions designed to explore more deeply people's personal experiences with adjustment policies and suggestions for alternatives. A summary of the results from these workshops was used to prepare for the presentations and discussions at the Opening National Forum.

In Ecuador, over 450 organizations from 20 of 22 provinces participated in regional workshops.

Delegates from each regional workshop later met in Quito at a national citizens' workshop to further discuss regional priority issues raised and to elect a national SAPRIN civil society steering committee. That committee, which has coordinated the involvement of more than 750 organizations in the Ecuador exercise, has consisted of a wide range of population groups and representatives of geographical areas. Peasants and rural workers, small-scale enterprise organizations, women's groups, organized workers and unions, low-income community groups, indigenous peoples, Afro-Ecuadorian communities and human rights activists are represented, as are organizing committees that have been active in six major regions of the country. In addition to organizing the Opening National Forum, the steering committee subsequently formed a technical team that worked with the government's and Bank's technical experts to design and oversee the research process under the auspices of the tripartite national steering committee.

El Salvador

FUNDE, the lead organization in El Salvador (and SAPRIN's Latin American regional centre) launched an outreach process in its country in late 1996, but momentum stalled when the government, in the person of the Finance Minister, backed out of its prior commitment to SAPRI. By the second half of 1997, SAPRIN had decided to move ahead with the exercise on its own in the void left by the withdrawal of the government and the Bank. Ten permanent round tables, or *mesas*, were organized around the various economic and social sectors in the country, each of which held a workshop between November 1997 and February 1998. The objectives of these workshops were to discuss the specific problems and priorities of each sector, inform the organizations and their members about adjustment policies and the SAPRI process, and obtain input as to the impacts people had felt from those policies and the perceived causes of the problems they identified. The results were presented as contributions to the discussions at the Opening National Forum. At the same time, several hundred people from a broad range of organizations across the country participated in an array of activities up to mid-1998 designed to educate groups on the overall economic situation and to address specific problems in different sectors, such as poor healthcare services and child poverty.

This organizing work led to the establishment of a 14-organization steering committee representing 13 different sectors and to the expansion of the SAPRI network to include 70 major networks and organizations representing more than 500 grassroots groups. Joining forces in this coalition were organizations representing rural cooperatives, a union federation representing urban workers, an association of small and medium-size enterprises, a network of organizations focused on the problems of children, the National Council of Churches, a national women's organization, and networks representing environmental, human rights and media organizations, as well as NGOs and universities.

Ghana

The Integrated Social Development Centre (ISODEC), which has acted as the lead organization in Ghana with the support of Third World Network–Africa, began a national outreach drive after SAPRI was formally launched in November 1997 following cabinet approval of the Initiative. By August of the next year, workshops had been held in all ten of the country's regional capitals. Organized through six regional SAPRIN structures and involving approximately 300 civil society organizations, as well as civil servants and district officials, these sessions provided information on SAPRI, identified issues of concern to civil society to serve as a basis for discussion at the First National Forum and selected representatives from the regions to attend the Forum. The broader SAPRI network has encompassed virtually all of the major NGOs, churches and trade union umbrella organizations in the country.

> **The Coordinating Council in Ghana represented organizations of workers, women, students, Muslims, farmers, fishermen, small and medium-scale industries, environmentalists and other NGOs.**

The Civil Society Coordinating Council (CivisoC) – composed of 21 members representing organizations of workers, women, students, Muslims, farmers, fishermen, and small and medium-scale industries, as well as environmentalists and other NGOs – was formed to manage the network's participation in the SAPRI exercise in Ghana. CivisoC formed four subcommittees to work in the areas of organization, media, finance and management, and chose seven of its members to participate in the tripartite national steering committee with government and World Bank representatives, as well as eight civil society experts to participate in the tripartite technical committee that designed and oversaw the research process.

Hungary

In mid-1997, Hungarian trade unions and NGOs engaged their government in discussions about joining SAPRI after World Bank overtures proved unsuccessful. As a result, the Office of the Prime Minister, in conjunction with the ministries of Labour, Industry and Finance, committed the government to participating in a national exercise. With this success, a group of socially concerned economists began an extensive outreach effort by first enlisting the participation of the largest trade union alliances. Three large farmers' organizations, the national alliance of small industries, and other key constituency groups, such as national organizations of Romas (gypsies), women, pensioners and the disabled, as well as organizations representing environmentalists, engineers and economists, were also brought on board. The Alliance of Social Associations (ASA), which coordinates a nationwide network of civic organizations, was then asked to reach out to the different regions of the country to broaden public knowledge of, and participation in, the SAPRI exercise. There were 11 well-publicized meetings, with media coverage and the involvement of local officials, organized for this purpose in ten of the nation's 19 counties in late 1997 and early 1998, in which approximately 725 people participated.

A total of 1,600 organizations have been represented directly or indirectly through the various coalitions actively involved in the network, and organizing centres were established in 16 of the 19 counties across the country. They have been coordinated by a 22-member steering committee. An information committee was established to access and review World Bank and government documents on structural adjustment programmes and policies in Hungary, and a technical committee of civil society experts was formed to help design and oversee the research process.

Uganda

The Ugandan SAPRI process began in January 1997 with a meeting convened by the African Women's Economic Policy Network (AWEPON) and attended by some 20 NGOs. The participants decided that the Uganda National NGO Forum, an umbrella group with nearly 100 members, should organize the initial stages of the local SAPRI exercise. The NGO Forum later convened an outreach meeting that was attended by representatives of more than 70 organizations. The outreach effort was assisted by the public launch of the tripartite initiative at a national conference held in Kampala in August that was attended by a broad array of civil society organizations as well as government officials. It served to introduce SAPRI to the participants, and saw the formation of a civil society steering committee and the start of the process of selecting issues to be addressed during the exercise.

The NGO Forum expanded its outreach efforts by making special, ultimately successful overtures to the nation's labour union umbrella organization and by undertaking organizing efforts in all parts of the country. Regional outreach peaked in early 1998 when SAPRI civil society teams visited 20 of Uganda's 45 districts to explain the exercise, solicit participation in the SAPRI process and gather views on adjustment-related issues. The teams specifically included farmers, traders, artisans, housewives, civil servants, civic leaders, trade union and cooperative members, middlemen, labourers and district officials. Two-day workshops were held in each district, in which approximately 1,000 people participated and contributed their ideas and experiences. These events were, in essence, hearings on citizens' perceptions of government policy in general and structural adjustment policies in particular. Regional structures were formed and have included associations of small-scale farmers, educators, healthcare workers, women, youth and the disabled, as well as environmental, human rights and religious groups, and development-related NGOs. They are coordinated by a 16-member civil society steering committee, delegates from which formed the tripartite SAPRI national steering committee along with representatives of the Ministry of Finance, the Ministry of Planning and the World Bank.

Zimbabwe

The SAPRI exercise in Zimbabwe began with a series of meetings involving national and international NGOs, labour unions, church groups, farmers' associations and the Chamber of Commerce. Because of the rural, dispersed nature of much of Zimbabwe, radio time was purchased and several programmes explaining the SAPRI exercise were produced and broadcast, while numerous televised panel discussions with representatives of the government and the World Bank were also used to spread the word about the Initiative. In addition, a series of six regional workshops were organized in late 1997 and early 1998 by the national networks of the Zimbabwe Council of Trade Unions (ZCTU) and the Zimbabwe Council of Churches. To extend the outreach further, the 50 or so participants from grassroots organizations in each of these regional events agreed to fan out into rural areas and replicate the workshops at the village level. There were 45 local workshops held in early 1998, in which a total of 2,000 people participated, thus facilitating the formation of district committees. These regional and district-level workshops were used to explain and solicit participation in SAPRI and to discuss thoroughly those aspects of the national adjustment programme that were of the greatest concern to participants. Local participation was extremely broad and even included soldiers and police in their roles as concerned civil servants.

Six regional and 45 district committees constitute the SAPRI network in Zimbabwe.

Although there had been participation by government representatives in SAPRI activities in 1997 and early 1998, as political tension increased and the economic situation worsened, the government disengaged from SAPRI. Following a two-day national meeting, in which it refined the issues raised at the local level for discussion at the Opening National Forum, the SAPRIN civil society steering committee spent the second half of 1998 and the first half of 1999 focused on re-involving the government. When these efforts failed, a series of civil society meetings with representatives from the six regional and 45 district committees that constitute the SAPRI network led to the decision to move forward with the exercise, regardless of the government's role. These local committees, along with the 100 or so national civil society organizations that have been active members of SAPRIN/Zimbabwe, became the backbone of the network decision-making structure, while the steering committee established various sub-committees to provide the necessary technical support and outreach. The steering committee, which includes the above-mentioned organizations, as well as women's organizations, the Confederation of Zimbabwe Industries and other constituency groups, has been coordinated by SAPRIN's lead organization, the Poverty Reduction Forum at the Institute of Development Studies, with the support of the ZCTU.

Mexico

During the first half of 1998, Equipo Pueblo, acting as the lead civil society organization in Mexico, organized a series of regional meetings and sectoral workshops in different parts of the country. These outreach meetings were designed to involve, in particular, marginalized groups – including women, children, indigenous people and others among the rural and urban poor – in the CASA process and discussions on national economic policy. A regional workshop brought together dozens of community groups and NGOs from the southern provinces of Chiapas and Oaxaca. Seminars were held with Mayan children on the outskirts of the city of Merida in Yucatan province, with youth in the poor neighbourhoods of Mexico City, with mothers involved in community childcare centres in the capital, and with a range of community groups in Guadalajara. In addition, a national workshop designed to address conditions in rural areas was organized with the participation of nearly 100 representatives of a broad range of rural-based social organizations from around the country.

Nearly 50 organizations became actively involved in the CASA exercise, including local and regional groups and many national organizations and networks. The Mexican network includes organizations working in the Mexico City metropolitan area, as well as in the four regions of the country where CASA focused its efforts: the northern border region; the central region (Queritaro, Guanajuato, Michoacan, Sierra de Hidalgo, Tlaxcala and Puebla); the south-east (Chiapas, Oaxaca and the southern part of Veracruz); and the western region (Jalisco, Colima, Nayarit and Guadalajara). They represent groups working in the *maquila* sector, small-business and producers' associations, rural organizations, associations of farmers and indigenous peoples, credit unions and microfinance institutions, trade unions, development organizations, neighbourhood groups, healthcare organizations and youth groups. A General Council was organized, with general coordination and the organization of specific activities delegated to a six-member coordinating committee.

The Philippines

When initial efforts to bring the government and the Bank on board to carry out a SAPRI exercise failed in 1997, civil society organizations in the Philippines began a CASA initiative. In early 1998, the Freedom from Debt Coalition took the lead in carrying out an extensive process of outreach with an economic literacy programme designed to involve actively a wide range of organizations representative of different national sectors. Special efforts were made to include people and their organizations in the poorest and most disadvantaged regions of the country, particularly northern Luzon, Visayas and Mindanao. A national assembly was held in March 1998, followed by a general organizing meeting in August. Thematic working groups were constituted, with the participation of a wide range of organizations involved in the network in order to help elucidate issues of concern to civil society, outline possible questions for research and prepare background materials.

> **When efforts to bring the government and the Bank into SAPRI failed, civil society organizations in the Philippines began a CASA initiative.**

Over 150 national and locally based organizations, including many coalitions representing hundreds of grassroots groups, affiliated themselves with SAPRIN and the CASA exercise in the Philippines. Among the groups that participated in a range of activities organized by SAPRIN were eight peasant associations, seven peace and human rights organizations, ten poor-people's associations, seven development organizations, six environmental groups, five health organizations, 15 labour unions, 12 church and other religious organizations, five educational associations, 28 women's organizations, five youth groups, three indigenous peoples' organizations, six political movements, five political parties, 13 debt relief advocacy groups, and four migrant-support associations. Of the 15 members selected to form the local SAPRIN steering committee, six were conveners of thematic working groups, three were regional representatives and six were members at large. The committee decided in 1999 to continue with the process as a CASA exercise when a newly elected government opted to remain officially outside the initiative.

National Public Fora: Infusing the Economic Policy Debate with Local Knowledge

The SAPRI consultative fora lay at the heart of the national exercises. It was the omission, civil society groups had long claimed, of a local-level, 'real world' perspective on the design, implementation and impact of adjustment measures that doomed those programmes to failure. In his first months at the reins of the Bank, Wolfensohn had already established consultation with civil society as part of his new approach at the institution, and SAPRIN set out to ensure that SAPRI would be a broad-based, highly decentralized, and effectively organized consultation on the critical issue of economic policy.

The approval by the Bank's board in February 1998 of the SAPRI Information Disclosure Policy Agreement unfroze some of the country exercises by allowing SAPRIN information teams to study documents related to structural adjustment in preparation for Opening National Fora. Within four months, a series of seven national fora – organized by SAPRIN committees in conjunction with the Bank and government – were launched, beginning in Hungary and Uganda in June and ending in Ecuador in January. Ghana, where the momentum in civil society organizing and government/civil society relations was broken by the 18 months it took the Bank to establish a policy for public review of adjustment agreements, did not hold its Forum until November. The Zimbabwe exercise, with its highly successful civil society mobilization, was another unfortunate victim of the delay, with the government, in a changing political climate, walking away from the table by the time the SAPRIN committee had prepared itself for the Forum in that country. After more than a year of informal discussions with various ministries, SAPRIN finally proceeded unilaterally with a Forum in Zimbabwe in September 1999, an event in which the Bank participated. Likewise, SAPRIN in the Philippines convened its Forum in July 1999 with members of Congress after failing to engage its government in the exercise. A Forum in Mali was also not held until the third quarter of 1999, but, in that case, organizational issues were the problem, issues that would eventually lead to the premature termination of that national exercise.

The Opening National Fora were designed for the presentation and discussion of local populations' experience with, and perspectives on, specific economic adjustment measures and their respective impacts. In all the fora except those in El Salvador and Mexico, Bank and government officials were present to learn from, and respond to, the information and analysis presented, while parliamentary representatives participated in the others. The respective local SAPRIN steering committees selected presenters who could represent the points of view of a broad range of economic and social groups. The issues were chosen in accordance with global SAPRI guidelines, which empowered the local SAPRIN technical teams to engage civil society organizations across the country in the generation of a long list of priority economic policy issues. The list was then narrowed before the final selection of three or four issues was made in each country with the Bank and government in the respective national tripartite steering committees. While the selection of the same issues for all the exercises would have made subsequent cross-country comparisons and synthesis much easier, the preservation of local choice was at the heart of the participatory nature of SAPRI.

The focus of civil society presentations was on specific consequences of particular policy reforms.

The impact of trade liberalization policies was selected by local organizations as one of the three or four most problematic issues for discussion in nine of the ten countries, including Mali. Trade policies were often chosen in conjunction with other adjustment measures – price liberalization, financial sector liberalization, industrial policy reforms, removal of agricultural input subsidies, investment liberalization, labour flexibilization – and related to a broad range of impacts, including their effects on local industries, small enterprises, rural producers, the agricultural sector, domestic production, employment and workers. Privatization – of public utilities and services and of the mining and industrial sectors – was another prioritized problem area identified by citizens' groups, arising in six countries. The focus varied from the impact on consumers, workers, the poor and vulnerable groups to effects on the environment, employment and the concentration of wealth.

Agricultural sector reform policies were also on the agenda in six countries, while the impact on workers of labour market reforms was discussed in four, and the liberalization of the financial sector and the problems of credit access for local producers in four. Public expenditure reform issues – including user fees, the elimination of subsidies, and the impact of reform on healthcare and education, social services, family economic security and social development – also emerged as a priority in eight of the national exercises. Overall, however, the greatest emphasis was placed in all the countries on the problems, dislocations and increased poverty and inequities generated by economic adjustment policies through the destruction of domestic productive capacity and through the failure to generate sufficient employment at a living wage.

The Opening National Fora themselves were well-attended, highly publicized events. Typically held over two days and organized around plenary sessions and work groups, these fora each brought together over 100 representatives of civil society organizations from around the country (SAPRIN budgets covered local transportation and lodging) and usually between 200 and 300 people in all. Presentations were made by civil society representatives on three or four specific adjustment-related issues, drawing on the knowledge, experience and analysis of local constituency groups. These were followed by discussion with World Bank and government officials and the broader group of participants. The information and analysis presented by these representatives from different sectors and population groups constitute some of the qualitative information synthesized in this book. Summaries of the country fora can be found on the SAPRIN website.

Participating government officials usually included ministers, state secretaries, department heads and/or other representatives from the Ministry of Finance, as well as from other economic and social ministries, although participation was uneven from country to country. In those countries in which governments were not officially participating, ministry staff sometimes informally attended the proceedings. The Fora also attracted parliamentarians, former cabinet ministers, members of local councils and other politicians. Washington and country World Bank representatives (including the resident representative in Zimbabwe) participated actively in the sessions. The local SAPRIN steering committees and technical teams were joined by representatives of the network's global steering committee, secretariat and/or regional centres, who took note of the information and analysis presented.

In Ecuador, the Forum was held amidst a financial crisis and widespread street protests against adjustment policies.

While civil society representatives often stressed the non-participatory, non-transparent and externally imposed design of adjustment programmes, as well as their overall negative effects, the focus of their presentations and discussion was on specific consequences of particular policy reforms. The Fora were designed as a learning experience for the Bank and governments, but the sessions invariably turned into debates, with the Bank defending its record and disputing citizen analysis. However, the Fora did help generate good local media coverage and clearly laid out the problematic areas that civil society felt required further investigation and a fundamental change in policy.

In Ecuador, where the Forum was held in an environment of widespread street protests against adjustment policies and amidst a serious financial crisis, SAPRIN representatives urged the government and the Bank to extend the SAPRI dialogue and be responsive to the broader society on the issue of economic policy. In Bangladesh, Professor Rehman Sobhan, former presidential adviser and chair of the joint Bank/SAPRIN national SAPRI steering committee, issued a similar challenge to the Bank and government at the end of proceedings in that country. He reminded them that public expectations had been raised as a result of the Forum and the Initiative and urged them to take the output from the exercise seriously or face a further loss of credibility and integrity amongst civil society and the local electorate.

Joint Research to Deepen Local Civil Society Assessments of Adjustment Policies

Immediately after the Opening National Forum in each of the SAPRI countries, local World Bank and SAPRIN teams sat down to begin determining the specific areas of field research in which to deepen the knowledge gleaned from the participatory events. In almost all cases, including those in which the Bank was not officially involved, the research issues selected were more narrowly focused versions of the questions explored in the Fora. The collaboration between the local Bank and SAPRIN teams intensified at this point, with their respective technical teams working jointly to develop local research designs within the framework of the global SAPRI methodology, as well as terms of reference (TORs) for jointly selected research consultants.

This process extended over several months, taking longer than expected in most countries. In an effort to ensure tripartite ownership of the research design and the TORs, much time was required for all parties to work together and reach agreement. Delays in finalizing TORs were in some cases due to political crises and events that diverted the government's attention from the technical process, causing the technical team to have to wait for the government's input before proceeding. In the case of Ecuador, for example, a worsening economic situation erupted into a major political crisis in early 1999, making government participation in the process inconsistent. With five different presidents and more than twice as many finance ministers in power during the period in which SAPRI was carried out, it was particularly difficult and time-consuming to keep the government actively involved. In Ghana, the government tasked representatives to the tripartite technical team without compensating them for their time, causing a delay of many months before a solution was found.

Once terms of reference were agreed upon by the tripartite teams, the joint selection of researchers began. In most countries, SAPRIN civil society technical teams found that the Bank intended to proceed with its usual method of hiring consultants, using a bidding process that drew from the same pool of institutions and researchers that are used by the Bank for its range of projects in each country. The civil society teams, however, made sure that this would not occur with the SAPRI research.

In Bangladesh, for example, the process began with civil society, on the one hand, and the Bank and government, on the other, putting forward suggestions for researchers for each policy area, with the intention of selecting candidates by mutual agreement. The Bank, however, continued to insist on including certain researchers it had worked with consistently in the past, who, for that reason, were not acceptable to civil society. It took several months and the involvement of the Bank and SAPRIN secretariats in Washington to resolve this conflict and ensure that independent researchers were chosen.

In Ghana, recruitment of researchers took about two months to complete. Advertisements were placed in the country's major newspapers and followed by special radio announcements. The publicity yielded an overwhelming response, as over 320 applications were received. The local joint SAPRI secretariat did the first screening, ensuring that applicants had complied with the minimum qualifications stipulated in the advertisement. Civil society's technical committee then took over and did a second screening that led to the shortlisting of 37 applicants. Thereafter, the tripartite technical committee became involved, as interviews were held to select the final list of researchers. A similar process occurred in Ecuador, where advertisements were placed in several newspapers. More than a month was given for proposals to be received, and it took two months to review and formally agree on the final selection.

In Hungary, a different approach was taken, as the SAPRIN civil society technical team could not agree with the Bank and government on a joint process to hire researchers. For that reason, the parties agreed that civil society would choose its own research team, while the Bank and government would hire a separate team to cover the same subjects, an option stipulated in the global standard operating procedures. Upon completion of their work, the results of each team had to be compared and integrated by the tripartite technical team.

Following the selection of researchers, several countries held national methodology workshops for the researchers and the civil society and tripartite technical teams in order to ensure that the researchers clearly understood the SAPRI methodology and to review their plans for carrying out the research process. Such workshops – organized in Bangladesh, Ghana, Uganda and Zimbabwe – emphasized the key aspects of the methodology and helped to link researchers with civil society organizations to ensure that fieldwork would be participatory and involve grassroots groups and affected populations around the country.

Research was based on an understanding of the structures and relations in society that have determined the selection, design and impact of adjustment policies.

These methodology workshops emphasized the gender-sensitive, political economy approach that was to characterize the research. The studies were to be based on an understanding of the structures and relations in society that have determined the selection and design of adjustment policies and through which these policies have had an impact on people's lives. This meant looking at the effects as a whole of a package of interrelated policies, rather than a search for a unilateral causal relationship. Thus, the research process needed to take into account the institutions, power structures and interests that affect economic behaviour, and seek a multidimensional analysis that considered factors such as gender, ethnic, cultural and age differences, as well as variations in the political, social and environmental context. At the same time, the participatory field research was to utilize workshops and a range of techniques through which various sectors of civil society could share their knowledge and perceptions of the impact of adjustment policies. Qualitative information, including that presented at the Fora, was to be as valued as quantitative information in the studies.

Specific research plans were developed once researchers were selected and the methodology workshops completed. Given the different experiences and conditions at the country level and the range of actors involved, national teams developed a variety of means they deemed best suited to their local context for applying this non-traditional methodology. The country studies were conducted using three basic tools of investigation:

- *Desk reviews.* Each research team compiled and reviewed existing literature, including previous research, official documents and statistics, as well as reports by international institutions. In most cases, this also involved analyzing data derived from various secondary sources.

- *Primary surveys.* Local stakeholder surveys were undertaken by some of the research teams, either using quantitative techniques or employing a mix of both quantitative and qualitative methods.

- *Participatory reviews and fieldwork.* A key strength of the whole exercise was the use of participatory methods, including a range of participatory appraisal techniques, semi-structured interviews, workshops and focus group discussions with a wide array of social actors, whereby the experiences and views of various stakeholders were collected and analyzed.

It was in the use of participatory methods that country teams were most innovative. Several different approaches were adopted.

In Bangladesh, one research team was contracted to carry out an extensive participatory study addressing all the selected adjustment policies together using Participatory Rural Appraisal (PRA) methodology. The study complemented the work of separate teams contracted to carry out four policy-focused and four issue-oriented studies. In addition, a series of focus group discussions and regional consultative meetings were held with a wide range of local and national civil society groups and sector-specific organizations to gather input for each of the research teams, both at the beginning and at the end of the research process. The results of all the research teams were integrated to produce the final country report.

In Ecuador, the two research teams that were contracted to carry out studies on the three selected policy areas worked together to ensure their research would be participatory. A series of workshops and in-depth interviews were conducted with social actors from a range of sectors, selected according to the policy areas being studied and the productive characteristics of each geographical zone. Causality diagrams were drawn to identify perceptions of the causes and effects of these policies, as well as their impact on the participants' communities. Information gleaned from these processes was then systematized by the research teams and used to identify the variables and indicators, along with their respective interrelations, that were the focus of the research. Thus, the workshops were the starting point for identifying the policies and themes to be analyzed, as well as for the study of causal relationships as indicated by the participants. Once the first results from the research were obtained, another series of workshops was held to obtain more input and validate the results.

In Hungary, parallel research processes were carried out by civil society and the World Bank and their results integrated in order to produce the final country report. Four civil society research teams involving 20 researchers from Budapest and ten regions of the country carried out investigations in the four policy areas selected. At the same time, nearly a hundred civil society representatives presented short case studies addressing these policy areas, using their own organizational resources. The local SAPRIN technical team then synthesized the four civil society research reports and the various NGO papers into a draft summary, which was taken to a process of consultation in a series of workshops held around the country with civil society representatives and experts. Input from these meetings was incorporated into the final country report together with the results from the four World Bank research reports that had been done separately.

In Mexico, a different approach was taken to ensure the participatory and integral nature of the research process. Fieldwork utilized the Participatory Action Research (PAR) methodology, which comes from the tradition of Paulo Freire and is used to enhance participation in research while giving citizens ownership over the process itself. Because PAR uses popular education as a means for achieving local empowerment, economic literacy was integrally linked with the research process. Workshops were conducted in two modules, each of which was utilized in three regions of the country. The modules began with a training of trainers, involving representatives of more than 40 community groups and NGOs, which was followed by a series of workshops carried out in the respective regions by the participating trainers. In the workshops, participants described the socioeconomic transformations experienced in their communities, as well as the reasons for such changes and their reactions to them, and identified possible relationships between these changes and the application of structural adjustment policies. The workshop results were synthesized and integrated with the work of researchers who carried out three thematic studies that also drew information from household surveys and interviews with civic leaders.

In Zimbabwe, where political violence made it difficult to carry out the extensive participatory fieldwork that had been foreseen, a series of workshops was organized utilizing participatory methodologies to facilitate discussions of the policies selected for study and their impacts. Some 15 full-day workshops, each with over 50 participants from a wide cross-section of social classes and age groups, were conducted in the country's eight provinces to elicit information from communal, resettlement, commercial-farming, mining and urban settlements. The results of these workshops were integrated into the overall findings by the researchers carrying out five thematic studies.

In Uganda, the national SAPRIN civil society network developed some 20 district-based structures that helped to mobilize local communities and organizations throughout the SAPRI exercise, as well as to ensure the participatory character of the research. Using these structures, workshops were organized to gather input from many groups around the country that helped to define, orient and validate the research process. The research teams that were contracted to carry out the three policy-focused studies and one issue-oriented study also worked with these local structures to elicit stakeholder involvement in the research. A similar process was followed in Ghana, where six regionally based civil society structures ensured stake-holder involvement and input in the four policy-focused studies carried out by researchers.

In El Salvador, the participatory nature of the research process was ensured through a series of workshops and focus group discussions that were held with stakeholders. In the first phase of the research on the three policy areas selected, thematic working groups were formed and consultations were organized in order to help orient each of the studies and provide a qualitative analysis based on the input and ideas of a broad range of civil society groups. Another series of workshops was held in the final phase of the research process at which initial findings were presented to the different sectors affected by the policies under study to seek feedback and outline the primary conclusions and recommendations. The results of these workshops were integrated into the final country report.

The participatory process in the Philippines was carried out in a similar manner. Thematic working groups were established for each of the four study areas to help guide the research and ensure its participatory nature. These thematic groups organized workshops at the local and regional levels with the affected population. In addition, researchers carried out key-informant interviews and utilized other participatory techniques to gather information on the impact of the policies under investigation.

The SAPRI/CASA research process extended over a two-year period – three years including the development of the country research designs and

TORs – and averaged 9–12 months per country. Foreseeing this eventuality, the SAPRIN secretariat continued to raise additional funds to support the completion of the country exercises. At an April 1999 meeting of the SAPRIN global steering committee in Bonn, the lead organizations in the SAPRI/CASA countries decided that some of these resources would be applied to further grassroots work that would deepen and dynamize the research process. The committee thus allocated funds to programmes of economic literacy and, in a few countries, the local-level exploration of economic alternatives. As a result, economic literacy workshops became an integral part of iterative processes of citizen review of interim research findings, with local-level groups being further informed on the subject while either validating or suggesting modifications in these results. Meanwhile, the alternatives work gave a forward-looking edge to some of the exercises, and, in countries like Ecuador, has provided the basis for the ongoing development of more appropriate economic policies.

After working with some of the researchers in the SAPRI countries to improve the quality of their respective draft papers, the national and SAPRIN technical teams recommended approval of joint Bank/civil society reports. Only in Hungary, where two distinct sets of papers had to be merged into a final product, was agreement on the reports difficult to reach, as elsewhere the research processes had been fully collaborative endeavours. The reports were sent to the national SAPRI steering committees, which delivered them to the Second National Fora.

The Fora brought together similar numbers of participants as attended the opening national events and also attracted significant media coverage. Civil society representatives typically suggested improvements, additions and modifications to the reports, but accepted them as imperfect compromises with their Bank partners. Many said that, left to carry out their own research and write their own reports, citizens' networks would have produced papers more sharp-edged and critical of the adjustment programmes in their respective countries, but that the SAPRI reports did capture for them the essence and many of the particulars of the problems faced by affected populations. Government officials, including those from finance ministries, were also accepting of the final SAPRI outputs and often supportive of civil society positions.

The national SAPRI reports were approved in principle by all the parties at the Second National Fora.

The Bank, too, publicly accepted the reports at the SAPRI Fora after expressing disagreements on particular points in some of the sessions. In fact, all the submitted reports were approved, at least in principle, by all the parties at the Fora, though often with instructions to the technical teams to integrate the Fora input as much as possible into the final documents, and, in a couple of cases, to have the researchers carry out additional work. In the case of Bangladesh, the independent SAPRI secretariat in that country was left the task after the Forum of incorporating some of the Bank's critiques of the joint report before its publication. Overall, however, there was general approval of, if not total agreement on, the assessments at the Fora, but the Bank did not commit itself as to what it was prepared to do with the country findings or to any concrete action.

World Bank Distances Itself from the Emerging SAPRI Findings

From the earliest stages of SAPRI it was clear that the commitment by President Wolfensohn to engage civil society in an equal and constructive partnership would not translate into an easy relationship with the Bank. The civil society negotiators understood that the president, in engaging some of the strongest critics of his institution, was involving them in a potentially long-drawn-out initiative, possibly without clear resolution. This belief received some confirmation in the negotiating process when the Bank attempted to convert SAPRI from the participatory exercise proposed by NGOs to a longer-term research programme. Nevertheless, it was felt by those organizations that, not only would SAPRI legitimize a voice for civil society in economic policy making and enable the mobilization of local organizations around the issue, but it would also, if professionally and objectively carried out in a truly participatory manner, yield findings that reflected the experiences and perspectives of people struggling under adjustment programmes.

> **The commitment by Wolfensohn to engage civil society in an equal partnership would not translate into an easy relationship with the Bank.**

While a mutually respectful relationship developed between the SAPRIN secretariat and the Bank counterpart in its Policy Research Department that allowed the professional organization of the Initiative during the project preparation stage, problems started to emerge, particularly in the Latin American Vice-Presidency, when it became clear that SAPRI would be a serious endeavour in which the Bank could be held accountable to findings. Governments, too, began to understand the risk of involvement, caught as they would be between the popular expectations that would be raised by such an assessment and the unlikelihood that the Bank and the IMF would allow them to change economic course in response to citizen pressure. El Salvador bailed out. Latin American emerging-market countries, buoyed by support from the Bank's Regional Vice-President, kept their distance. And the Bank's Managing Director, acting for Wolfensohn, reflected the institution's ambiguous commitment to the Initiative by failing to resolve these disputes, end Bank bureaucratic delays, and ensure broad-based government involvement, beyond finance ministries, in the field exercises.

Regardless, on the strength of the global guidelines and the country local-level organizing, the field exercises effectively moved to the Opening National Fora before it became clear that the 'new' Bank's commitment to meaningful consultation was also in question. Refusing to consider seriously as important knowledge, the personal and institutional testimony to the real-life impact of adjustment policies presented at the Fora, Washington World Bank staff made no effort (or none that it could report on to SAPRIN) to integrate this vast amount of potential learning into internal decision-making processes at headquarters.

During the subsequent country research processes, the Bank changed its SAPRI leadership within the DEC. With that change, SAPRIN's relationship with the Bank became increasingly untenable. For six months, as the country investigations began to yield draft findings, the Bank persisted in an attempt to move the Second SAPRI Global Forum out of Washington and away from the high-profile public format previously agreed upon. Round-table discussions with Bank staff would, in this scenario, replace a public consideration of findings and follow-up action with Wolfensohn and Bank management. Attempts by SAPRIN to reach a compromise that retained the essence of the original agreement failed, and the Bank moved to block the release of European government funds destined for SAPRIN and the completion of the country exercises. After extraordinary means were used, successfully, by SAPRIN to obtain the release of the funds, the Bank announced that it would soon be terminating its involvement in SAPRI.

Recognizing both its obligations to SAPRI participants, who expected that their articulated experience with structural adjustment policies would be given due consideration in Washington, and the lack of Bank seriousness in meaningful engagement with populations affected by its policies, SAPRIN's global Steering Committee decided to participate in a round-table meeting at Bank headquarters in July 2001, before the institution's imposed deadline, but also to organize a public Global Forum, or Fora, at which it would release the final results of the joint Initiative. While the Bank had insisted upon, and fully participated in, collaborative efforts throughout all phases of the SAPRI process, it chose to leave it to SAPRIN to synthesize the joint national reports into a final global report. SAPRIN's multi-country team sorted through mounds of completed and semi-completed national reports and rapidly summarized four years of work from nine countries. It presented this draft synthesis to Bank officials at the round-table meeting in accordance with the latter's agreement and commitment to discuss, at the highest levels of the institution, concrete changes in macroeconomic policy and policy making based on field findings and conclusions. SAPRIN received no such feedback from Bank management at the meeting. In fact, senior Bank managers failed to participate in discussions of the report's findings with the twenty SAPRIN representatives who had travelled to Washington for the meeting, and the Bank officially withdrew from SAPRI as the report was delivered.

Elaborating the Results of the Global Policy Assessment

While the Bank chose to disengage from SAPRI, SAPRIN moved to ensure that the findings from this joint investigation with the Bank into the effects of structural adjustment reached interested parties in official circles and in civil society. The draft synthesis, prepared hurriedly by SAPRIN representatives from ten countries to meet the Bank's imposed deadline, was expanded with the integration of additional material from the country reports and National Fora and infused with the rich and diverse learning gleaned from the country exercises and from SAPRIN's interaction with the Bank. The completed report, *The Policy Roots of Economic Crisis and Poverty*, was released in April 2002 in Brussels at a press conference and a public forum at the European Union. The significance of the report and its findings as products of a public and transparent process over which the World Bank had co-ownership led to the decision to update and publish the report in the form of this book.

While it is a synthesis of the results of nine sets of country studies in seven policy areas, this book does not pretend to be exhaustive in presenting the work undertaken, as it was not possible to include all that was produced in each country or to do justice to some issues that were extensively covered in particular investigations. Neither is this work meant to be a standard cross-country analysis, as not every study contained the same depth of information or addressed the same set of issues. Furthermore, given the different experiences and conditions at the country level and the range of actors involved in the SAPRI and CASA processes, as well as the fact that the national teams developed a variety of means they deemed best suited to their local context for carrying out broad consultations and applying the non-traditional SAPRI methodology, each national investigation had a richness uniquely its own that was not easily comparable across countries.

Most researchers will agree that there is no single best way of examining complex realities and interdependent relationships. The SAPRI endeavour undertaken with the Bank was designed methodologically to shed a different light on the impacts of adjustment by, for the most part, leaving aside a traditional macroeconomic analysis that relies on aggregate averages and, instead, basing its analysis on the perspectives and assessments of the stakeholders and social actors themselves. It draws its validity, not from statistical or econometric analysis, although such methods were used for aspects of the country studies, but rather from the valuable information gleaned from a broad-based and highly participatory process of public consultations and research designed to highlight the differentiated nature of policy impacts, particularly with regard to those sectors and populations at the margin. It is intended to be a unique complement to the increasing number of studies on structural adjustment, many of which have raised serious questions about these programmes.

The SAPRI endeavour draws its validity from the participatory process of public consultations and research.

The book is organized around the adjustment policies prioritized by local populations for examination as to their impact on particular sectors and groups. *Chapter 2* presents an assessment of trade liberalization measures and focuses on their impact on the manufacturing sector, particularly the differentiated effects on various subsectors and population groups. *Chapter 3* discusses liberalization measures in the financial sector, assessing their distributional impact and their effect on a country's productive apparatus, particularly small and medium-size enterprises. *Chapter 4* looks at how adjustment policies overall have affected employment and assesses, in particular, the impact of labour market reform and flexibilization policies on working people. The privatization of both public utilities and publicly owned industries is examined in *Chapter 5*, which looks at the varied economic outcomes of this measure, as well as its differentiated effects on employment, access to essential utilities and the distribution of wealth. *Chapter 6* focuses on the agricultural sector, assessing the impact of a range of adjustment measures on farmers' incomes and production, as well as on food security, with an emphasis on how the effects vary depending on socio-economic group. Reforms carried out in the mining sector are addressed in *Chapter 7*, which examines the net economic outcome, as well as the social and environmental impacts on local and indigenous communities. *Chapter 8* assesses public expenditure reform and discusses trends in public spending on services, particularly education and healthcare, with a focus on access to quality services by low-income groups and effects on poverty and inequality. Finally, *Chapter 9* addresses the relationship between adjustment pro-grammes and poverty and inequality, a common denominator across all the countries involved in this investigation. Given the almost total absence of an analysis of this relationship in current Bank-supported poverty assessments, these findings take on added significance. The chapter concludes with the suggestion of new policy approaches that emanate from civil society's participation in this process and with an assessment of the World Bank's conformance with the commitments of its president to take follow-up actions on the findings of SAPRI.

CHAPTER 2

Trade Liberalization Policies and Their Impact on the Manufacturing Sector

Trade liberalization, an integral element of the structural adjustment package promoted by the Bretton Woods institutions, is based on the neoclassical notion of high relative supply elasticities that elicit speedy and sizeable responses in investment and output under improved price incentives and free markets. The neoliberals justify liberalization of trade on the premise that competition from imports leads to specialization and efficient allocation of resources while cleansing the economy of inefficient producers, thus removing the burden on society of sustaining such entities. With greater openness, small economies, it is argued, tend to have higher shares of trade in their gross national product (GNP) than do large countries and gain more than those nations that restrict trade. Furthermore, it is said, trade liberalization enhances the welfare of consumers and reduces poverty as consumers find opportunities to choose from a wide variety of quality goods and cheaper imports.

The trade–welfare nexus, however, is not automatic; rather it depends on factors such as the sequencing and phasing of liberalization, as well as built-in mechanisms for distributing such benefits. Critics of conventional wisdom contend that the world trading environment is grossly uneven and characterized by unequal exchange, transfer-pricing practices, manipulation of prices by monopolies, imperfect competition, etcetera. Under such circumstances trade liberalization, in the absence of policies and institutions to ensure equitable distribution, results in hardships and an increase in poverty.

It is against this backdrop of ongoing policy discourse that the World Bank adopted its trade and industrial policy reforms, derived from the neo-classical critique of import-competing industrialization.

This chapter seeks to summarize the information and analyses on the impact of trade liberalization contained in seven of the country assessments prepared under SAPRI and CASA. The five SAPRI countries are Bangladesh, Ecuador, Ghana, Zimbabwe and Hungary, while Mexico and the Philippines are the CASA countries.

Trade liberalization measures were launched in most of these countries during the mid- or late 1980s and continued into the early 1990s. In this context, the major analytical approach deployed in the country studies is 'before and after' or 'pre- and post-' comparison. Given the fundamental mandate of SAPRI, however, the studies have highlighted the concerns of the disadvantaged segments of society in these countries, whose voices are not usually heard at the policy level. All country research utilized a range of participatory techniques, including focus group discussions and interviews to collect data from business and labour leaders, as well as workers and communities most affected by trade liberalization. In addition, a primary survey was carried out in Ghana to assess survival strategies of firms. In Zimbabwe, case studies were done in four different industrial sectors: woodwork and furniture, textile and clothing, crafts, and metal.

This section provides a brief overview of key characteristics of the sample countries. The second section presents the design of the reforms, including the policy instruments utilized at the country level. The next section analyzes the impacts of trade policy reforms at the aggregate and sectoral levels. This is followed by discussion of the distributional impacts of these reforms before the chapter ends with a few concluding observations.

The countries under study are diverse, ranging from upper-middle-income to low-income, posing a challenge to any attempt to reach general conclusions. Three countries – Bangladesh, Ghana and Zimbabwe – fall in the low-income category, as classified by the World Bank, while by the same measure the Philippines and Ecuador are lower-middle-income countries, and Mexico and Hungary are upper-middle-income (Table 2.1). As regards population, Bangladesh is the most populous nation and has the lowest *per capita* gross domestic product (GDP) amongst the seven sample countries. Mexico has the highest *per capita* income and merchandise exports and imports in absolute terms.

All the countries have one thing in common – merchandise imports as a percentage of GDP are above the level of product exports. With regard to degree of openness (the ratio of the sum of exports and imports to GDP), at one extreme is Hungary (106.5 per cent), as that country's total volume of exports and imports was greater than the corresponding GDP in 1998. At the other end of this range lies Bangladesh, where exports and imports together account for a quarter of its GDP.

Merchandise imports were greater than product exports in all the participating countries.

Such a diverse set of sample countries implies that the initial conditions under which trade liberalization was carried out were also significantly

Table 2.1 • SAPRI/CASA Countries: Profile by Selected Indicators

Country classification by level of income		Population (millions) 1999	GDP US$m 1999	GDP per capita US$	Merchandise exports		Merchandise imports		Degree of openness
					US$m 1998	Exports as % of GDP	US$m 1998	Imports as % of GDP	
A. Low income	Bangladesh	128	45779	358	3831	8.96	6974	16.30	25.26
	Ghana	19	7606	400	1700	22.66	1850	24.66	47.33
	Zimbabwe	12	5716	476	2111	35.73	2772	46.92	82.65
B. Lower-middle-income	Philippines	77	75350	979	8068	12.39	31496	48.38	60.78
	Ecuador	12	18712	1559	4203	21.26	5576	28.21	49.47
C. Upper-middle-income	Hungary	10	48355	4836	22995	50.29	25705	56.22	106.51
	Mexico	97	474951	4896	40711	10.35	130811	33.27	43.62

Note: Bangladesh is the only Least Developed Country.
Source: World Bank. *World Development Report 2001.* Washington, DC: World Bank.

different. For example, in the case of Hungary, trade liberalization measures were part of systemic changes, whereas in most of the other countries they were part of a package to address external disequilibrium (and, partly, internal crisis). It may be also noted that in some cases trade liberalization took place in connection with the concerned country – the Philippines, Mexico and Zimbabwe, respectively – joining the World Trade Organization (WTO), its predecessor, the General Agreement on Tariffs and Trade (GATT), or a regional trading bloc.

Design of Trade Policy Reforms

Objectives of the reforms

The major objectives presented at the outset of the process of trade and industrial policy reform in the SAPRI/CASA countries were: achievement of efficiency in the traded goods sector; facilitation of the import of industrial inputs to encourage industrial production; provision of export credit; and encouragement of growth and diversification of non-traditional exports

Table 2.2 • General Objectives of the Trade and Industrial Policy Reforms as Outlined in the Policy Framework Papers

Areas of reform	Policy objectives
Tariff structure	• Improvement of efficiency in trade and enhancement of gains from trade • Reduction of disparities of effective protection to enhance efficiency in domestic production
Import restrictions	• Facilitation of import of raw materials, intermediate goods and capital goods to stimulate domestic industrial production
Export promotion	• Stimulation of growth and diversification of non-traditional exports • Improvement in export finance • Promotion of backward linkages
Exchange rate management	• Strengthening of the balance-of-payments position • Unification of dual exchange markets to reduce distortions
Investment sanctioning	• Liberalization and simplification of investment procedures to encourage greater flow of foreign investment

Source: D. Bhattacharya and R. A. M. Titumir *Bangladesh's Experience with Structural Adjustment*, Bangladesh, (2001). http:www.saprin.org/bangladesh/research/BDS.pdf

(Table 2.2). These objectives were to be achieved through pursuing strategies such as: rationalization of the import regime; reduction of customs duty rates and levels of effective protection; simplification of the tariff structure and removal of special tariff concessions and exemptions; liberalization of imports; and elimination of export subsidies.

Policy design

The policies pursued to liberalize trade were not new, but the bundling of such policies in a package resulted from the adoption by developing countries of structural adjustment, a new macroeconomic approach of the 1980s that relied completely on market forces and private enterprise. The principal instrument of trade liberalization was and is the rationalization of the import regime, which contains measures such as the elimination of import quotas, the reduction and unification of tariffs, and removal of special tariff concessions and exemptions. The World Bank reasons that tariff structures in developing countries require a massive restructuring with a view to removing an anti-export bias that, according to these institutions, discourages the development of an export-oriented economy. It is argued that the elimination of quotas and the reduction of the level of protection are intended to make the domestic economy and surviving firms more competitive in export markets, though the drastic lowering of protection has real costs in exposing local producers to fierce competition. The implementation of a flexible exchange rate policy is another integral and complementary part of trade liberalization, as frequent downward adjustments of national currencies maintain the competitive advantage of exports and discourage excessive imports.

Table 2.3 provides a summary of instruments that have been utilized to liberalize the trade regimes of the seven sample countries. The rest of this subsection reviews these policy instruments and their pace of implementation at the country level.

Bangladesh

The government of Bangladesh adopted trade policy reforms in 1986–7 under a three-year, medium-term adjustment programme, though elements of the reform agenda started to appear in the World Bank-sponsored Import Programme Credits of the mid-1970s. Trade policy reforms have included the elimination of quantitative restrictions, rationalization of the tariff structure, simplification of import procedures, exchange rate liberalization and various measures to stimulate export growth.

The speed of liberalization in Bangladesh has appeared to be fast by South Asian standards. The numbers of the four-digit Harmonized System Codes subject to quantitative restrictions have been reduced from 478 in 1985 to

Table 2.3 • SAPRI/CASA Countries: Scenario of Trade Liberalization

Country	Period	Instruments
Bangladesh	• During 1972–86, the government contracted 13 Import Programme Credits with the World Bank. • In 1986–7 the government adopted a medium-term adjustment programme administered under a three-year arrangement of the IMF's Structural Adjustment Facility (SAF). • An Extended Structural Adjustment Facility (ESAF) was in force during 1990–3.	• Rationalization of the import regime (e.g., elimination of quantitative restrictions) • Reduction of duty rates of customs • Reduction of levels of effective protection • Simplification of the tariff structure • Removal of special tariff concessions and exemptions • Liberalization of imports • Elimination of export subsidies
Ghana	Economic Recovery Programme (ERP), 1983	• Tariff adjustments • Liberalization of imports • Liberalization of the exchange rate • Deregulation of controls on domestic market prices • Institutional reforms of revenue-generating bodies, such as Customs and Excise
Philippines	• In the 1980s, the Philippines government embarked on structural adjustment. • A five-year Tariff Reform Programme (TRP1) began in 1981. • Another trade liberalization programme was implemented in 1986–9. • Tariff Reform Programme (TRP2) was launched in 1991 for five years. • The third phase of the Tariff Reform Programme began in 1996.	• Phased abolition of quantitative restrictions on import items, and reduction of tariffs, from 100 per cent to 50 per cent • Abolition of export tax • Reduction of import restrictions, removal of import licensing requirements or outright import bans • Introduction of anti-dumping and countervailing duty mechanisms
Hungary	• The Hungarian Socialist Workers' Party decided to begin rapid import liberalization in July 1988 with the launch of a four-year programme (January 1989–1992) to liberalize the nation's trading regime.	• Import liberalization • Releasing state authority on trade activities to enable any competent enterprise to engage in foreign trade • Transition from ruble to dollar accounting

Zimbabwe	• Three phases of trade liberalization started in 1991 within the context of the Economic Structural Adjustment Programme (ESAP) of the Bretton Woods institutions. • Further liberalization followed within the contexts of WTO, regional blocs and bilateral agreements. • ESAP was succeeded by the Zimbabwe Programme for Economic and Social Transformation (ZIMPREST) in 1998–2000.	• Removal of export incentives • Phasing out of the import-licensing regime • Elimination of foreign currency controls • Reduction of tariffs to a band ranging from 0 to 30 per cent • Removal of surtax and raising of the minimum duty to 10 per cent
Ecuador	• In 1980 trade liberalization policies were introduced. • From 1990 to 1995, financial liberalization policies were adopted through a package of economic, legal and institutional reforms aimed at either weakening or dismantling prior public regulations and controls. • In 1990, labour reform policy was undertaken.	• Devaluation of exchange rates in favour of export-related enterprises • Reduction of tariff rates to eliminate the protection given to domestic enterprises • Expanding the capital account liberalization programme • Liberalization of labour policy
Mexico	• The onset of the unravelling of the state's functions as a direct producer and regulator of the economy took place in 1982. • Entry into GATT in 1987 and NAFTA in 1994 required implementation of a series of trade liberalization measures.	• Import liberalization of basic goods • Reduction of protectionist barriers

124 in 2000. There were 24 tariff slabs in the early 1980s, which were brought down to five. The number of banned items was reduced from 135 in 1990 to only five at the end of the decade. The maximum tariff rate was dropped from 350 per cent in 1991 to 37.5 per cent in 2000. The tariff structure has been further compressed by reducing the number of end-user-based tariff concessions. The share of zero-rated items in total imports (excluding export processing zones and the system of back-to-back letters of credit) rose from 11 per cent in 1992 to 33 per cent in 1999, although it declined to 25 per cent in 2000.

During the 1990s, direct export incentives were further strengthened. The special bonded warehouse facility has been extended to all exporters and deemed exporters. The duty drawback facility allows exporters to get refunds of duties/taxes paid on imported inputs. The import of raw materials and capital machinery has been made duty-free for fully export-oriented industries. Cash compensation of 25 per cent of the freight-on-board value of exports is provided in lieu of the duty drawback and bonded warehouse facility. Exporters also enjoy income tax rebates, tax holidays of five to seven years or accelerated depreciation allowances at the rate of 80–100 per cent. The ceiling for foreign currency retention by exporters has been increased to 40 per cent. Export procedures have been simplified by allowing export without a letter of credit but on the basis of a purchase contract, agreement, purchase order or advance payment.

Trade liberalization has increased economic openness and reduced the anti-export bias. The economic openness index rose from 19 per cent in 1991 to about 35 per cent in 1999. The unweighted average customs duty rate was reduced from 88.6 per cent in 1991 to 16.7 per cent in 2000. The unweighted average nominal protection rate for all tradables declined from about 87 per cent to 24.7 per cent during the above period. The average effective protection rate came down from 75.7 per cent in 1993 to 24.5 per cent in 2000. The sharpest reduction in the unweighted average tariff has occurred for capital goods (69 per cent), followed by that for intermediate inputs (52 per cent), consumer goods (48 per cent) and primary commodities (48 per cent). A similar trend is observed for weighted average tariffs.

The Philippines

Reversing its previous import substitution strategy, the Philippine government moved to liberalize its trading regime in the 1980s. Trade liberalization was progressively pushed through in three phases.

The Marcos administration in 1981 began a major trade reform programme, known as the Tariff Reform Programme (TRP1), with a five-year import liberalization plan to reduce import restrictions and an indirect tax realignment scheme. All tariff rates were reduced to a range from 0–50 per cent, which significantly brought down both the average nominal tariff and tariff dispersion across industries. The average nominal tariff fell from 42 per cent in 1981 to 28 per cent at the end of TRP1. This was part of the government's first structural adjustment programme under the World Bank's structural adjustment loans SAL I and II, and a standby credit from the IMF.

The Aquino administration undertook extensive import liberalization that continued and intensified the trade reform process during 1986–9. The export tax on all products except logs was abolished. Import restrictions, mainly in the form of import-licensing requirements or an outright import ban, were reduced. The number of restricted import items as a percentage of the total number of lines in the Philippine Standard Commodity Classification was reduced from around 35 per cent in 1985 to 7.5 per cent in 1989. Tariff restrictions on 1,471 items were lifted during that period.

Reversing its previous import substitution strategy, the Philippines government moved to liberalize its trading regime in the 1980s.

In 1990, the government attempted to carry out a new Trade Reform Programme through Executive Order (EO) 413. A new tariff system was conceived that included the narrowing of the tariff range to 3–30 per cent, the elimination of specific duties and the simplification of the tariff nomenclature. However, an order was signed on 30 August 1990 suspending the implementation of EO 413.

Subsequently, the government launched a tariff reform programme in 1991 with the issuance of Executive Order 470, also called Trade Reform Programme 2 (TRP2). Tariff rates were realigned over a five-year period. The restructuring involved narrowing the range of the tariff rate structure through a series of reductions in the number of commodity lines with high tariffs and an increase in the commodity lines with low tariffs, within the range of 10–30 per cent, by 1995. Outside this range, there were 43 lines coming in at zero rate and 208 lines with 50 per cent tariff. The duty-free items were mainly capital goods. Those with 50 per cent tariff were mainly agricultural and industrial products covered by the Board of Investments local-content programmes.

The Ramos administration continued to liberalize trade, consistent with its policy thrust of global competitiveness. The third phase of the Trade Reform Programme was implemented with Executive Order 264. In 1993, several executive orders were issued to further liberalize the trade regime. With the ratification in 1995 of the Uruguay Round of GATT, the Philippines committed itself to binding 2,800 industrial and 744 agricultural tariff lines.

Zimbabwe

Beginning in 1991, Zimbabwe undertook unilateral measures to liberalize its trade regime within the context of the Economic Structural Adjustment Programme (ESAP), with assistance from the World Bank and IMF. These measures were followed by further liberalization within the multilateral context (WTO) and the regional framework (Southern African Development Community, SADC, and the Common Market for Eastern and Southern Africa, COMESA), as well as at a bilateral level. Zimbabwe entered its second phase of trade liberalization within the Zimbabwe Programme for Economic and Social Transformation (ZIMPREST), the successor to ESAP, as well as the new WTO trade negotiations, the Lomé Convention, SADC and COMESA.

The main objective of ESAP in the area of trade was liberalization, including the abolition of quantitative controls and the reduction and harmonization of tariffs and duties. Specific objectives of the trade liberalization programme have included: removal of export incentives; phasing out of the import-licensing regime; elimination of foreign currency controls; reduction of tariffs to create a tariff band ranging from 0 to 30 per cent; removal of surtaxes; raising the minimum duty to 10 per cent; and achieving an export growth rate of 9 per cent a year over five years beginning in 1991.

The *first phase,* spanning 1991–3, began with the devaluation of the Zimbabwean dollar in August 1991, followed by continued depreciation of the currency. The *second phase* (1993–5) started with the placing of most goods on an Open General Import Licence (OGIL) and the removal of export incentives. All imports were placed on OGIL except those that are regarded as strategic, such as fuels. The *third phase* in 1995 coincided with the implementation of commitments Zimbabwe had made within the framework of the WTO – tariffs were significantly reduced and non-tariff barriers were converted into tariff equivalents, allowing the controls to move towards using only tariffs for protection. The foreign exchange regime was further liberalized, leading to currency convertibility. Important export incentives that served as lifelines for some firms were removed, with the exception of the duty drawback and export-financing schemes. The final phase of trade liberalization saw the implementation of the Export Processing Zones (EPZs) programme. ZIMPREST sought to further deepen trade liberalization measures adopted under ESAP.

During the ESAP period, Zimbabwe fully implemented the trade policy liberalization component of the economic programme. Since 1998, however, there has been a divergence between official policy and practice. Within ZIMPREST (1998–2000), and even the Millennium Economic Recovery Programme (MERP), the official position on trade has been further liberalization, yet in practice the government has taken several measures that indicate trade policy reversals. These include the tariff ratio-nalization programme of 1998, Zimbabwe's mid-loading of tariffs within the SADC trade protocol, the removal of several tariff exemptions, and the proposed re-introduction of price controls.

Ghana

In Ghana, trade policy reform has been central to the adjustment process, which was activated in the context of economic crisis in the late 1970s and early 1980s. The reforms have included tariff adjustments, the liberalization of imports and foreign exchange, deregulation of domestic market prices, and controls and institutional reforms that particularly affected revenue-generating bodies such as Customs and Excise. Trade liberalization in Ghana was carried out in two phases. The first phase was effected under the Economic Recovery Programme I (ERP I, 1983–6), which was aimed at economic stabilization, while the second was implemented as part of the Economic Recovery Programme II (ERP II, 1986–91), which was geared towards consolidation and expansion.

Ecuador

Trade liberalization policies were introduced in Ecuador at the beginning of the 1980s. Acting in response to global economic circumstances, as well as to domestic crisis, the government used exchange rate policy through various devaluations to control imports and foster exports, particularly primary products from the agrarian sector. The sucre–dollar exchange rate increased 899 times from 1980 to 2000, at which time the economy was dollarized. Beginning in 1986, the government implemented measures to open the country's trade regime by lowering and partially unifying tariffs in order to eliminate protection for some domestic economic activities and reducing the list of banned imports from 600 to 200.

Trade liberalization was accelerated in the first half of the 1990s. Measures were adopted to eliminate quantitative restrictions and dramatically reduce tariffs, decreasing the range of effective protection from a maximum of 75 per cent to 35 per cent, as well as to eliminate all existing surcharges. By 1994, a 0–20 per cent tariff range was in effect (except for autos, which main-tained a 37 per cent tariff), with an average tariff rate of 11 per cent.

At the same time as tariff reforms were implemented, measures aimed at deregulation dismantled non-tariff barriers in order to further open the trading system in preparation for the country's entry into the WTO. Various administrative procedures were simplified, lists of import excep-tions were phased out and administrative requirements were eliminated for the import of agricultural products, machinery and other inputs. Export taxes on traditional products were eliminated, and port taxes were reduced by 25 per cent, with each port then given the freedom to establish its rates independently.

In summary, by 1995, extensive reforms had been successfully put in place to liberalize the trade regime in Ecuador. Prior to 1990, average tariffs were greater than 40 per cent, while non-tariff barriers were estimated to be more than 55 per cent of products' value. Following the reforms, Ecuador was considered to have one of the most open trade regimes in Latin America.

Mexico

Trade liberalization began in Mexico in the mid-1980s with the reduction of protectionist barriers, particularly on basic goods, as a means of increasing supply and putting downward pressure on prices to control inflation. The process accelerated with the country's entry into GATT in 1987, when a series of measures were implemented that unleashed a flood of imports, leading to a trade deficit that reached nearly US$4.7 billion in late 2000. The increase in imports displaced national production for the domestic market, as liberalization policies were not accompanied by industrial or credit policies to modernize production, level the playing field or otherwise provide support for the large number of micro, small and medium-scale enterprises that had made up a large part of the country's productive apparatus. The implementation of the North American Free Trade Agreement (NAFTA) with the United States and Canada in 1994 has exacerbated this situation. The myth of Mexico as a growing exporter is unmasked by the fact that the vast majority of manufacturing inputs are imported, while only 15 per cent of exports (oil and agrarian products) have a high level of national content.

Hungary

In Hungary, preliminary steps towards market orientation were taken before the political change that began in the late 1970s. Economic change accelerated with the reformist government that assumed power at the end of the 1980s, and rapid deregulation and liberalization took place during 1988–90. The trade liberalization programme in Hungary was undertaken as a part of the 1989–92 Four Year Programme.

Hungary embarked upon the liberalization process with such speed that the World Bank itself, in its evaluation of the adjustment loan, SAL I, in June 1993, said that 'in the area of trade liberalization, Hungary's speed of adjustment was comparable to that of countries which applied shock therapy (Czechoslovakia and Poland)'. Hungary embarked on something unprecedented, both in the transition economies and in a wider international context: the exceptionally rapid elimination of quantitative restrictions on imports without the temporary enhancement of customs protection amidst a declining level of tariffs.

Summary

The foregoing review of the policy designs of trade liberalization in the seven sample countries clearly brings forth their standard features. Irrespective of their contextual diversities, a one-size-fits-all type of reform programme was implemented in all the countries. Second, although trade liberalization measures were designed as a part of an overall policy package, they were the part of the package that was most expeditiously implemented in all the sample countries. Third, none of the liberalization programmes had any built-in provisions for compensation: they had neither safety net schemes nor support mechanisms for the people who would potentially be affected by reform-induced policy shocks.

Trade liberalization was implemented as a one-size-fits-all type of reform programme in all the countries.

Macro and Sectoral Outcomes of Trade Policy Reforms

Keeping in mind the stated objectives of trade liberalization under Bank/Fund-sponsored adjustment programmes, the present section traces the outcomes of the reforms at the aggregate level in the following areas: (1) export growth and diversification; and (2) growth in industrial capacity and competitiveness.

External trade

The original stated goal of the trade policy reforms had been to integrate developing economies into the world economy through pursuance of an export-led development strategy as opposed to the inward-looking one of the post-World War era. The policy reforms were carried out on the promise that the economies would benefit from dynamic efficiencies generated by free trade.

Although the studies showed that exports grew in most of the countries following trade liberalization, this export growth was very narrowly based on a few national resources and items produced with low-skill labour. Moreover, export growth was underpinned by continued import growth and falling terms of trade. As a result, trade deficits as well as current account deficits increased, with a consequent adverse impact on the size of external debt. Furthermore, trade liberalization was paralleled by a proliferation of informal trade, as well as by an increase in cross-border illegal trade. Finally, in many countries the benefits of export growth went primarily to transnational corporations at the cost of domestic producers.

Export growth following trade liberalization was very narrowly based, resulting in trade and current account deficits and worsening debt.

A number of constraints have been identified to explain the lack of export competitiveness of domestic manufacturing firms. They include: poor infrastructure; high transaction costs of entering the international market; lack of technical experience in competitive marketing; difficulties in obtaining export finance; restrictive policies occasioned by the business environment; and lack of capacity to take advantage of the trade regime of the WTO.

Export growth and GDP share

Trade liberalization policies were supposedly aimed at expanding the growth rates of exports. In most of the sample countries, export growth accelerated during the post-liberalization period. Yet, while the share of total exports of the sample countries in GDP rose when compared to the pre-adjustment period, the rate of increase was far from satisfactory and has not been able to put any dent in the trade deficits of these countries.

In Ecuador, for example, the share of exports in GDP rose from 21.5 per cent in 1980 to 25.8 per cent in 1990. At the same time, however, the total value of exports fell from US$2.52 billion in 1980 to US$2.35 billion at the end of the decade, failing to meet an anticipated export growth. The increase in exports' share of GDP can be accounted for more by an absolute fall of GDP rather than by a better performance of the exporting sector in the 1980s. Participants at the SAPRI Opening National Forum explained that, while large exporters have depended on devaluation rather than improved productive capacity to enhance their competitiveness, much of this competitiveness has been lost to the taking of large profits.

Bangladesh had only limited integration with the world economy prior to adjustment, and exports accounted for just 7.4 per cent of GDP. The period following adjustment reforms saw a modest increase in exports, with their overall contribution to GDP reaching only 9.7 per cent.

As the Zimbabwe Opening National Forum participants stressed, domestic businesses have often been insufficiently prepared to compete in global markets when liberalization measures have been taken. The result in Zimbabwe has been the failure to generate the foreign currency anticipated and to stimulate the economy. Real GDP growth during 1992–7, the period following trade liberalization, was 3.2 per cent as compared with a rate of 5.3 per cent in the period 1985–91, prior to the implementation of the structural adjustment programme.

While overall performance of manufacturing exports has not been strong, some countries experienced a modest export growth in the post-adjustment period. In the Philippines, the share of exports in GDP was 23 per cent in 1982 and grew to 52 per cent in 1997, recording a much better supply response than other countries in the study.

Diversification
The disaggregated data on the trade performance of the sample countries show either a high degree of concentration in a subsector or growth emanating from subsectors that already had established markets. It is evident, however, that traditional sectors have not performed well at all. More importantly, a large segment of the leading manufacturing activities suffered significantly, provoking output contraction, retrenchment of employees and bankruptcy of enterprises.

Manufacturing activities suffered significantly, provoking output contraction, job loss and enterprise bankruptcies.

In Ecuador, a marked differentiation was observed in the exports of primary and manufactured products. In the 1980s, exports of manufactured goods declined more than 40 per cent, from US$626 million in 1980 to US$367 million in 1990. This drop in Ecuadorean manufactured exports, an important impact stemming from adjustment policies during the decade, occurred within a period in which the world trade of manufactured goods was growing at three times the pace of trade in primary products. At the same time, Ecuadorean exports of primary commodities (bananas, cacao, etcetera) grew at an annual average rate of 2.7 per cent, increasing from US$1.85 billion in 1980 to US$2.34 billion in 1990. While other countries, including neighbours such as Colombia, were developing and strengthening their industry, Ecuador was concentrating on increasingly intensive exploitation of its natural resources. Instead of relieving the country's external debt burden, this pattern of trade had the opposite effect, as the ratio of external debt to total exports rose from 183 per cent in 1980 to 490 per cent in 1990.

In Zimbabwe, three major outcomes relating to manufacturing export performance emerged during the ESAP period. First, agro-processing emerged as a high-growth subsector in 1990–5, with dairy products recording 18.5 per cent average growth, meat products 21 per cent, grain foodstuffs 40.2 per cent, other foodstuffs 11 per cent and beverages 86.2 per cent. This indicates the potential of Zimbabwe's agricultural base to generate export competitiveness in an open market economy and in the absence of serious externalities. Second, traditional and high-technology industries emerged as low-growth subsectors. The worst performers among traditional exports were: iron and steel, with 21 per cent *negative* growth; ferro alloys, with 6.7 per cent growth; textiles, with 7.3 per cent growth; and clothing, with 11.2 per cent growth. High-technology exports, such as machinery, electrical machinery and transport equipment, experienced slow growth, revealing the country's technological weaknesses. Finally, resource-based manufactured exports such as metal products, leather, hides, wood and furniture responded positively to economic liberalization. Exceptional growth of 130 per cent for jewellery exports is a result of the very low initial base.

In Bangladesh, the share of ready-made garments (woven, as well as knit) in total manufactured exports climbed from 54.6 per cent in 1990/1 to 75.8 per cent in 1997/8, indicating that export-oriented manufacturing activity over time was highly concentrated in the clothing-assembly sector. Thus, Bangladesh's apparent success in export promotion remains a 'single activity wonder' underpinned by the peculiar global textile trade regime (in this case, the quota system of the Multi-Fibre Arrangement, due to expire in 2005).

Ghana's manufactured exports earned US$3.5 million in 1986 and increased to US$14.7 million in 1991. This tends to suggest that there was dynamic growth of manufacturing in a more competitive environment in which, as expected, there was a shift of resources from inefficient to efficient enterprises. However, disaggregated data show that the growth came mainly from domestic resource-based firms that already had established markets (the leading performers were the wood and aluminium companies that already had long experience in international trade). Available information from the Ghana Export Promotion Council relating to non-traditional exports shows that the absolute value of the exports involved was extremely small.

In the Philippines, the major winners in terms of growth rates and export share were electronic and electrical equipment and parts, as well as the machinery and transport equipment sector, which has a very high import content. Among the losers were garments, footwear, wood manufactures, baby carriages, toys, games and sporting goods, basketwork, wickerwork and other articles of plaiting materials, and miscellaneous manufactured articles. Garment exports dropped drastically, their share of exports falling from 21.7 per cent of the total in 1990 to just 8 per cent in 1998, thus being replaced by machinery and equipment as the second top export earner. Meanwhile, the garments sector saw intensified competition from imported products from China and South and South-east Asia in the domestic market.

Import growth and trade deficit

Imports have been robust during and after adjustment. There has been a general trend of higher growth in imports *vis-à-vis* exports in the sample countries. In Ecuador, for example, imports grew impressively from US$1.6 billion in 1990 to US$5.1 billion in 1998. In other words, imports grew at an annual average rate of 15 per cent, which was significantly higher than the annual average rate of growth of exports (5.6 per cent). The resulting deterioration in the trade balance emanating from trade liberalization, it was pointed out at the Opening National Forum in Quito, has intensified with the flood of Asian exports into the country.

Consequently, there were causes for concern in the mismatched export–import growth that negatively impacted the trade balance and created pressure on foreign exchange reserves. In the Philippines, for example, the share of imports in GDP was 28 per cent in 1982 and grew to 64 per cent in 1997. The share of the trade deficit in GDP rose from 9 per cent to 12 per cent in 1994. In Bangladesh, imports were 19 per cent of the GDP for the entire two decades. In recent times, import levels have been rising and have been drawing down the country's foreign exchange reserves.

Composition of imports

Regarding the composition of imports, it is worth highlighting that imports of final goods and consumer goods are on the rise, while there has been a deceleration in the growth of imports of intermediate inputs and capital goods. This result indicates a decline in domestic manufacturing sectors that tend to have a greater value added.

In Ecuador, imports of consumer goods grew from US$229 million in 1990 to US$1.3 billion in 1998, a six-fold increase. Imports of non-durable goods increased from US$97 million in 1990 to US$660 million in 1998. These trends in imports are contrary to what the trade liberalization programme meant to bring about, namely, an improvement in the trade balance. The data provided by the Superintendent of Companies of Ecuador show that firms increased their imports of final goods – excluding raw materials. Thus, the total value of these goods, which could easily have been produced locally if there were adequate conditions in support of domestic industry to do so, reached US$2 billion in 1998. For example, the total expenditure on imported consumer goods increased from US$160 million in 1990 to US$738 million in 1995 alone. In other words, while the growth of exports hardly doubled between 1990 and 1995, imports of consumer goods quintupled.

In Bangladesh, the drop in imports of capital goods and intermediate inputs relative to finished products indicates a reduced capacity and lack of investment in the industrial sector, particularly in medium- and large-scale industry, given that the country is still dependent on imported machinery and equipment. The growth rate of capital goods imports in 1989/90 was 55.9 per cent, while the average annual growth rate between 1990/1 and

1997/8 dropped to about 11 per cent. Although the average annual growth rate of imports of intermediate inputs between 1990/1 and 1997/8 was nearly 8 per cent compared to 4.8 per cent in 1989/90, this can be explained by an increase in capacity utilization in the export enclave sector, primarily ready-made garment (RMG) producers. Thus, the deceleration in the growth of imports of capital goods and decline in the share of imports of intermediate inputs in total imports indicate a drop in growth of domestic manufacturing, with the exception of garment industry assembly plants that produce little value added.

Balance of payments

In the sample countries, export growth was outweighed by the expansion of imports, generating pressure on the balance of payments. In the Philippines, current account deficits shot up during the 1993–6 period, approaching 7 per cent of GDP in 1997. Only the remittances of Filipino overseas workers and decreased foreign-debt interest payments stopped it from going higher. In Mexico, there was a deterioration in the trade deficit, which amounted to about US$6 billion in 2000. During the mid-1980s, the current account deficit of Bangladesh moved to nearly 10 per cent of GDP, and, although it has since been declining on the average largely due to remittances by migrant workers, no clear patterns in the current account balance can be observed.

Terms of trade

The aim of any trade strategy is to achieve terms of trade in favour of domestic producers. During the 1990s, Bangladesh's terms of trade declined compared to that of the pre-adjustment period. In Ecuador, the terms of trade actually fell steadily during most of the 1980s, shifting from 100 in 1980 to 15.7 in 1988. Afterwards, the terms of trade index improved slightly, increasing to 16.9 in 1989 and 17.8 in 1990. As a consequence of the deterioration of the terms of trade, in 1990 Ecuador was compelled to export five times the value of 1980 exports so as to obtain the same revenue as that needed to cover the total volume of 1980 imports.

Manufacturing sector

The trade policy reforms were based on the assumption that a regular supply of imported inputs at cheaper prices, together with competition from imports of finished products, would goad the manufacturing sector to move at a faster pace. The reforms were carried out on the premise that exposure of local firms to international competition would improve their efficiency and the quality of their products, all to the benefit of the consumer. To a large degree, therefore, trade policy reforms would be successful in placing the reforming countries and their firms on a path to global competitiveness.

The Bretton Woods institutions claim that these reforms have contributed positively to export performance and enhancement of technology transfer.

It has been observed, however, in the SAPRI/CASA country experiences that, across the board, liberalization and the lack of sequencing of the trade reforms resulted in unnecessary damage to the local manufacturing sector. Fast and radical import liberalization was implemented at a time when local manufacturers were faced with severe supply-side constraints characterized by resource and management limitations. When these factors combined with exchange-rate losses suffered by many firms, and with a high cost of credit, local companies were unable to adjust to fierce external competition. As a result, it is observed that many local firms – especially small and medium-size enterprises – went out of business.

Thus, against a backdrop of narrowly based export growth, the industrialization process has faltered in all the sample countries. Fluctuating and fractured industrial growth led to either a fall in, or stagnation of, the share of the sector in GDP. More importantly, in most countries the phenomenon of deindustrialization was highly evident in the small and cottage subsector. Furthermore, a withering away of the import-competing industries was observed, while very few new areas for local manufacturing firms were visible. Exchange rate depreciation was unable to contribute effectively to the export competitiveness of the industrial sector.

Manufacturing growth and share in GDP

Reflecting an indifferent manufacturing growth observed in the seven countries under review, the performance of the manufacturing sector has not been impressive in terms of its contribution to the respective national outputs.

In Zimbabwe, manufactured value added, which peaked in 1991, fell by 12 per cent in the next seven years. The high interest rates and cost of foreign currency penalized manufacturing. The manufacturing production index (1990 = 100) indicates a decline in output of more than 20 per cent since trade liberalization commenced. Manufacturing production has been the main victim of liberalization policies introduced in 1991. During the 1990s manufacturing's share in GDP fell to less than 16 per cent for the first time since 1960, compared to an average of 25 per cent in the 1970s and 1980s. The sector has stagnated since the introduction of ESAP and the relaxation of import controls.

Manufacturing production in Zimbabwe was the main victim of trade liberalization policies, with a decline in output of more than 20 per cent.

In contrast, in Bangladesh the average growth rate of the manufacturing sector between 1993 and 2000 has been 6.8 per cent, compared to 3 per cent during the 1980s. Yet the country's manufacturing growth rates experienced high fluctuation during the 1990s. For example, for the manufacturing sector as a whole, the growth rate fell from 8.6 per cent in 1993 to 8.2 per cent the following year, but then rose to 10.5 per cent in 1995. Subsequently, the growth rate showed a declining trend for the rest of the decade, except for 1998 when it was 8.5 per cent.

At the same time, the share of total manufacturing output in GDP in Bangladesh increased only marginally, from 13.8 per cent in 1993 to 15.4 per cent in 2000, at the average annual rate of only 0.2 per cent. From the point of view of structural transformation of the economy, this can hardly be considered as healthy or satisfactory. When looking at large and medium-scale industries, it is found that their share in GDP rose from 9.8 per cent to 11.1 per cent between 1993 and 2000, implying an average annual rate of increase of 0.18 per cent. This can likewise hardly be viewed as dynamic performance. The share of small and cottage industries in GDP has virtually stagnated, rising from 4 per cent in 1993 to 4.3 per cent in 2000.

In Ghana, after the launch of the Economic Recovery Programme in 1983, the performance of the domestic manufacturing sector improved with the availability of imported inputs. The real annual growth rate of manufacturing value added rose from 12.9 per cent in 1984 to 24.3 per cent in 1985, but then fell back to 11 per cent in 1986 and 10 per cent in 1987. Since 1987, when domestic manufacturing accounted for 9.4 per cent of real GDP, the domestic sector's performance has been rather unimpressive in terms of growth, share of real GDP and industrial output.

Sectoral composition and scale of firms

Disaggregation of the manufacturing sector by activity category points to several fluctuating patterns in terms of size, spatial distribution and market orientation. Overall, import liberalization reduced or wiped out certain domestic manufacturing activities and forced many small and medium-scale enterprises out of business.

In Zimbabwe, the slowdown in manufacturing output was largely attributable to the weak performance of textiles, clothing, footwear, wood and furniture, paper, printing and publishing, and transport and equipment. The textile industry was hit particularly hard by the liberalization of trade and the consequent influx of cheap imports that forced many small and medium-sized enterprises to reduce production, go out of business or switch from manufacturing to importing in order to survive. Imported second-hand clothing flooded the local market at a time when wages were falling and consumers were forced to seek the cheapest products available, Opening

National Forum participants explained. As locally manufactured textiles were pushed out of the domestic market, several clothing and textiles firms went under and employment and wages fell significantly. The Zimbabwe Congress of Trade Unions estimates that over 15,000 people lost their jobs in this subsector from 1992 to 1997. Electronics manufacturers and workers suffered similar fates. The Forum participants stressed that there should have been a serious assessment of the ability of Zimbabwean industry to compete before trade barriers were dropped, as well as a recognition of the crippling effect that the high cost of borrowing would have on those firms that did try to upgrade their competitive capacity.

At the Opening National Forum in Mexico in 1998, it was estimated that 17,000 to 20,000 small businesses had been forced into bankruptcy as a result of trade and financial sector liberalization, dealing a severe blow to the country's productive apparatus. The precipitous removal of trade and investment barriers has caused many such Mexican enterprises to be displaced by foreign companies and the domestic content of finished goods to be reduced.

In Hungary, tens of thousands of small shops lost their viability as suppliers, it was explained at the SAPRI Opening Forum in that country, with the demise of much of the small and medium-sized enterprise sector at the hands of the country's fast-paced open-trade policy. Employing about 70 per cent of all Hungarian workers, this sector did not have the time or support needed to develop the capacity to compete with the flood of cheap, high-quality imports.

The fast-paced open-trade policy in Hungary led to the demise of much of the small and medium-sized enterprise sector.

In Bangladesh, the average growth of large and medium-scale industries during the 1990s was 7 per cent, while the growth rate of small and cottage industries was 6.4 per cent. These average growth rates may be somewhat misleading, however, as a pattern of uneven and inconsistent growth is observed for large and medium-scale industries, as well as for small and cottage industries. The growth rate of large and medium-scale industries declined from 9 per cent in 1993 to 8.3 per cent in 1994, but then rose to 11.4 per cent in 1995. Growth in the following years showed a somewhat declining trend, except for 1998; the growth rates in 1997, 1999 and 2000 were less than half that registered in 1993. For small and cottage industries, the growth rate increased consistently from 7.7 per cent in 1993 to 8.3 per cent in 1996, but then declined equally consistently to 4 per cent in 2000, although it had plummeted to 0.8 per cent in 1999 (after flood damage).

Meanwhile, in Bangladesh the share of import-substituting manufacturing output in total manufacturing output has declined rapidly over time, as seen when this ratio is compared with the ratio of total manufacturing output to GDP: manufactured exports rose from 5.2 per cent of GDP in 1990/1 to 11.7 per cent in 1997/8. Some major import-substituting industries – such as cotton textiles, sugar and paper – experienced a regression in the 1990s. During the period 1991/2–1997/8, production of cotton textiles, sugar and paper shrank by 24.2 per cent, 14.8 per cent and 48 per cent, respectively. The participants in the Opening National Forum pointed to the country's rapid reduction of tariffs, which has opened a floodgate of imports from better-financed transnational corporations, as a principal reason for the country's inability to develop its indigenous industries. At the same time, export-oriented manufacturing activity has become concentrated in the assembly of ready-made garments, whose share in total manufactured exports climbed from 54.6 per cent in FY1991 to 75.8 per cent in FY1998.

In Ghana, the firms that fared well were those with a strong local resource base (wood and beverages), cheap input sources (aluminium) and high, 'natural' protection from transport costs (cement). Also included in this group were firms that the government considered core industries, which thereby benefited from public investment in upgrading equipment (the petroleum refinery).

Capacity utilization

The modest industrial (export) growth experienced by the SAPRI/CASA countries in the face of low investment flows to the sector has been largely achieved through improvement in the capacity utilization rate. Yet increases in the capacity utilization rate have been marginal.

In Ghana, capacity utilization in the manufacturing sector increased from a low level of 18 per cent in 1984 to 40 per cent in 1988 and then fell to 38 per cent in 1989. These levels, however, are still deemed unacceptably low. Further growth in manufacturing activity requires more investment to refurbish and modernize run-down facilities. A significant proportion of production capacity had been run down to such an extent that it could no longer be used. Yet fiscal and monetary policies have not been able to encourage the investment needed to revamp existing capacity, let alone fuel an expansion of capacity. Since such investment was slow to materialize, the rate of growth of manufacturing value added fell to 5.1 per cent in 1988, 3.1 per cent in 1989 and 2.5 per cent in 1990.

In Bangladesh, the average annual growth rate of imports of capital machinery and parts during the period 1990/1–1997/8 was 11.2 per cent, compared to a growth rate of 51.5 per cent in 1989/90. The share of capital goods imports in total imports has dropped from 18.8 per cent in 1992 to

14.9 per cent in 2000. These figures seem to indicate that while an increase in industrial capacity has occurred in the 1990s, this growth has not taken place in a sustained manner, with the result that the share of capital goods imports in total imports has declined.

Concurrently, the average annual growth rate of imports of intermediate inputs in Bangladesh between 1990/1 and 1997/8 was nearly 8 per cent, compared to 4.8 per cent in 1989/90. This indicates an increase in capacity utilization during the 1990s. On the other hand, the observed decline in the share of imports of intermediate inputs in total imports between 1991/2 and 1999/2000 seems to indicate that either (1) the rate of increase in manufacturing capacity utilization outside the export enclave (basically producing ready-made garments) has been lower than within the enclave, or (2) intermediate goods produced by local industries have to some extent replaced their import. The first inference is in fact supported by the rapid increase in bonded imports of fabric by the RMG industry under the back-to-back letters of credit system and a large increase in imports by industries located in export processing zones. The average annual growth rate of fabric imports within the export enclave between 1990/1 and 1997/8 has been 19.6 per cent, with a clearly discernible upward trend.

Structural transformation

Trade liberalization seems to have unleashed a structural shift away from manufacturing in favour of the service sector. At the same time, local enterprises have found it difficult to enter new areas of specialization.

In Ecuador, the service sector is in the process of replacing the production of goods at the margin. The share of industrial firms in the total number of companies registered in the country decreased from 20.4 per cent in 1985 to 11.6 per cent in 1998. The share of construction companies decreased from 6.8 per cent to 5 per cent in the same period. On the other hand, the share of commercial, transport and communications, and service companies increased from 61.6 per cent to 73.3 per cent. The reduction in the share of industrial firms in the total number of companies does not imply *per se* a proportional drop in overall industrial production. Yet a decline in the sector's importance can be observed through its share in total national assets and sales. While the industrial sector owned 40 per cent of total assets in 1985, it controlled only 24 per cent in 1998. Industrial sales as a part of total sales declined from 40.4 per cent to 31.4 per cent in the same period, thus showing that overall industrial production has in fact shrunk following liberalization. Opening National Forum participants noted that the country had suffered a dramatic deindustralization as a result of trade liberalization, which spurred cheap imports, and related adjustment measures (see Chapter 3).

The service sector is replacing the production of goods in Ecuador, as industrial production has shrunk following liberalization.

In Ghana there is hardly any sign of local enterprises entering new areas, even within the category of local resource-based manufacturing for export. It had been anticipated that the natural cost advantage would stimulate local entrepreneurs to invest in this export subsector.

Ownership of the emerging sectors
A wide range of incentives is being provided to attract foreign investment in the sample countries, as a result of which the relatively developed countries are witnessing a shift of ownership in the production sector in favour of transnational corporations.

In Hungary, industrial output is recovering quickly owing to the activity of transnationals, which are mainly in operation in the customs-free zones. The Hungarian economy can well be characterized by performance differences between the customs-free and customs-zone enterprises. Companies in customs-free zones, which employ only 2 per cent of the 2.1 million workers in the manufacturing sector, produce two fifths (43 per cent in 1999) of the total exports.

In Mexico there has been displacement of domestic producers by transnationals in export activities, as 70 per cent of exporting enterprises are foreign-owned corporations.

Exchange rate depreciation and competitiveness
Trade liberalization is expected to promote export growth by reducing policy-induced anti-export bias. An overvalued exchange rate discourages exports, however, and can frustrate the achievement of the goal of trade liberalization. In other words, an 'appropriate' exchange rate policy complements trade liberalization by enhancing export competitiveness, and at the same time it helps to contain import growth in the face of ongoing import liberalization.

Box 2.1 Impact of Trade Liberalization: Voices of the People of Bangladesh

It is necessary to prepare the economy and the society before making any policy change. By preparation I mean to make necessary changes in social conditions, working culture, technological preparedness, skilled workforce, access to capital markets, administrative and judicial reform, etcetera. Bangladesh has liberalized its trade regime without such preparation. – *An entrepreneur*

Due to liberalization without preparing the industrial base in the country, many finished products are now coming into the local markets that our entrepreneurs can produce as well. As a result, many small industries (for example, *khadi* of Comilla) are being wiped out from the market. Our producers can produce good quality biscuits. However, biscuits are being imported. Consequently, many of the local biscuit-producing industries are being forced to close down. – *An entrepreneur*

As a small country, we should have been able to expand our export-oriented industries. But the government has not been able to provide necessary support for investment. The Ministry of Industry is not doing anything substantial for industrial development in the country. Government should have taken the initiative to popularize our indigenous products (for example, organic food products like *khoi-muri-chira-gur*, etcetera) in the international market, which didn't happen. As a result we are falling behind in export. – *An entrepreneur*

Ours is the country of *khoi-muri-chira*. We can produce them cheaply and easily and have them fresh. However, we are importing corn flakes, which is not necessary at all. – *An entrepreneur*

We are now unemployed. We have tried hard but nobody is willing to provide us with employment at this age. Even when they come to know that we were workers of a closed industry, then they think that we are not good workers. We also do not find any self-employment opportunity that we can carry on. – *A worker at AB biscuit factory, Tongi*

My salary was Taka 2,000. I was able to bear the necessary expenditures of my children. In fact, I was able to manage two private tutors for my children. One of my daughters is a student of class ten and the other one is the student of class five. I have lost my job. Now I find it very difficult to send my daughters to school. I don't know what I should do now. I have tried my best to find another job but couldn't find any. I will probably have to stop sending my daughters to school. My husband is a low-paid worker. The wage he gets is not sufficient to maintain our family. So, I am now in a crisis after I have lost the job. Some of my old colleagues are even working as maidservant. Some of them are facing torture from their husbands. Families of some of them have also been broken down due to losing their jobs. – *A female worker*

I was a labourer of AB Biscuit Industries of Tongi. The factory is now closed for the last eight years. I am unemployed. I am not getting any other job and I do not find any self-employment opportunity to carry on. Now I cannot support

educational expenses of my children. My elder daughter is a student of class seven. Her admission fee is Tk. 500 but I am unable to pay the fee. I could not send my only son to school. He is 11. He is now sent to a workshop to do something for the family. I am now in a sea of problems.
— *A female worker, AB biscuit factory*

My husband tortured me physically after I had lost my job. He is unemployed. I have one child. I am now living in my brother's house. I have invested the money that I received but the return is insufficient to maintain my family.
— *A female textile worker,Tongi*

In the competitive market, the entrepreneurs are less careful about the environment of the workplace. There is no proper system of discharging industrial effluents in many industries. Workers have no voice in this regard as they are concerned to keep their employment sustained. — *A labour leader*

Hundreds and thousands of workers are now becoming unemployed due to closing down of both state-owned and private industries, but the government is virtually not doing anything for them. The workers who have lost their jobs are now living a substandard life. Many of them have been compelled to withdraw their children from schools. Their children have now become child labour, sex labour. They have become maidservants. They are now breaking the bricks on the streets. Should the government do anything for them?
— *A female worker*

We can now have many foreign goods cheaply. But government should take care of our own industries as well. — *A rural consumer*

Female workers are also in worse situation with respect to using the money that they got at the time of retrenchment as compared with their male counterparts. Male workers could spend or invest that money on their own but the female workers had to give that money to their husbands. Many of them can't even ask where and how that money was spent or invested. Some of their husbands have also fled away with that money, deserted them and married again with that money. Some of their husbands have left them saying that 'I married her only because of her job, now she has lost her job, I don't need her anymore.' How awful the situation can be for those who are the victims of such desertion.
— *A female worker*

Whether export growth is likely to be significantly stimulated by devaluation depends on the price elasticity of supply at home and the price elasticity of demand abroad for the export commodities. An estimation of the export supply function linking export value with relative price and capacity output of the tradable sector as determinant variables in Bangladesh found statistically insignificant sensitivity of export supply to price, but significant strong sensitivity to capacity output. The estimate revealed a high sensitivity of demand of Bangladesh's exports to the income growth of trade partners. The price elasticity of export demand was, however, found to be low, with a 10 per cent decrease in export prices likely to raise demand abroad for Bangladesh's exports by about 5 per cent. Studies by other investigators report similar general findings about the supply-side constraints and relatively low price elasticity of demand for Bangladesh's exports. Another recent study, however, found consistently high values of price elasticity of demand for Bangladesh's exports. Overall, available evidence indicates that devaluation can increase exports of Bangladesh to some extent, provided supply-side constraints are addressed. The SAPRI study argues that devaluation should not, however, be relied upon to ensure competitiveness, as compensatory measures against inefficiencies elsewhere in the economy only delay removal of the inherent problem.

Meanwhile, Ghana's substantial realignment of nominal exchange rates, a critical component of the structural adjustment programme, has not had a significant impact on export volume. The export response of Ghana's manufacturing sector apparently depended on factors additional to exchange rates.

Distributional Impacts of Trade Policy Reforms

All reform programmes have their 'winners' and 'losers'. A political economy analysis of the impact of trade liberalization measures under adjustment reveals that the most disadvantaged segments of society had a disproportionate share of the burden of adjustment. It was evident that the employment growth occurring subsequent to trade liberalization was no match for the volumes of new entrants to the labour market. The marginal increase in employment was highly concentrated in the non-manufacturing sector, and within the manufacturing sector it largely flowed into the export-oriented industries, many of which depended on low-skill assembly plants. The loss of employment occurred mostly in the domestic market-oriented sector. Real wage rates declined as a rule, and informalization of labour became more pervasive.

Most employment loss was in the domestic market-oriented sector: real wages declined, informal labour increased.

Effects on employment

General employment scenario

In the Philippines, the combined effect of the liberalized trade climate, an overvalued peso and capital liberalization has proven to work against labour. Overall, the number of employed persons in the formal sector has increased by less than six million per decade between 1980 and 2000, the period covering the process of trade liberalization. This average of barely more than half a million jobs generated annually is way below what the economy must generate – over a million jobs per year – to absorb an average of 700,000 new entrants to the labour force, over and above the existing jobless individuals. The Asian crisis reduced employment growth drastically in 1997 and 1998. Employment growth in the Philippines was a mere 112,000 in 1997, reaching 27.53 million from 27.42 million in 1996, followed by a further diminutive growth of 325,000 in 1998. It only bounced back again above the one million mark in 1999, adding 1.636 million workers for a total of 29.49 million in a country with a population of about 77 million. In 2000, however, the total number of employed persons plunged downward again, dropping by 1.314 million to 28.198 million.

The trends in employment and unemployment in Bangladesh indicate that the labour force has grown at a faster rate than the creation of job opportunities following trade liberalization. According to the Labour Force Survey, overall employment increased from 50.1 million in 1989 to 54.6 million in 1995/6, while the number of unemployed persons grew from 0.6 million to 1.4 million during the same period. Previously, in the post-independence period between 1974 and 1989, open unemployment had declined consistently from 8.68 to 1.18 per cent. The observed increase in open unemployment, from 1.96 per cent in 1990/1 to 2.50 per cent in 1995/6, has occurred during the period when the process of import liberalization was accelerated. Furthermore, unemployment of women has increased at a faster rate than that of men.

In Zimbabwe, the rate of growth in employment decelerated from an annual average of 2.4 per cent during the period 1985–90 to 1.5 per cent during the period 1996–9. The average rate of formal sector employment growth under adjustment was half the rate of growth of the labour force, implying that new jobs have not been created fast enough to absorb new entrants into the labour market. According to *Standard Chartered Bank Business Trends* (September 1998), a total of 140,000 new jobs were created between 1990 and 1997, certainly far behind the level of new entrants into the labour market, estimated under ZIMPREST to be 183,000 annually. Another data source, *Gemini Technical Reports* (1991 and 1994), indicates that some 196,000 jobs were created in the micro- and small-enterprise sector between 1991 and 1993 in both the formal and informal sectors. Without dwelling on the definitional overlaps of the above-mentioned two sets of figures, it may be concluded that the incremental new jobs were basically 'low quality' jobs created largely in the informal sector.

Apart from the pressure from new entrants, liberalization has had casualties among those who are already employed. In Zimbabwe, the first of these casualties were those engaged in firms that supplied the domestic market and were unprepared to face competition from abroad. Removal of protection saw the exit of such firms during the early phase of the economic reform programme. Particularly affected, as mentioned earlier, were the textile and clothing sectors, in which several large companies (such as Cone Textiles and Julie White), as well as small firms, were closed and over 20,000 employees laid off. The second category of the labour force that suffered was employees in firms that supplied overseas markets but were unable to do so when export-incentive schemes were eliminated by the reforms. The last casualties included workers retrenched as a result of privatization and civil service rationalization. This final group received some compensation through the so-called social dimension fund that enabled a number of unemployed workers to start their own informal business operations.

In Ecuador, open unemployment in urban areas has increased. The jobless rate was 6 per cent in 1990, 9 per cent in 1992, 10 per cent in 1996, and 14.4 per cent in 1999. The greatest increases in unemployment rates took place in the lower-income population groups. At the bottom quintile, which comprises the poorest population, unemployment rates shifted from 10 per cent in 1989 to 15 per cent in 1992 and from 17.7 per cent in 1996 to 24 per cent in 1999. At the higher end of the income distribution scale, which comprises the top quintile, the average unemployment rate remained below 5 per cent during the 1990s. Furthermore, with respect to the total number of unemployed people, the share of those who permanently lost their jobs is higher than the share of those who were unemployed for the first time. This pattern was particularly notable from 1991 onwards, which marked the beginning of labour market flexibilization under Ecuador's adjustment programme.

The greatest increases in unemployment rates in Ecuador took place in the lower-income population groups.

Hungary is an extreme case. The number of employed fell by 1.5 million from 5.5 million to 4 million between 1989 and 1995, and stabilized at about 37 per cent of the total population and 52 per cent of people of working age. In the observed history of Hungary, including the years of crises, world wars and revolutions, at no time was the workforce reduced to such an extent. While in the previous 40 years unemployment was unknown, under liberalization formal unemployment increased at the national level to 13 per cent and, in some regions, reached about 17 per cent. Employment opportunities have been especially difficult to find for young people seeking their first jobs and for those over 40 or 50 years of age.

Experiences in other countries also show that there is a demographic attribute of the newly employed that favours young workers. As a result, retrenched workers have had great difficulty obtaining new jobs. In general, although there were some routine increases in job creation in most of the SAPRI/CASA countries in the post-trade-liberalization period, the level of employment growth remained susceptible to both external and internal shocks. It is also significant to note that this employment increase bypassed the manufacturing sector.

Sectoral distribution of employment: loss in the manufacturing sector

In the Philippines, the rise in the share of employment of the commercial and service sectors is consistent with the course of the inflow of investment into real estate, financial institutions, wholesale and retail trade, and private services. Even though agricultural employment has increased in absolute terms, there has been a declining share of agriculture in employment throughout the 1990s, dropping from 45 to 40 per cent of total employment. At the same time, there have been only incremental and marginal increases in manufacturing's share even during the relatively higher employment years of 1995, 1996 and 1999. It is apparent that the liberalized trade climate did not have any significant impact on job creation. Rather, with the increased competition from cheaper imports, local industries that have been forced to shut down, streamline or cost-cut have added to the level of unemployment and underemployment. Furthermore, as pointed out at the Opening National Forum in Manila, increased foreign control and freer mobility of industries have facilitated the movement of factories to other Asian countries where wages are lower. This, said the Forum participants, has helped fuel the growth of the informal sector and forced many skilled workers to migrate overseas.

The sectoral distribution of employment in Bangladesh shows that the absolute level of employment has fallen sharply in the industrial sector between 1989 and 1995/6. For industry as a whole, employment has declined from 7.8 million to 5.2 million, a fall of 33 per cent. The contraction in employment has been sharper in the manufacturing sector, where employment shrank from 7 million in 1989 to 4.1 million in 1995/6. As a result, the manufacturing sector's share of total employment was reduced from 14 per cent to 7.5 per cent during the above period. This sharp reduction in employment in the manufacturing sector as a whole has occurred primarily in the small and cottage industries, much of it in informal sector industries in both urban and rural areas.

In Zimbabwe, most of the jobs created in the period 1990–7 were in large-scale agriculture (40 per cent), followed by education (29 per cent) and other service sectors (23 per cent), reflecting a lack of industrial development. These statistics indicate that liberalization brought some gains to workers in non-traditional agriculture, such as agro-processing and large-scale horticulture, as well as in the financial sector, at the expense of the industrial labour force.

Out of the entire sample of the empirical survey conducted in Ghana, a marginal majority (51 per cent) of the firms experienced an increase in job creation since the inception of the structural adjustment programme. This increase in employment, however, occurred mostly in large-scale manufacturing firms. Nearly two thirds of medium-sized firms experienced a decline in employment generation. While these figures indicate the location of the new jobs, they do not say anything about the magnitude of the employment increase.

Informalization of employment
In Zimbabwe, the formal sector has shown limited capacity to absorb new entrants who, unlike in the past, have good formal training and education. Market-oriented economic reforms introduced in 1991 have been responsible for shrinking demand for labour, retrenchments and a fall in real wages for those who remained in the formal sector, according to the UNDP's *Zimbabwe Human Development Report 1998*. Contraction in formal sector employment has resulted in the growth of an informal sector to absorb retrenched workers and new entrants into the job market, as well as to provide supplementary incomes for those who remain in formal employment, as their real incomes have been on a downward trend for a long period. Women are supplementing declining real wages by selling food products and second-hand clothing through informal cross-border trade and by making clothes and crochet handicrafts.

> **Goods produced by informal industry in Bangladesh have faced competition from imports, and many small enterprises have been forced to close down.**

Although the importance of the informal sector in creating employment in Bangladesh has declined slightly since the mid-1980s, the sector is estimated to have accounted for about 88 per cent of total employment in the country in 1995/6. In sharp contrast, the share of the informal manufacturing sector in total manufacturing employment has fallen dramatically from nearly 82 per cent in 1983/4 to only 4.6 per cent in 1995/6. Goods produced by informal industry have faced competition from imports as a result of liberalization, and many of these small enterprises – including small engineering workshops, rural industries, bakeries and biscuit factories – have been forced to close down due to the easy inflow of foreign goods.

Effects on consumers

In some cases, a positive feature of trade liberalization has been the increase in the availability of a wide variety of quality goods and services on the domestic market. In such a situation, the removal of restrictions on accessing consumer goods has meant that real prices of basic goods have remained relatively low due to intense competition between wholesalers and retailers, as well as between informal and formal firms and operators.

In other cases, however, import liberalization, coupled with the devaluation of national currencies, has led to higher prices in the face of stagnating purchasing power. For countries whose productive sectors are highly import-dependent, such as Ecuador, this has meant a rise in production costs, as well as an increase in inflation levels, all of which leads in the long run to a loss of competitiveness. In Ghana, according to the Opening National Forum participants, trade liberalization and devaluation have combined to raise food prices. In an environment of increasing lay-offs and stagnating wages, this has hit the poor particularly hard. Food security among the poor has simultaneously been undermined by a decline in domestic food production caused by the increased devotion of land to export crops in response to devaluation and related measures. At the Forum in Hungary, it was pointed out that the entry of foreign supermarkets with their cheap imported goods has reduced the national consumption of local products, such as milk, that are of high quality in Hungary.

Gender implications

Trade liberalization has also had a gender bias. The study in Zimbabwe found that women have been the main victims of retrenchments in the formal sector and, as a result, have been forced to stay home or engage in informal businesses in which incomes and other benefits are at a minimum. According to a survey conducted in Ghana, over 50 per cent of the female-owned firms suffered a contraction of production during the period under review, significantly more than their male counterparts. It could be said that female-owned firms were more sensitive and vulnerable to the forces that brought about change in employment, production output and market size. In the agricultural sector, Ghanaian women, who produce 60 per cent of the country's food, have suffered disproportionately from the flood of cheap imports and from other liberalization measures, according to the Opening Forum participants. They also expressed concern about the fate of rural manufacturing, particularly small-scale food processing, much of which is also done by women.

While the incremental employment gains observed in the export-oriented industries are usually highly feminized – women hold 90 per cent of the 1.7 million assembly plant jobs in the apparel sector in Bangladesh, for example – the vagaries of the market and adjustment-related labour market reforms make employment in such industries extremely precarious. A case in point is the Philippines, where the 1980s export boom in the garment sector, in which women comprise 75 per cent of the workforce, gave way by the mid-1990s to a precipitous decline in foreign sales. By then, labour flexibilization measures allowing greater subcontracting of workers had reduced job security, as well as wages, benefits and working conditions, from the already low levels that have characterized this sector. A similar situation exists with the *maquila* sector in Mexico, which employs mostly women in low-paying, unskilled jobs with poor working conditions and no benefits or job security.

Income inequality

Income inequality has been accentuated in almost all the sample countries in the post-adjustment period. The increase is possibly most stark in the case of Hungary, where the economic transformation that involved the liberalization of trade polarized society. A broader middle class did not develop, and important segments of middle-income sectors that in the past enjoyed stable living conditions suffered setbacks. A large part of the population can be regarded as the losers in this transformation.

Income inequality has been accentuated in almost all the sample countries.

The proportion of the population living on less than the minimum necessary for subsistence in Hungary was about 15 per cent in 1991, 22 per cent in 1992, 25 per cent in 1993, 32 per cent in 1994, 30–35 per cent in 1995 (based on a downwardly amended minimum level) and 35–40 per cent in 1996. A complete readjustment of income levels followed the political change in the country. The difference in *per capita* income between the lowest and highest income brackets (the 10 per cent of the population at each end of the scale) increased from 4–4.5 times before 1990 to 8–9 times in 1999. The steep growth of income in the highest 10–20 per cent category was accompanied by the tragic impoverishment of the low-income sectors.

Ecuador is another case in which income inequality has worsened dramatically. The Gini coefficient (which measures the extent to which the distribution of income among individuals or households deviates from a perfectly equal distribution: 0 being perfect equality and 1 being complete inequality) increased from 0.44, where it stood from the mid-1970s until 1988, to 0.57 in 2000. This indicator would be much worse if it were also able to take into account the concentration of assets and property rather than simply reported income.

Conclusion

The seven countries in which SAPRI and CASA assessments were done on the impact of trade liberalization, although diverse with regard to their income levels and economic conditions, have all experienced greater growth of imports, in terms of value of merchandise, than of exports. As a result, trade and current account deficits have increased, causing higher levels of foreign debt. This situation has been exacerbated by declining terms of trade, which has meant that more exports have been required to purchase the same amount of imports. Furthermore, most export growth has been highly concentrated and typically based on a just a few resources and items produced with low-skilled labour.

Import liberalization has led to the failure of local enterprises and the destruction of domestic productive capacity. This has resulted in an employment loss in important sectors of local economies, thereby reducing the purchasing power of large segments of society and overriding presumed consumer benefits from the opening up of trade. Export-led growth has not become a driving force in the countries reviewed, while those gains registered from what growth there has been in exports have tended to be concentrated in few hands, exacerbating existing inequalities.

> **Import liberalization has led to the destruction of domestic productive capacity and employment loss in important economic sectors.**

The failure to recognize the negative impacts of trade liberalization programmes on significant sectors of society has made these programmes economically inadequate, socially unacceptable and politically unviable, as well as technically inefficient. This failure is due in good part to a lack of meaningful participation of national stakeholders in the articulation, design and implementation of economic policies, a point that was driven home at the Opening National Fora. Furthermore, absence of any feedback mechanism involving the affected constituencies largely deprived the programmes of the ability to make any mid-course corrections and reduce their economic and social cost. In sum, there have been the following consequences in the countries studied:

* *Trade liberalization, having been pushed through indiscriminately, has allowed import growth to surpass that of exports and destroyed the conditions necessary for*

the sustainable growth of domestic firms. At the same time, greater import growth and falling terms of trade have resulted in trade and current account deficits that have worsened the external debt situation.

- *Many local manufacturing firms, particularly innovative, small and medium-size ones that generate a great deal of employment, have been forced out of business.* Leading manufacturing activities have suffered from indiscriminate import liberalization, provoking a reduction in output, bankruptcy of enterprises and loss of employment. While import–competing industries have tended to disappear, very few new areas for local manufacturing firms have replaced them. The decline in domestic manufacturing has followed the flooding of local markets with cheap imports that have displaced local production and goods. The situation has been exacerbated by the absence of an industrial policy to support domestic firms in dealing with new conditions or with shocks in international markets.

- *Exchange rate depreciation, unable to contribute effectively to the export competitiveness of domestic industries for which it was intended, has increased the price of imported inputs and raised production costs, which particularly hurt manufacturing firms producing for the domestic market.* Lack of access to affordable credit and to technology transfer, as well as depressed demand resulting from loss of employment and a fall in wages, have also contributed to the devastation of local industry.

- *Export growth has been concentrated in a few activities that do not create links to the local economy and has typically been very narrowly based on a few resources and items produced with low-skilled labour.* Many traditional manufacturing sectors have been unable to compete in a liberalized market. Furthermore, in many countries the benefits of export growth have gone primarily to transnational corporations at the expense of domestic producers.

- *The most disadvantaged segments of society have borne a disproportionate share of the burden of adjustment.* Employment growth occurring subsequent to trade liberalization has been no match for the volumes of new entrants to the labour market. The limited employment that has been generated is highly concentrated in export enclaves or in similarly low–waged services. Employment losses have occurred mostly in the domestic market-oriented sector. Overall, real wage rates have tended to decline, income inequality has increased, and job insecurity and informalization have become more pervasive.

- *Trade policies have been rendered technically inefficient and socially costly by the lack of meaningful participation of national stakeholders in their articulation, design and implementation.*

In the light of these findings, several initial recommendations can be made. An industrial policy should be in place to address the structural constraints causing inefficiency and enhance the competitiveness of domestic enterprises before undertaking any further opening of a country's trade regime. Trade reform measures should take into account the conditions of domestic producers and should be paced and sequenced in order to create a level playing field that will help to stimulate local production and ensure that domestic enterprises can face competition from foreign goods. Industrial inefficiency should not be solved by killing industries through imports. Rather, efficiency-enhancing measures should be adopted to enable industries to confront import competition successfully.

Industrial inefficiency should not be solved by killing industries through imports but through measures that enhance competitiveness.

In each country, certain industries and sectors of the economy are an important source of employment and play a key role in domestic development, particularly for poor and middle-income segments of society. Trade policy should support a country's strategic sectors and employment-generating industries, serving to build a strong industrial sector that can provide the base for economic development. Trade reform should be nuanced rather than indiscriminate. Finally, future reform processes should be designed by governments with the participation of a wide range of sectors and population groups to ensure that policies are consistent with national development aspirations.

CHAPTER 3

Financial Sector Liberalization: Effects on Production and the Small Enterprise Sector

Financial sector liberalization was an integral part of the structural adjustment and economic stabilization programmes in four of the SAPRI countries under study, namely, Bangladesh, Ecuador, El Salvador and Zimbabwe. There are a number of similarities among these countries in terms of both their rationale for embarking on the reforms and the processes and instruments utilized to achieve adjustment goals. Although the magnitude of the impact of the reforms has varied, there has also been much similarity in the nature of that impact.

Concerns about financial sector inefficiencies, the failure of some of the sectoral policies that had been in place, and the desire of international and national financial interests to wrest control of the sector from the state were major motivations behind the shift towards a more market-based approach to management of the sector in these countries. In Bangladesh and El Salvador, where the role of the state was very extensive prior to reforms, banks were reported to be near collapse and reforms were implemented in an effort to rescue the system from bankruptcy. In Zimbabwe, on the other hand, state control of the sector was more limited, but government policies had nonetheless created problems of inefficiency in the allocation of resources. In Ecuador, liberalization was expected to increase savings and foreign investment in order to reactivate the economy.

Financial reforms have failed to work for the poor, who have been further marginalized from the credit and financial system.

In terms of reaching out to the economically disadvantaged, pre-reform financial systems were not achieving this goal. In all four countries, however, the evidence indicates that subsequent financial reforms have also failed to work for the poor and other economically disadvantaged groups and that, on the contrary, these groups have been further marginalized from the credit and financial system through market forces of exclusion.

Background and Process of Financial Sector Liberalization

Financial sector liberalization, part of the package of economic stabilization and adjustment measures, was in many ways similar in the four cases studied. All the country programmes were characterized by a shift from state control of the sector towards a market-driven system. Interest rates were liberalized, entry barriers and ceilings on credit were removed, and measures to improve supervision of the sector were partially adopted.

In Bangladesh, financial sector reform was a core element of the structural adjustment package. The sector reforms were backed by a number of adjustment credits and a large-scale technical assistance programme. With the nation's independence, the government had nationalized and reorganized all financial institutions with the exception of a few foreign bank branches. After 1976, as policy related to the role of the private sector changed, the government decided to denationalize and privatize its banking institutions in order to generate competition and improve the level of operational efficiency of the sector.

The financial sector reform measures in Bangladesh were much more comprehensive than in the other three countries. Notably influenced by an overriding concern to improve the performance of banks that were experiencing difficulties, these measures included: (1) market determination of interest rates; (2) an end to directed lending to priority sectors; (3) strategies to improve performance by setting overall recovery targets for state banks; (4) introduction of legal and administrative changes to help enforce action against defaulters; (5) strengthening of rural credit institutions; (6) strengthening of bank supervision; and (7) improvement in the loan classification system to identify non-performing assets and provide adequate provisioning for bank lending operations.

Prior to the introduction of structural reforms in El Salvador in the 1990s, the financial sector was heavily controlled by the state. The banks had been nationalized in 1980 in the context of a civil war in order to avoid a total collapse of the financial system. Interest rates were fixed by the government, credit ceilings were established to ensure that certain levels of resources were channelled to specific sectors, and there were restrictions as to who could carry out banking business. The sector was segmented, with the different forms of financial institutions being confined to providing specific types of banking services.

Despite government support to the financial sector, the economy's poor performance deepened the lack of confidence in the Salvadoran banking system, resulting in capital flight out of the country. This situation provided justification for the re-privatization of the banks in 1990–1, as it was argued that private intermediaries would guarantee greater efficiency and competitiveness.

Instead, however, the country's most conservative businessmen used their political influence and economic power to manipulate the financial sector reform process to serve their own interests, taking particular advantage of the deficiencies in the legal and regulatory mechanisms. For example, in order to privatize the banks, the government was forced to assume financial responsibility for all bad debts through the creation of the Fund for Financial Restructuring and Strengthening (FOSAFI). The privatization process was supposed to democratize the ownership of assets through the sale of bank stocks to a large number of new stockholders, including bank workers and small investors. Yet the process was manipulated by the country's élite to regain control of the majority of financial assets, while taxpayers footed the bill for the bad debt.

El Salvador's most conservative businessmen used their power to manipulate financial sector reform to serve their own interests.

Other modifications undertaken in the sector during the first half of the 1990s in El Salvador included the redefinition of the role played by the state development banks and the creation of the Multisectoral Investment Bank (BMI) – a second-tier state institution whose stated mission was to promote growth in all the productive sectors, foment the development of small and medium-scale enterprises (SMEs) and generate employment.

In Zimbabwe, financial sector liberalization was an integral part of the Economic Structural Adjustment Programme, introduced by the government in 1991 to restructure the economy along more market-oriented lines. A set of laws was established to create new money-market instruments and financial services, set effective prudential norms for financial institutions and eliminate credit-market segmentation supervisory mechanisms. A gradual approach was adopted to increase the levels of competitiveness and efficiency by allowing a limited number of new domestic and foreign entrants into the financial sector. The development of a stock market exchange was accompanied by the creation of a Security Exchange Commission, a regulatory body that was intended to monitor trading operations. Deposit and lending rates were deregulated and credit controls were removed. The capital market was opened to foreign participation, barriers to entry into the money and financial markets were eliminated and foreign exchange controls were relaxed to allow banks greater freedom in the control and use of foreign currency. Finally, there was a reduction in the prescribed asset ratios of insurance companies and pension funds from 60 to 55 per cent.

In Ecuador, between 1990 and 1995, the government implemented financial liberalization policies through a package of economic, legal and institutional reforms. The structure of the financial system was recast and its regulations and oversight mechanisms were modified according to the economic wisdom prevailing at that time, with the aim of allowing market forces to allocate the country's scarce resources. Among other measures, the government proceeded to expand capital account liberalization gradually, which was expected to both foster capital inflows and help national businesses obtain higher profits from their offshore investments.

From the beginning of the liberalization process, deposits in the Ecuadorean financial system were increasingly short-term and made in dollars. By the time the extraordinary growth of short-term deposits ended in 1996, there had been a severe process of divestment from productive activities. Ecuadorean society's scarce capital was diverted from productive sectors, such as agriculture and industry, in search of higher rates of return achievable through interest rates. These resources could have been used for enhancing national production and, thereby, for generating more and better quality employment opportunities.

With symptoms of financial crisis evident by 1996, a new series of reforms was undertaken to bolster the earlier measures. These included the creation of a deposit insurance agency in 1998, which, with the collapse of the banking system beginning in 1999, channelled public funds to bail out the private banks that failed as a result of irresponsible and corrupt lending practices under liberalization.

Impact of Financial Sector Reforms

Change in the role of the state
In all the countries studied, financial sector liberalization has been understood as a process of weakening or dismantling prior public regulations and controls. The implementation of measures aimed at either authorizing interest rate liberalization or expanding capital account liberalization has led to several negative, lasting consequences.

The reformed institutional framework created through structural adjustment policies to regulate the sector has been shown to be incapable of effective oversight of private financial intermediaries. Following deregulation, governments have not succeeded in instituting a minimum set of adequate regulatory procedures aimed at either correcting market failures or curbing private speculative behaviour. Besides fostering different sorts of financial crises, the lack of adequate public controls has enhanced the financial sector's inefficiencies.

As deregulation has allowed private élites to consolidate financial assets, banking systems have shown little interest in financing the development of diverse productive sectors.

At the same time, the removal of government controls has further weakened the state as an institution, while strengthening, both politically and economically, a small group of private interests in the countries reviewed that are not prone to comply with the authority of the state. After two decades of structural adjustment, governments do not have enough authority and legitimacy to even pursue complementary and corrective reforms.

Financial deregulation has allowed private élites to consolidate financial assets in a few private hands. As a result, banking systems show little interest in promoting the development of a country's diverse productive sectors, much less satisfying the needs of SMEs. Lacking resources, the state cannot attend to these producers either. As a result, development banking practically does not exist in the sample countries.

El Salvador is a clear case of a small group of private interests benefiting from non-competitive practices that were enabled as a result of financial sector reform. After the privatization of the banking system was completed, the financial system came under clear oligopolistic control. Five banks came to control the lion's share of the financial market. Furthermore, the dismantling of the development banks has occurred without alternatives being created for those sectors they served. The Multisectoral Investment Bank was established in 1994 to promote the growth of productive sectors, but it has functioned with highly questionable lending criteria that significantly favour commercial banks and their limited group of large clients. Rural and small-scale businesses, in particular, have been hurt. Participants at the SAPRI Opening National Forum thus called for the resumption of development banking, as well as special government programmes, to foster the growth of small and micro enterprises, including start-up and women-owned companies, and to ensure diversification of the economy.

In Bangladesh, the large amounts of non-performing assets and the continued non-compliance of provisioning and capital requirements of the banks indicate the Central Bank's inability to enforce effective supervision. The new legal system also has not proved to be effective in recovering money from loan defaulters. In Zimbabwe, the absence of an effective regulatory and supervisory framework allowed for influence peddling and inefficiency in the newly deregulated banking sector. New banks appeared to be licensed on the basis of political patronage, and there was wide speculation that the collapse of the United Merchant Bank in 1996 was due to 'connected' lending practices and mismanagement that led to massive defaults. This undermined confidence in the banking system.

Liberalization led to a financial crisis in Ecuador, and over US$7 billion in public funds were spent to bail out the banking system.

In Ecuador, the legal framework created as a part of financial sector liberalization in the period 1990–5 led to a full-scale financial crisis in 1999, the consequences of which the government was unable to control. Instead of promoting a more stable macroeconomic environment, liberalization policies pushed the Ecuadorean economy into a severe recession. In 1996, within a year of the completion of the reforms, one of the country's largest banks folded. Since then, the Ecuadorean financial sector has been lurching from one crisis to another. Assessed in terms of the initial objectives of the structural adjustment policies, the results of financial liberalization have been negative. The Ecuadorean state has been unable to regulate the financial sector effectively and was forced to assume the costs of the 1999 financial crisis that resulted. When taking into account both explicit and implicit financial costs, over US$7 billion in public funds had been spent by early 2001 to bail out the banking system, 75 per cent of which had to be put under state control. In July 2001, the Ecuadorean financial system was once again on the verge of collapse after one of the largest banks taken over by the state following the most recent crisis folded, and another was teetering down the same path.

Efficiency
Structural adjustment reforms were supposedly designed to lower the cost of credit by enhancing the financial system's efficiency. The evidence, however, shows that this has not been the case.

In Bangladesh, with the spread between lending and deposit rates being an indicator of financial efficiency, SAPRI researchers found that the margin of financial intermediaries has widened in the post-reform period. The efficiency of credit allocation in terms of the advance–deposit ratio of all banks was reported to have declined from 0.91 in 1990 to 0.82 in 1998; the advance–deposit ratio after adjusting for reserves indicates the same trend. The loan–output ratio, which is another indicator of the efficiency of credit allocation, further substantiates the argument that there was inefficient allocation of resources. From 1987 to 1998, this ratio corresponding only to agricultural lending fell from 0.677 to 0.428.

In the Latin American cases, the spread between interest rates for borrowing and savings has been widening.

In the Latin American cases, the spread between interest rates for borrowing and savings has also been widening. In El Salvador, during the years following the privatization of the state-owned banks, the reference borrowing rates corresponding to short-term loans experienced monthly increases and reached a high of 20.2 per cent in 1996. In recent years, the spread has stabilized, showing an average margin differential of 4.5 percentage points. Nevertheless, the interest rates available in El Salvador remain significantly higher than those prevailing in the US market. This indicates that the Salvadoran state has favoured speculative over productive investment.

In Ecuador, the high margins of financial intermediaries have been quite evident. As one of the consequences of these spreads, 17,352 legally registered firms transferred nearly US$722 million to the private financial system in 1996. This amount, which was paid in interest and commissions for previous loans, was greater than all the labour costs that these companies had incurred during the same period and more than five times the income tax revenue they paid to the Ecuadorean state. In fact, the amount of funds transferred from productive enterprises to the financial system over the last decade, when combined with the amount of public funds used to bail out the banking system, is approximately equal to the country's total foreign debt burden.

Concentration of credit: pattern of allocation

As indicated earlier, financial sector reforms have been based in part on the idea that liberalization of financial systems would increase efficiency within national economies. More specifically, it was assumed by some that the introduction of market forces would create financial markets capable of efficiently allocating capital by mobilizing savings with a minimum waste of social resources. In reality, however, the processes observed in the sample countries depict a quite different situation.

Broadly speaking, financial liberalization has reinforced patterns of economic growth that are based on strengthening non-competitive practices. Oligopolistic practices have not only been preserved but also enhanced by the side-effects of financial liberalization, the most important of which are speculative behaviour and non-productive borrowing.

This has been accompanied by the increasing concentration of financial and non-financial assets, both sectorally as well as regionally. Instead of helping those producers who really need capital for maintaining or expanding their operations, financial intermediaries have preferred to work with the largest firms – those usually located in wealthy urban areas. In particular, the type of resource allocation fostered by financial liberalization has exacerbated the structural conditions for the reproduction of rural economies. During the post-reform period in Bangladesh, for example, more than 70 per cent of the total available funds in the banking sector was directed towards 1 per cent of borrowers. The bottom 95 per cent of borrowers received only one seventh of the total available funds. In Ecuador, 63 per cent of loans have been monopolized by only 1 per cent of the financial system's clients since 1995. In El Salvador, where one of the stated purposes of the bank privatization process was the democratization of participation by stakeholders, privatization in fact permitted greater concentration of banking assets in the hands of the traditionally most powerful families.

Financial sector liberalization has made a major contribution to the growth of non-productive activities. In Ecuador between 1987 and 1999, nearly 34 per cent of loans granted by the banking system was extended to the commerce and service sectors. Another 28 per cent of total loans was destined for consumption. With regard to the placement of credit in El Salvador, between 1992 and 1997 the sectors that showed the greatest growth were commerce (253 per cent) and services (739 per cent). In Bangladesh, an analysis of the sectoral distribution of credit advances from 1990 to 1998 indicates that no improved allocation of resources in favour of productive sectors occurred in the post-reform period.

In Bangladesh, more than 70 per cent of the total available funds in the banking sector was directed towards 1 per cent of borrowers.

In addition to increasing the concentration of loans in the hands of a few economic agents, liberalization policies have encouraged a regional concentration of credit, a process that particularly affects small and medium-sized farming economies located in a country's less developed regions. In Ecuador, about 90 per cent of loans have been made to clients in two geographical regions where the most wealthy and powerful élite reside. Small and medium-scale firms located outside these regions had little or no real opportunity to access loans. While the share of rural deposits in Bangladesh increased after the 1980s, the net flow of agricultural credit was negative, indicating that rural capital was actually transferred to urban areas. In El Salvador, the regional concentration of credit was indirectly ascertained through an analysis of the structure of deposits. The research showed that four of the 14 departments of the country held 91 per cent of the total checking accounts. Furthermore, credit lines provided by the Multisectoral Investment Bank are directed in large part towards the development of free trade zones.

Distributive effects: lack of access to affordable credit by SMEs

As a consequence of financial sector liberalization and the resulting concentration of loans, access to affordable credit by small and medium-scale enterprises has worsened. This has weakened the conditions for the survival and development of SMEs, which are an important source of employment generation in the countries studied. The high cost and short repayment period of loans and a series of obstacles to qualify for financing, in addition to the relative paucity of financial assets directed to meet the needs of this sector, were found to have limited access by SMEs to much-needed funds.

As a consequence of financial sector liberalization, access to affordable credit by small and medium-scale enterprises has worsened.

The difficulties faced by small and medium-scale producers are related to the entire functioning of the formal financial system, which is based on standard procedures not capable of coping with the diversity of economic situations and agents. With interest rates high, with the lending policies of private financial intermediaries characterized by short-term preferences, and with the largest share of the credits provided by these institutions concentrated among few, powerful economic agents, SMEs have experienced increasing difficulties in obtaining credit, particularly long-term loans. The package of liberalization policies has restructured national productive systems in such a way that long-term, non-export-oriented activities are becoming increasingly unfeasible.

Since the financial sector liberalization process began in Ecuador, SMEs have been forced to pay such high interest rates that their profits have been wiped out. At the workshops carried out with small and medium-scale business owners from different cultural and economic backgrounds, most producers indicated that they were afraid of acquiring debts within the formal financial system. In addition, with interest rates as high as 70 per cent engendering a great deal of speculation, there has been little credit available to SMEs for productive investment. The lack of credit for SMEs can be seen by the fact that after financial sector reforms were introduced not only did the number of loans greater than US$8,000 increase the most, but the average amount of such loans rose from US$17,600 in 1994 to US$90,000 in 1999. Furthermore, 95 per cent of loans between 1995 and 1999 had a maturity of less than one year, while only 5 per cent of the total loans provided by the financial system had maturities ranging from one to five years, making business development virtually impossible. As a result, almost 4,600 firms were dissolved or liquidated from 1990 to 1996. This pattern has continued, and over 2,000 small-scale producers went out of business in

1999 alone, contributing to the devastation of national production and the deindustrialization of the country.

In Ecuador, high interest rates contributed to the devastation of national production and the deindustrialization of the country.

In El Salvador, the situation is quite similar. For several years following the privatization of the banking system, the reference interest rate on loans of up to a one-year term experienced a monthly increase, rising by nearly 50 per cent to 20.2 per cent in 1996, before declining somewhat and stabilizing, although still at a higher rate than prior to reforms. Furthermore, as Opening National Forum participants pointed out, banks are charging higher commissions when they approve loans, special rates on overdue loans, and interest on top of interest. In addition to high interest rates and these attendant charges, according to an analysis of the experiences of community-based groups in accessing credit, the primary obstacle to accessing formal-sector credit is the imposition of restrictive requirements that are not in tune with the particularities of the diverse sectors that need credit (in terms, for example, of type of ownership, working capital needs, means of commercialization). Since structural adjustment policies were introduced, it was explained at the Forum, more collateral has been required to receive credit and some assets are no longer accepted by banks as collateral. Such is the case with the purchase contracts of artisans. Overall, only 23.3 per cent of the total loan portfolio of the banking system was directed towards micro, small and medium-scale enterprises.

In a survey carried out by researchers in Bangladesh, 76.9 per cent of rural producers pointed to the bankers' rent-seeking behaviour, expressed through high interest rates, as the major reason why they, the producers, do not seek loans. In speaking of other causes for not pursuing credit, 53.7 per cent of non-borrowers mentioned their inability to fulfil loan requirements, 44.05 per cent mentioned the time-consuming process of borrowing as an important reason, and 32.74 per cent of respondents complained of complex loan procedures. Specific difficulties include excessive collateral requirements, delays in processing loan applications, expectations of bribes and even harassment by bank officials. As a result, producers have been forced to obtain financial resources through non-formal means, such as moneylenders, at even higher interest rates.

Small businesses are numerous in Bangladesh and form a large majority of firms in the domestic market. It is estimated that there are 523,000 small industrial enterprises in the country, employing about 2.3 million people, or about 82 per cent of the total industrial labour force. As a result of financial sector reforms, directed lending to the small- and cottage-industry sector, which accounted for about 7 per cent of the banks' total demand and staff time, was eliminated. Of the 59.6 per cent of these small businesses that regularly seek finance for their working-capital needs from banks, only half actually succeed in obtaining loans. Many rely on trade credit, available at a much higher rate of interest than that provided by banks. Between 1987 and 1998, the loan–output ratio for small industry declined from 0.859 to 0.398.

In Zimbabwe, interest rates rose following the implementation of adjustment policies and remained high throughout the 1990s, increasing five-fold to nearly 50 per cent by the late 1990s and diverting investment from productive to speculative activities where returns have been 33–37 per cent. The high interest rates increased systemic risk in the financial sector and created the greatest difficulties for SMEs and the poor generally in accessing credit. While even larger businesses could not afford these rates, Opening National Forum participants explained that they could at least reinvest earnings from previous years. It is small businesses, especially those in the informal sector that desperately need start-up capital, that are most affected.

According to a 1993 survey, the proportion of SMEs in Zimbabwe's manufacturing sector had declined from a high of almost 70 per cent in 1991, as the number of enterprises involved in commerce increased. At the same time, only 0.7 per cent of these producers were receiving credit from a formal lending institution. Those in rural areas have been the most disadvantaged, in part because of the cost of travel to the institution where loans must be processed. Although a few banks set up small-business units designed to serve those producers who were previously excluded from access to the formal financial system, their operational procedures replicate standards that perpetuate the marginalization of poor customers.

Gender

The gender impact of financial reforms was examined in Bangladesh and El Salvador. While it is clear that women have more limited access to the financial sector than do men in Zimbabwe, it was difficult to assess more definitively what the full impact of the reforms has been since reports of the financial institutions do not disaggregate their statistics according to gender.

In Bangladesh, women's access to banking services was measured in terms of their share of the total number of accounts, of total deposits and of total credit provided by financial intermediaries. Although women were contributing 26.26 per cent of the total deposit amount, their share in credit was only 1.79 percent. Stated differently, irrespective of the types of bank branches (women's branch, branch headed by a female manager, or branch headed by a male manager), women have been contributing much more than they have been receiving in terms of credit access. Even in women's branches, female customers are getting only 21.52 per cent of the total loanable funds. On a related point, the share of female employees in the banking sector, though increasing from 4.74 to 6.23 per cent, is still far lower than it is in the government sector.

In El Salvador, despite the proliferation of gender-related credit programmes promoted by NGOs and governmental agencies, most women are unable to satisfy loan requirements. Either they are not property owners or they lack documentation and business records. In addition, access to credit by women in the informal sector continues to be rather limited. Only 23 per cent of women surveyed reported having received loans, while the rest indicated a lack of access to credit. Women are caught in a vicious circle. Unable to guarantee loan repayment in accordance with criteria established in the formal banking system, women do not receive loans to invest in their businesses, thus reducing their ability to continue their business activities at levels that would allow them to move from subsistence to accumulation.

Conclusion

The non-participatory manner in which financial sector liberalization policies were designed and implemented has not only allowed, but also fostered, a reform process that has been biased in two senses. First, in practice, these reforms have been aimed primarily at achieving interest rate and capital account liberalization, weakening or dismantling existing regulations and controls. Second, as a consequence of this shortsighted view of financial sector reform, the reform process has been captured by a few private élites, foreign and domestic, who act as profit-seeking, monopolistic agents.

A major consequence of these biases has been a sectoral reform that preserves economic inefficiencies, produces political destabilization and promotes social exclusion. These general features and outcomes of financial sector liberalization emerge from several concrete findings:

- *Liberalization has not improved the level of economic efficiency within the financial sector.* As can be clearly seen in the four countries where studies were undertaken, the spread between borrowing and savings rates has increased. This demonstrates that banking systems are either incapable of lowering their operational costs or are reaping exceptional profits. Furthermore, corruption and bribery have undeniably blossomed under liberalization, affecting both public and private financial intermediaries.

Financial sector liberalization has promoted short-term speculation rather than investment in productive activities.

- *Financial sector liberalization, in practice, has promoted short-term speculation and investment in non-productive activities, as well as borrowing for the purpose of consumption.* Reforms have facilitated the search for quick profits and have helped channel resources away from productive sectors. Rather than promoting macroeconomic stability, the liberalization of interest rates and capital accounts has allowed capital to become increasingly volatile, flowing easily off-shore, and has contributed to economic crises and increased vulnerability to external shocks. The national and regional crises that have at times resulted have crippled financial systems and productive capacity. Consequently, the structural weaknesses of national economic systems have been reinforced.

- *The weakening of the state and its regulatory role has left it incapable of addressing inefficiencies, abuses and exclusionary practices in the sector.* Financial liberalization has strengthened small, private-interest groups *vis-à-vis* the state and has reinforced patterns of economic growth based on non-competitive practices. In the absence of effective regulation, oligopolies have been preserved and in many cases enhanced. The institutional framework created through the reform process has failed to provide effective oversight of private financial intermediaries. Yet, governments have been left without the authority and legitimacy to pursue complementary and corrective measures to regulate private-sector control over financial resources or to curb speculative behaviour. At the same time, state support for development banking has practically ceased to exist.

- *Reforms have allowed financial assets to become more concentrated in fewer private hands, rather than fostering broad-based productive investment that would stimulate national economies.* Instead of helping producers that need capital to maintain or expand their operations, financial intermediaries have directed financing towards large (usually urban) firms and extended the largest share of loans to a few, powerful, economic agents. This has hindered the development of small and medium-sized enterprises, an important source of employment generation in the countries studied, as well as rural economies as a whole, thereby exacerbating existing inequalities. In concentrating lending activities in geographic regions where upper-income groups reside, banking systems have also discriminated against producers in low-income regions, thus further reinforcing patterns of unequal development.

- *Important sectors of the economy and population groups have been unable to access affordable credit.* Small and medium-size firms, rural and indigenous producers and women have very limited access to the formal financial system, as high interest rates resulting from liberalization and obstacles to qualifying for financing have prevented them from borrowing. Access to long-term loans has become particularly difficult for these sectors, as liberalization policies have reoriented national productive systems away from long-term, non-export-oriented activities and stimulated short-term investment. Furthermore, reforms have not taken into account the fact that standard procedures established by private financial institutions are not capable of dealing with the diversity of economic situations and borrower needs. As a result, many small-scale enterprises have gone into bankruptcy or been forced to seek credit from non-formal sources, such as moneylenders, that can assure neither a sufficient volume of credit nor affordable interest rates.

The failure of these adjustment policies and their negative impact on the poor have been due to a number of factors, notably:

• the inherent limitations of the market process in addressing the needs of the poor and other disadvantaged groups;

• poor sequencing of sector policies, whereby the regulatory environment has lagged behind the market reforms, thus allowing profit-seeking, non-competitive private élites to capture and turn the reform process to their benefit;

• inadequate legal and regulatory frameworks that neither curb the dominant influence of these élites nor allow for the entry and participation of smaller and informal institutions that are more geared towards serving the poor; and

• lack of ownership and participation in the design of the sector reform programmes by the intended beneficiaries, and undue influence exercised by foreign and national élites and international financial institutions.

On the basis of these findings stemming from the sample countries, some basic recommendations can be made to ensure that financial systems serve the interests of national development above those of small, private groups. Financial sector policies should promote investment in production, particularly for the domestic market where small and medium-scale enterprises that account for much of a country's employment generation operate. They should facilitate lower interest rates, reduce the gap between savings and borrowing rates, and include support for employment-generating enterprises through the establishment of development banking mechanisms.

Financial sector policies should promote investment in production, particularly for the domestic market, and small and medium-scale enterprises.

Alternatives to financial sector liberalization must address specific conditions in each country and should be developed with broad participation by affected population groups and economic sectors. It is necessary to create conditions to enhance financial services that reach not only formal, large-scale economic entities and the urban and export-oriented sectors, but also small, informal ones, many of which serve the domestic market. This requires regulatory and supervisory frameworks that prevent financial instruments from being captured by profit-seeking élites, stem speculative practices, and allow financial institutions capable of serving the poor to enter into, and survive in, the formal financial system.

Any financial sector reform should be carried out within a broader development framework that has at its centre the criterion of equity. The market by itself does not ensure opportunities for the poor to escape poverty. Accordingly, it will be necessary to design policy packages that can specifically address the needs of those who are unable to gain access to, or take advantage of, market opportunities.

CHAPTER 4

Employment under Adjustment and the Effects of Labour Market Reform on Working People

Wealth is generated by human labour, without which there is no income, whether in cash or in kind, no consumer goods, no technology, no capital nor organization. Without labour there would be neither production nor distribution of wealth, nor would markets exist. In other words, it is not the market that determines the existence of this labour; on the contrary, without labour, markets cannot exist.

Labour can be employed in many different ways. In developed economies, where the relationships between supply and demand are clearly articulated, work is usually salaried. Such is not the case everywhere, however. The labour market can coexist with many types of workers and employment, including small-scale rural producers, independent merchants, the self-employed, and non-paid family workers. Paradoxically, within the logic of the market, some activities necessary for the reproduction of society remain outside all economic considerations. Non-remunerated housework underpins work performed outside the home by other household members. Such work, however, is considered to be 'non-economic', and whoever performs it is almost always classified as part of the economically inactive population.

That is to say that, from a market point of view, labour is reduced to a simple relationship of supply and demand. The economic policies that have predominated since the beginning of the 1980s have placed emphasis on the labour market rather than on the value of work itself. Within structural adjustment programmes, labour has been defined in terms of individual productivity and competitiveness, with little regard for social and labour rights or social equity and collective well-being. The isolated, competitive individual supplants the collective and cooperative effort.

Structural adjustment, including specific labour market reforms, has significantly affected labour and living conditions in all of the participating countries.

The national investigations into the impact of a broad range of adjustment policies – including privatization, deregulation, and trade and financial
sector liberalization – indicate that structural adjustment has significantly
affected labour and living conditions in all of the countries participating in
the SAPRI and CASA exercises. This impact has been deepened by specific
labour market reforms undertaken as part of structural adjustment
programmes in numerous countries. These policies and their effects on
employment, wages and working conditions have been examined in
Ecuador, El Salvador, Mexico and Zimbabwe. The studies are illustrative of
the international trend towards reducing the concept of work to that of the
labour market, reorganized through the concept of flexibilization.

This chapter first presents a brief description of the differing, as well as
similar, characteristics of the four countries. It then discusses two types of
impacts that adjustment has had on employment: those caused by general
economic adjustment strategies; and those derived from specific labour
market reforms. Finally, it summarizes the findings and recommends a change
in course.

Country Characteristics

The countries under consideration have very different points of departure.
Their geographical and population sizes, as well as that of their markets, are
contrasted in Table 4.4 below.

Mexico, which possesses over three quarters of the total population of
the four countries studied, also generates 91 per cent of the combined GDP.
It is classified by the World Bank as a high-middle-income country, while
Ecuador and El Salvador are listed as lower-middle-income nations and
Zimbabwe as a low-income country.

Table 4.1 • Selected Countries: Population, Territory and GDP

	Population (millions)		Territory (thousands of km²)	GDP (millions US$, 1987)		GDP per capita		
	1980	1997		1980	1997	1980	1997	Average annual growth
Ecuador	8.0	11.9	256,370	11,733	19,768	1,467	1,661	0.7%
El Salvador	4.6	5.9	21,041	3,574	11,264	777	1,909	5.4%
Mexico	67.6	94.3	1,958,201	223,505	402,963	3,306	4,273	1.5%
Zimbabwe	7.0	11.5	390,580	6,679	8,906	954	774	(1.2)%

Source: World Bank, *World Development Indicators 1999*, Washington, DC: World Bank.

Macroeconomic evolution, expressed in GDP *per capita*, shows not only very different initial structural characteristics but also different types of development. Under an orthodox adjustment regime since its Economic Reform Programme was launched in 1991, Zimbabwe's growth has slowed significantly. Likewise, Ecuador's GDP *per capita* appears to have fallen in real terms during the past two decades of economic liberalization and particularly during the recent period of economic crisis. In contrast, El Salvador grew significantly in the 1990s after the Peace Accords were signed in early 1992. Its GDP *per capita* was scarcely half of Ecuador's in 1980, but by 1997 surpassed it by 15 per cent. Mexico's dynamic can be located somewhere in between Ecuador's and El Salvador's – a weak level of growth *per capita* that does not keep up with the growth rate of the economically active population.

Because of these differing conditions, each country's specific characteristics were taken into account in the participatory consultative exercises. But, in spite of such differences, all of the countries where employment and the labour market were studied have shared a number of basic structural characteristics.

- All four countries have had an extremely heterogeneous[1] market structure (Zimbabwe's reached dualism and enclave formation), with economic control exercised by a handful of businesses and the majority of work performed outside the formal hiring schemes usually found in developed economies. For example, in Mexico, out of an economically active population of 40 million, fewer than 18 million were enrolled in the social security system. (The law requires that all labour contracts enrol workers in this system; therefore, those not enrolled either work in the informal sector, are self-employed or are unpaid.)

- At the same time, all the countries have shown a high concentration of income, wealth and factors of production. Above and beyond the countries studied here, Latin America and Africa are historically the two regions with the highest concentrations of wealth. In Zimbabwe, 70 per

---

[1]   In economic development theory, heterogeneity refers to disparities in development within a country's economy. A heterogeneous economy tends to include the following: a sector producing raw materials or primary goods – whether for export, domestic markets or direct consumption – with low levels of technology and poor working conditions; a modern industrial sector that is generally linked to transnational firms; an urban informal sector involved in small-scale production, commerce and services; and a *maquila* or assembly-plant sector that produces goods for export using mostly imported inputs. Adjustment policies applied in a heterogeneous economy tend to increase competition on an unequal playing field and thus will have differentiated impacts, benefiting most those sectors that are better off and further exacerbating inequality.

cent of the land belonged to fewer than 1 per cent of producers, who have also controlled 85 per cent of the water resources. It should be pointed out that racial and labour discrimination against indigenous peoples in some areas of Latin America, as well as against blacks in parts of Africa (Zimbabwe, for example, given the enduring effects of its colonial inheritance), is translated into conditions of total disparity in economic development. In Zimbabwe, at the end of the last decade, the white population comprises 2 per cent of the population while receiving 37 per cent of national income.

• The four countries studied here are among those with the highest concentration of income in the world. Out of 96 countries appearing in the World Bank's *World Development Report 1999*, Zimbabwe has the eighth-poorest distribution of wealth, Mexico is in fourteenth place, El Salvador in twenty-first and Ecuador in thirtieth – although, with the breakdown of the financial and monetary systems at the end of the 1990s in Ecuador, this situation has clearly worsened.

• Latin America experienced a situation of massive external debt, which led to the debt crises of the 1980s in Ecuador and Mexico. This was one of the factors that spurred the adoption of structural adjustment policies. During that same period, El Salvador's war economy enjoyed significant assistance from the United States government. Since then, its foreign exchange needs have been met largely by migrant workers, especially those living in the US, who send money home.

• Associated with the debt during the 1980s was a growing fiscal imbalance frequently linked to cases of public sector corruption and inefficiency. To give an idea of the extent of fiscal crisis in these countries, Zimbabwe's deficit was 9.6 per cent of GDP in 1980 and Mexico's was 16.5 per cent in 1981.

• On top of this, the 1980s showed a profound deterioration in the terms of trade for raw materials, which particularly affected Ecuador and Mexico in the area of oil.

• In the case of Zimbabwe, a fundamental element to consider is that of HIV/AIDS. Life expectancy at birth dropped from 61 to 48 years, and one fourth of the population became infected. The lack of concern shown by many, including the World Bank, with regard to the spread of the disease in sub-Saharan Africa during the 1980s should be noted.[2]

---

[2]   AIDS has had an immediate impact on employment due to reduction of the healthy working-age population and the growing rate of dependency. In addition, HIV/AIDS presents an ethical problem in terms of market criteria: how can you invest in human capital

In summary, these are highly indebted countries that are finding it difficult to meet their financial commitments. They have had growing fiscal imbalances, highly concentrated income distribution structures and markets controlled by oligopolies. Such were their characteristics in the early 1980s, and it was obvious that substantial modifications to their economic organizational structures were necessary. However, the types of changes implemented have not reduced labour disparities existing before adjustment. On the contrary, the heterogeneity of these economies has substantially increased. It would almost seem that the main common denominator among these countries is their internal structural heterogeneity.

Adjustment Programmes, Employment and Poverty

Employment and the labour market have been significantly affected by structural adjustment policies that directly impact the productive sectors.

Employment and the labour market have been significantly affected by a broad range of structural adjustment policies that have direct impact on the productive sectors of the economy. The impact of these policies on employment is a reflection of their effect on the country's productive apparatus. Furthermore, as discussed later, decisions made by governments under adjustment to liberalize the labour market are often carried out through specific labour market reforms: that is, legal changes regulating labour relations.

Employment is a function of the level and structure of economic activity and productivity. That is to say:

- An increase in demand for goods and services tends to increase a sector's economic activity. With constant levels of productivity, if this demand is not met by imports, employment rises. In effect, in order to produce more, additional labour is needed, whether by increasing time worked by those already employed or by adding new workers.

- If demand increases as a result of a net increase in those productive sectors requiring little labour per unit of capital, accompanied by decreases in highly labour-intensive sectors, then, even when production increases, employment declines.

---

[2] cont. in an HIV-infected population when you know beforehand that the investment's profitability will be less than in the case of non-infected persons?

• Increased productivity has a double-edged effect: it directly results in technological unemployment (substitution of workers by technological modernization), but also indirectly generates employment linked to the new technologies and provides a stimulus to production that will, in turn, generate new jobs.

Just as production and productivity depend on an economy's overall functioning and its relationship to the rest of the world, so employment's behaviour is linked to the entire economy's performance and the primary economic strategies promoted by public policy. As a result, the effects of structural adjustment on employment cannot be determined by specific labour market policies alone but also depend on the economy's evolution, the restructuring of its productive apparatus and the effects this generates in terms of overall changes in employment patterns.

Economic activity
In the countries studied, economic restructuring has not led to greater modernization and competitiveness even after 20 years of adjustment. As well as being irregular and insufficient, the growth of GDP has been concentrated in the development of the leading businesses, sectors and regions. This has exacerbated the gap between these and the sectors left behind, as well as the heterogeneity already existing before adjustment. In addition, the concentration in the distribution of generated wealth has tended to increase, and, as a result, the consumption capacity of growing segments of society is deteriorating even further. In the face of such imbalances within the real economy, financial equilibrium has been given precedence. Nevertheless, even in this domain, Ecuador and Mexico have experienced major problems, including disastrous banking crises.

Economic restructuring has not led to greater modernization and competitiveness after 20 years of adjustment.

Ecuador's GDP grew at an average annual rate of 2.5 per cent from 1980 to 1997; however, population growth was 2.4 per cent, and, thus, growth *per capita* was practically at a standstill. For the following two years, up to 1999, GDP *per capita* decreased at an average of 6.2 per cent annually and only rose two per cent in 2000.

Mexico's economic performance under adjustment has also been inadequate. The mean rate of yearly GDP growth from 1980 to 1997 was barely 1.3 per cent, while the average rate of population growth was 2 per cent. Recovery began in 1997, indicated by an annual GDP *per capita* of 2.7

per cent from 1997 to 1999. However, these cycles of recovery have been short and unstable, and a process of deceleration, rooted in the US economic downturn, began during the last third of 2000.

El Salvador experienced profound economic stagnation during the 1980s because of the civil war. Recovery during the 1990s following the Peace Accords was accelerated, with GDP *per capita* growing at 2.9 per cent per year, with the help of a lower population growth rate (1.5 per cent). However, the situation has reversed since 1997, with GDP *per capita* increasing by barely 0.9 per cent over the following three years. On top of this, the country experienced the adverse impacts of Hurricane Mitch at the end of 1998 and, in particular, the earthquakes in 2001.

Finally, Zimbabwe was the country that grew most rapidly over the last two decades (2.9 per cent annually). However, strong growth in the 1980s, before structural adjustment policies were applied, was followed by a weakening during the 1990s, when growth reached only 1.6 per cent annually. Also, Zimbabwe had a higher population growth rate (2.96 per cent) than the other countries studied, and by the end of the twentieth century its situation was similar to that of 1980 in terms of economic activity, as GDP *per capita* had stagnated. When the effect of the HIV pandemic and the recent political crisis are added to this mix, the panorama becomes more critical.

Restructuring of the productive apparatus

Given that the primary determinant of employment is production, and that much productive activity is concentrated in micro, small and medium-sized businesses, it is important to examine the restructuring of the productive apparatus resulting from adjustment policies.

In Ecuador, the impacts on employment of restructuring both production and the financial sector have been significant. A reorientation of policy to foster an export-based economy produced constraints on the domestic market, particularly small and medium-scale businesses, and strengthened large enterprises. From 1992 to 1998, several thousand workers were shed by the country's thousand largest firms (in terms of economic activity), which accounted for 75 per cent of GDP while employing 35 per cent of workers in formally registered enterprises, even as the amount of these firms' investment per worker increased by 50 per cent. Thus, large firms in the export sector were further concentrating capital while failing to generate employment.

Policy reforms led to massive closures of small businesses that employ the majority of Ecuador's workforce.

At the same time, the SAPRI investigation in Ecuador notes the massive number of closures of micro, small and medium-sized businesses, which make up the vast majority of the country's registered enterprises and employ the majority of its workforce. From 1990 to 1996, 4,600 businesses went bankrupt (1,675 of them closed in 1995 alone), leaving a total of 17,352 formally registered enterprises. As a result, thousands of workers joined the ranks of the unemployed, as 96 per cent of registered firms account for 65 per cent of employment in all firms, although they produce less than 25 per cent of GDP. Participants at the SAPRI Opening National Forum blamed this massive loss of jobs in part on the flood of imports that has emanated from Ecuador's trade liberalization.

The Forum participants also pointed to the country's credit policy and to interest rates that have reached as high as 70 per cent. The concentration of capital has contributed to the weakening and/or failure of businesses that were unable to compete in the new international context by directing credit towards monopolistic productive structures. Since 1992, 1 per cent of borrowers in Ecuador have received 68 per cent of the available credit, and the country's banking system has constrained lending that would have preserved and created jobs in the most labour-intensive sectors. To add insult to worker injury, the subsequent bail-out of the banking system then channelled public resources away from employment creation to protect a financial system that did not generate employment in such sectors.

Similarly, in Mexico, only 25–30 per cent of industries existing in 1982 are still in operation. Between the economic crises of 1982 and 1995, micro, small and medium-sized businesses stagnated, despite an apparent economic upturn, partly as a result of high interest rates and the dismantling of the country's development banking system. Trade liberalization, with the influx of imports that it has brought, and the reorientation of economic strategy towards exports, have considerably weakened these firms, as only 1 per cent of Mexican companies participate in international trade, with 700 companies controlling 75 per cent of all exports. Working conditions in the smaller businesses are particularly precarious, and their possibilities of modernizing and becoming successful in the export sector are practically non-existent. National Forum participants also pointed to the massive loss of jobs caused by the privatization of state-run enterprises.

The Mexican rural sector has felt the effects of structural adjustment policies through Article 27 of the country's constitution, which now allows the sale of *ejidos* (collective farms). This change has bolstered the profitability of agriculture, especially for export, while neglecting the domestic market, community organizational structures and efforts to attain domestic food security. This situation has resulted in a new dynamic of renting and potential selling of land and the displacement of small-scale farmers. Because of technological breakthroughs and crop substitution, a growing percentage of farmers find it necessary to migrate for economic reasons, whether: (1) as agricultural day labourers under conditions of monopsony for export companies; (2) to the country's urban-industrial centres where their knowledge and culture do not coincide with labour demand; or (3) to the United States as undocumented workers under precarious working conditions after risking their lives to cross the border. Rural women migrating to the cities usually become domestic workers. In short, from having been owners of their own land, small farmers have become day labourers or sweatshop workers in *maquiladoras*,[3] with the resulting deterioration in wages and working conditions.

In 1991, the Economic Reform Programme, financed by the World Bank, was implemented in Zimbabwe with the usual adjustment policies, including privatization and trade liberalization. As in the Latin American countries, liberalization brought about massive shutdowns. The SAPRI study drew out the analysis and perspectives of the Zimbabwean people on these changes through a series of consultations and found that, as businesses closed, the formal sector shrank and the informal sector expanded, there were fewer opportunities to obtain employment and poverty increased, while there was a growing phenomenon of people holding multiple jobs. An oversupply of overqualified workers was also observed. Paradoxically, in spite of the closings and greater vulnerability of micro, small and medium-sized businesses due to economic restructuring, this sector has experienced the most growth, given the small amounts of capital such businesses need to operate and how easily they can enter the informal sector. This phenomenon also indicates the high birth and death rates of these businesses and the fact that, while they are vulnerable to crisis, they also serve as a refuge from it.

Liberalization in Zimbabwe brought about massive closings of companies, fewer opportunities to obtain employment and increased poverty.

Employment in Zimbabwe was also affected by actions taken to correct public finance problems. In order to eliminate an existing fiscal deficit, 25 per cent of public workers were laid off. While the situation before adjustment was in some ways untenable, given the accumulation of the

---

[3] *Maquiladoras* are assembly plants in which most of the inputs are imported (in Mexico, about 98.5 percent). They enjoy an especially favourable tax environment, and production is focused on exports. Enclaves are formed to utilize 'comparative advantages' offered by the host countries: low salaries; fiscal breaks; lax controls on pollution (whether tacitly or implicitly defined); possible donations of electricity; and locations that may be conveniently close to consumers in the large international markets.

deficit and low job creation within a highly regulated structure, the adjustment programme failed to meet the challenge of modifying economic policy so as to generate fiscal equilibrium and employment.

Furthermore, there has been a 'maquiladorization' of industry, particularly in Mexico and El Salvador, while a similar process has taken place in Zimbabwe since 1996. As businesses in this sector do not generate either forward or backward productive linkages within the country's economy, they become enclaves and generate employment only in the production of the final product. They can also destroy existing businesses and the jobs of those providing inputs for the now-displaced firms, while dampening domestic investment. A case in point is El Salvador, where adjustment has brought about stagnant production, particularly in regard to manufacturing for the domestic market. Thus, gross employment generated by the *maquiladoras* can produce a negative sum in the net generation of employment, and increasing underemployment and informality.

This type of industrialization is also linked to the depression of wages and, with labour markets deregulated, to a high level of vulnerability of its predominantly female employees to arbitrary lay-offs, harassment and poor working conditions. Participants in the National Fora in these three countries zeroed in on this exploitation. Due to the removal of labour regulations and, with it, the disappearance of a functional grievance system, women in Zimbabwe, for example, who are sexually harassed at work, are far less likely to report an incident for fear of being fired, it was explained at that country's SAPRI Forum. At the Mexican National Forum and at other consultative workshops in Mexico, participants told of how the relaxation of regulations on hiring and firing has enabled employers to require a certification of non-pregnancy, for example, for employment and to refuse to provide maternity leave. They expressed concern that the *maquiladoras*, as significant sources of job creation in Mexico and as principal employers of women, are exploitative workplaces, as reflected in their low pay, paucity of benefits, poor working conditions and failure to respect basic labour rights.

> **'Maquiladorization' in Mexico and El Salvador was linked to depression of wages and increased vulnerability for its predominantly female employees.**

In sum, there has been a concentration in production for export (much of which is not labour-intensive or employs mostly unskilled workers in low-paying jobs), a breakdown in the integration of industrial sectors, employment dislocation, and, with a policy of reducing public expenditures paralleling business closings and lay-offs, a further concentration of employment in the service and informal sectors.

Unemployment and poverty

The increasing movement towards the service sector in all the countries studied has paralleled a sharp fall in agricultural employment for both men and women and the inability of the industrial sector to absorb these workers. Only in El Salvador has there been an increase in industrial employment and that has been minimal (and mostly in the *maquila* sector) compared to the loss of agricultural work. Furthermore, there has been an increase not only in female employment among those still employed, but in child labour and elderly workers, all in a situation of deteriorating working conditions and income levels.

Unemployment levels are not specifically dealt with in this chapter since the operative defining criteria for unemployment are significantly different for each country. While open unemployment stood at about 2.3 per cent in Mexico in 2000, in El Salvador it was 7.3 per cent, 14.4 per cent in Ecuador in 1999, and 22.3 per cent in Zimbabwe in 1993. This does not mean that there was nearly full employment in Mexico, as only active full-time job seekers are counted, leaving out laid-off workers who have immediately joined the informal sector, taken unstable jobs, or are not actively seeking work. In Zimbabwe, labour force surveys are not undertaken on a regular basis, and, when they are, methodologies and types of data collected are so different that they defy comparative analysis. The Zimbabwe Congress of Trade Unions estimated unemployment at between 35 and 50 per cent in 1997. The government's Central Statistical Office concedes its own estimates

Table 4.2 • Proportion (%) of Men and Women Employed by Sector, 1980 and 1990–97

	Agriculture		Industry		Services	
	1980	1990–7	1980	1990–7	1980	1990–7
Men						
Ecuador	44	39	22	20	34	41
El Salvador	56	50	20	22	24	29
Mexico	43	35	30	25	28	40
Zimbabwe	63	58	19	13	18	29
Women						
Ecuador	22	16	16	16	63	68
El Salvador	9	7	18	19	73	74
Mexico	19	12	28	20	53	69
Zimbabwe	85	81	4	2	12	17

Source: World Bank, *World Development Indicators, 1999*, Washington, DC: World Bank.

are low, as neither discouraged job seekers who have not been actively looking for a job nor those who have worked even one hour in the previous week are included in the figures. Unemployment in Ecuador was found to be much higher for the poorest 20 per cent of the population than for the richest 20 per cent, standing at 24 per cent and less than 5 per cent, respectively, in 1999. At the same time, underemployment was estimated at 50 per cent.

At the end of the 1990s in Ecuador, about two thirds of workers were either un- or underemployed, with 66 per cent of the population living on less than two dollars a day. Those employed were working longer hours, but new jobs were not being created. As a consequence, the informal sector grew by 5 per cent between 1998 and 2000. Meanwhile, the country's thousand largest companies (in terms of economic activity) employed fewer workers in 1998 than they had six years earlier (147,147 compared with 150,000). Yet, given the trend towards monopolization resulting from the impact of liberalization on competition, these companies have played a growing role in the country's economy. As a result, the formal sector has become increasingly powerful while generating less employment and producing ever-greater exclusion.

Many references are made in the Ecuadorean study to the widening breach between the formal, export sector and the traditional sector linked to the domestic market that has occurred as a result of privatization and trade and financial sector liberalization, a point driven home by National Forum participants as well. The impact on the marginalized communities participating in the study has been significant. Through a series of consultations and case studies, the SAPRI investigation found that, in the case of urban marginal populations (Bastión Popular and Itchimbia), instability in the residents' employment situation has increased perceptibly. Many people have gone from having a steady job to underemployment or unemployment. This has resulted in the modification of family survival strategies, with a significant increase in the number of household members (especially children) participating in economic activities. While the percentage of women employed nationally with respect to men grew from 38 per cent at the end of the 1980s to 48.6 per cent in 1992 and 50.1 per cent in 1999, open unemployment of women increased from 9 per cent to 13.2 per cent to 19.6 per cent during the same time period. The women's groups consulted as part of the SAPRI research explained that this increase of women in the labour force does not indicate an improvement in gender equity, but rather a tendency for employers to seek women for jobs that are low-paying and lacking in benefits and job security.

In El Salvador, a strong relationship was also detected between the deterioration of the employment situation and an increase in poverty. In

1998, open unemployment had risen to 7.3 per cent, urban under-employment was 17.4 per cent and informal sector employment reached 26 per cent. For the country as a whole, two thirds of the economically active population earned less than the minimum wage, and half of those employed worked 45 or more hours a week. These figures for informal and precarious employment explain how very high levels of poverty can coexist with relatively low levels of official unemployment. Nearly 19 per cent of the population was deemed to be living in extreme poverty and 25.7 per cent in relative poverty, meaning that 44.6 per cent of the Salvadoran population lived in poverty conditions.

In El Salvador, two thirds of the economically active population earned less than the minimum wage.

The social impact is exacerbated by the differential treatment of women. Of the 83 per cent of *maquiladora* workers in El Salvador who are women, 42 per cent receive less than the minimum wage, 67 per cent receive no severance pay, 53 per cent suffer from abusive treatment and only 3 per cent of pregnant women are given paid maternity leave. The social fabric has deteriorated through a process of exclusion, and the combination of policy-induced labour instability, marginalization and poverty is seen as a determining factor in the increased migration out of the country. Family structures have suffered, said National Forum participants, as a result of this instability, low salaries and long workdays. So have health, nutrition and the ability to find affordable and adequate housing. More and more children, they reported, are entering the workforce in an effort to supplement declining family incomes. These children are usually forced to drop out of school to take jobs that pay 'apprentice' salaries far below the minimum wage, although their duties are similar to those of adult employees.

The population in Mexico has been affected in a similar manner, especially the most vulnerable groups, with similar consequences in terms of employment instability, poverty and migration. Furthermore, the wave of privatization of state enterprises and public services that began in the 1980s (in 1992 alone, more than 1,000 state-owned enterprises in the industrial, financial and communication sectors were sold, merged or transferred) generated massive firings of over 500,000 state employees. These lay-offs were not accompanied by job creation programmes in the newly privatized enterprises, nor were incentives or aid given to the fired workers.

Although unemployment in Mexico was officially at 2.3 per cent in 2000, employment for nine million members of the economically active population was precarious, and 50 per cent of those able to work were making their living from the informal economy. Forty per cent of Mexicans get by on less than two dollars a day, and in the poorest regions labour instability has aggravated social conditions. Forum and workshop participants spoke of the increasing difficulty that heads of households have in maintaining steady jobs due to flexibilization measures in the labour market, and they asserted that those who are able to do so generally find that their incomes are insufficient to cover the basic needs of their families. Many are forced to seek a second job, which is difficult to find given the unemployment problem, or to revert to situations of underemployment or employment in the informal sector. These would-be solutions often involve a significant expansion of the working day, as well as greater job instability and income insecurity.

Other alternatives sought, particularly by low-income families, include the incorporation of additional family members, often children, into the labour market and migration to urban centres or to the United States. These survival mechanisms, said the Mexican Forum participants, provoke changes in the social and family structures that, in turn, generate additional hardship for large segments of the population, with women and children often bearing the brunt of the burden. Families often cannot afford to keep children in school, owing to both the direct costs of school materials and the opportunity cost of education. Children are increasingly needed to bring in additional income or, particularly in the case of girls, to take responsibility for household chores for which their mothers no longer have time, including the care of younger siblings. Longer working days for both parents, Forum attendees explained, often leave children with inadequate parental guidance and, when combined with intra-household tensions from added responsibilities and reduced purchasing power needed to cover basic needs, fuel social problems such as domestic violence and juvenile delinquency. The CASA study documented an increase in child malnourishment and infant mortality rates in the southern provinces (Oaxaca, Guerrero and Chiapas), while child labour is on the rise. By the age of 12, or upon entering secondary school, the school desertion rate increases considerably, especially for girls, while at the same time, out of 3.6 million agricultural day labourers, 1.2 million are under 18 years of age.

In Mexico, children were increasingly entering the work force to bring in additional family income.

Similarly, in Zimbabwe, after a decade of adjustment, employment creation had stagnated before the current political crisis took hold. Average annual employment growth rates fell from 2.9 per cent between 1991 and 1995 to only 0.3 per cent from 1996 to 1999. By the end of the 1990s, 68 per cent of the population was surviving on less than two dollars a day, as even those workers who did find full-time jobs were no longer guaranteed a living wage, said participants in the Opening National Forum. The collapse of wages has meant that many workers live far below the poverty line, they reported.

Labour Market Reforms and Flexibilization

Under adjustment programmes, labour market policy is being adapted to the free market model. Among the 'active' policies designed to adjust the labour supply to the needs of the market are those that increase the flexibility of the labour market. They address hiring and firing practices, as well as working conditions, including union organizing. Greater labour flexibilization can be effected by relaxing regulations in labour codes or as a result of negligence on the part of authorities and businesses with regard to the prevailing norms of formal employment. For example, while Ecuador and Zimbabwe instituted new laws regulating relationships between business owners and workers, practices changed ahead of the law in such countries as El Salvador and Mexico.

Economic policy reforms have accompanied the technological revolution of the 1980s as well as shifts in the forms of work organization and industrial relations. That is to say, adjustment policies have facilitated technological change and changes in the organization of work; these changes, in turn, have generated incompatibilities between the new economic policies and preexisting labour legislation. Labour codes were based on the welfare state model, and in Latin America, although this often meant a corporative type of state, labour relations involved aspects usually found in industrialized countries: the Taylor principle of specialization of tasks with standard procedures and times; production of homogeneous, identical goods; and the expansion of society's capacity to consume. With the implementation of adjustment, the technological revolution and changes in industrial relations, however, such legislation has become obsolete for the new groups in power.

> **Labour code reforms have increased labour flexibilization through the use of temporary, part-time, seasonal and hourly contracts, as well as the contracting out of work.**

The changes in labour law and practice have been justified using the free market argument that greater investment and employment will be attracted by: (1) fewer regulations concerning labour stability (limited or temporary contracts) and firing practices; (2) greater flexibility in labour conditions (hourly contracts, workers performing numerous functions); (3) lower labour costs (reducing social security payments, bonuses, vacations, minimum wage, costs of firing workers); and (4) less ability for workers to organize. While these conditions might produce short-term competitiveness for countries undergoing adjustment because of the low costs they can offer to attract investment, workers experience a deterioration in working and living conditions and a loss of collective capacity to defend their rights, eroding their stake in the companies' futures. The result is greater poverty and social problems, which can lead to social unrest and limit the attractiveness for investors. Furthermore, these practices have also hindered the development of a quality-based competitiveness that would produce greater labour stability and directly improve the living standards of workers.

In order to reinforce the market-based economic programme in Ecuador, from 1991 the labour code in that country was reformed to increase labour flexibilization and remove regulations governing employer–employee relations. Among the elements introduced, which further weakened labour unions, were the use of temporary, part-time, seasonal and hourly contracts, as well as the contracting out of work through an intermediary so that the employee establishes no labour relationship with the company. These hiring schemes avoid adding personnel to the company's permanent payroll, thereby freeing it from paying benefits or having to adhere to regulations governing regular, full-time personnel. The SAPRI study in Ecuador shows that 72 per cent of large and medium-sized businesses and 16 per cent of small businesses had turned to employing temporary workers, and 38 per cent of them laid off permanent staff in response to the economic conditions during the last half of the 1990s. Fixed-term contracts were also introduced, renewable at the company's discretion, thus tending to replace the use of indefinite contracts. At the same time, labour reform increased restrictions on the right to strike, collective bargaining and the organization of workers. Employers are no longer required to bargain collectively with workers, only one union is permitted in public sector workplaces, and the number of workers necessary to form a union has been doubled.

In El Salvador, modifications of legislation annulled clauses containing positive discrimination towards women, such as those outlining special conditions for pregnant women. Under the principle of 'equality' and based on Agreement 111 of the Labour Code, protection for women and for future Salvadorans (unborn children of pregnant women) was withdrawn. All regulations making distinctions between the sexes when hiring workers were eliminated, including those regulations protecting women from being hired for dangerous or unhealthful work. The Second National Forum in El Salvador spotlighted the degrading situation faced by women who – as in Mexico – now have to prove that they are not pregnant in order to be hired in the *maquiladoras,* or are being forced to sign illegal contracts in which the employee must agree to being laid off if she becomes pregnant.

Within the context of the adjustment programme in El Salvador, the country's weak labour laws concerning all workers have also been exploited by employers. The effects have been an increased absence of employment contracts, greater work instability, salaries below minimum wage, work weeks of over 40 hours, informalization of work done mostly by women, who endure double and triple workloads (as mother, wife and employee), reduced access to social security benefits, and failure to respect the right to organize or to uphold the rights of union members. There has been a negative impact not only on worker rights, but also on the ability of unions to fight for those rights.

Modifications of legislation in El Salvador annulled clauses containing positive discrimination towards women.

Those attending the Opening National Forum in San Salvador addressed this troubling pattern. They pointed to the increased use of temporary, part-time workers, to longer working days with no overtime pay, to the replacement of unionized employees with non-union workers, to the exploitation of women as *maquiladora* and domestic workers, and to an increasing reliance in the countryside on temporary day labourers.

There have as yet been no significant legal changes made in labour legislation in Mexico, but the country's corporative union structure served the interests of the government and the political party in power from 1929 through 2000, including the process of economic liberalization that they have promoted since 1982. It has permitted constant violations of existing rights, especially those of women, as documented in the Mexican study. The International Labour Organization (ILO) notes that Mexico is among member countries most frequently accused of violating the right of workers to free association (that is, in labour unions), discrimination against the female workforce, and non-compliance in the payment of social and economic benefits.

National Forum and workshop participants in Mexico expressed strong bitterness over the impact of those labour market reforms that have been made. Measures intended to create flexibility in the labour market have modified employer–labour relations by giving the former greater discretion in determining employment conditions. This has meant greater use of part-time labour and temporary contracts and the absence of benefit packages. As a result, according to the participants, there has been an increase in job instability. Flexibilization has also meant a relaxation of labour market regulation, oversight and enforcement mechanisms. This has led to a failure to recognize unions, respect collective bargaining contracts, and enforce labour rights, causing a serious deterioration in working conditions. Experiences were recounted of refusals to grant pregnancy or sick leave, failure to pay minimum salary or overtime, employment requirements that women not become pregnant and dismissal if they do.

Forum participants in Zimbabwe noted that the government, upon signing its first stabilization agreement with the IMF in 1983, abandoned the relatively high minimum wage that it had established, along with laws supporting collective bargaining, shortly after independence three years earlier. By the end of the decade and the institution of an adjustment programme, the government had begun to look at the labour market as any other market in need of deregulation. Wage flexibility was introduced, some restrictions on worker lay-offs were abolished, and competition in the area of labour organizing was promoted. In 1991, Zimbabwe began to restructure a highly protective legal framework established in 1985. The Labour Relations Act was reformed so that salaries would be determined by the market and defined in individual contracts, as well as to facilitate employers' ability to fire workers. Meanwhile, requirements that employers inform authorities before firing workers disappeared, as did mechanisms for conciliation and arbitration between workers and management and recognition of collective bargaining contracts.

Wages and Working Conditions

Impact on wages
Since stabilization and adjustment policies were first implemented, the reduction of wages and salary costs has constituted an important strategy for containing inflation and production costs. It has also served as a mechanism allowing a country to achieve competitiveness *vis-à-vis* the rest of the world by controlling labour costs.

As early as the mid-1980s, the Inter-American Development Bank noted that it has been working people, through their significant sacrifice in labour stability and the standard of living as a result of the reduction of real wages, who have borne the burden of policies to improve Latin America's current account. While corrections made to the external deficit in most countries have been fleeting and financial crises have abounded, Mexico and Ecuador being prime examples, wage deterioration has not reversed itself under adjustment regimes in the countries studied.

The Mexican minimum wage has lost 69 per cent of its purchasing power under adjustment.

The Mexican minimum wage has lost 69 per cent of its purchasing power since the beginning of adjustment in 1982, and the number of people living in extreme poverty (those unable to obtain the basic food basket) rose from 6 million to 30 million between 1994 and 2000. Salaries were restricted in order to maintain competitiveness and reduce demand. Meanwhile, corporativist (official) unions have defended business and government projects that maintain low salaries and replace collective with individual labour contracts, leaving the unions without any real power or independence. According to the leader of Mexico's Business Coordinating Council (and presidential adviser from 1988 to 1994), 'The day our country pays salaries above a competitive level, national industry will be priced out of the market and any hope of creating new jobs will disappear'.

Table 4.3 • Ecuador: Average Monthly Salaries (in 1998 US$) in Urban Areas by Economic Sector and Gender

	1987			1997		
	National average	Informal sector	Formal sector	National average	Informal sector	Formal sector
Total	242	191	293	199	136	279
Men	282	218	315	231	165	301
Women	175	149	243	147	92	238

Sources: Banco Central del Ecuador, *Información Estadística Mensual No. 1776*, April 1999.
Instituto Nacional de Emples (INEM), *Encuesta Permanente de Hogares*, 1987.
Instituto Nacional de Estadistica y Censos (INEC), *Encuesta de Empleo, Desempleo y Subempleo en el Sector Urbano*, November 1997.

In Ecuador, the average real income of those employed in urban areas dropped by 18 per cent between 1987 and 1997, from US$242 to US$199. The decrease was much more dramatic for those employed in the informal sector. Overall, it was pointed out at the Opening National Forum, adjustment took away more than one half of workers' incomes over the course of the 1980s and 1990s and substantially increased unemployment and underemployment. The increasing instability of employment and deterioration of wages as a result of adjustment, and flexibilization measures in particular, have also been facilitated by dollarization and inflation. When the national currency – the sucre – was eliminated, the minimum wage, strictly speaking, fell to about six dollars per month, and take-home wages, when all nontaxable benefits were included, did not exceed US$75. This represented, in real terms, a 19 per cent loss in purchasing power between 1998 and 2000 alone. During two decades of structural adjustment, Forum participants stressed, poverty and inequality have increased substantially in Ecuador.

The deterioration of salaries in Zimbabwe has been worst among the least skilled workers.

National Forum participants in Zimbabwe reported that flexibilization had decreased real wages to such a point that even those who have managed to find full-time jobs are no longer guaranteed a living wage. This collapse in wages has meant that many workers live far below the poverty line. The deterioration in salaries has been worst among the least skilled workers. The ratio comparing salaries of unskilled European workers with those in Zimbabwe is 25 to 1, for example, while it is 4 to 1 for skilled workers. Zimbabwe is experiencing growing inequality, the Forum participants said, with the burden of adjustment falling largely on workers and peasants.

Declining working conditions and job security and protection
In Ecuador, violations of the right of free association and discrimination against women's labour were cited in research consultations as impacts of adjustment policies and the accompanying preferential treatment given to business owners by government and its sanctioned unions. Only 2 per cent of workers enjoy social protection or have signed collective contracts. In the participatory workshops, workers talked of the fear of losing their jobs now that labour reforms have rendered their situation in the workplace more precarious at a time when the great mass of unemployed had rendered them all fully 'interchangeable'. In addition to the limitations on labour organizing and the right to strike that were a direct result of labour reform, the precariousness of employment (in terms of stability and security) unleashed a 'permanent fear' of job loss and the resulting willingness of workers to renounce their labour rights and accept whatever conditions they were offered while refraining from joining unions. Depending on the sector (public, private or informal), 45–66 per cent of workers in Ecuador are willing to give up labour rights in return for keeping their jobs. In addition, a process of polarization throughout the workforce can be seen in terms of the length of the work week, with the hours worked by those in the lowest-income deciles rising and the hours worked by those in the highest-income brackets having dropped. Those attending the Opening National Forum emphasized that the weakened respect for the rights of workers has left them increasingly unprotected and open to abuses by employers. They also pointed to the precipitous fall in real wages and the concomitant and explosive rise in poverty that have ensued.

Deterioration in working conditions and a decrease in union activity due to labour market reforms were also noted in Zimbabwe, where, in spite of wage deterioration, the number of strikes dropped radically after 1997 (from

230 in that year to 130 in 2000). Flexibilization has also increased in Mexico through such mechanisms as subcontracting (formerly illegal) by large industry and due to industrial development concentrated in *maquiladoras*, rendering employment conditions more precarious for significant numbers of workers. El Salvador follows the same model as Ecuador and Mexico: fewer collective contracts; labour flexibilization practices (beyond those that have been legally defined); and gradual liberalization of the economy to allow the market to set salaries as if they were just one more price.

The precariousness of employment in Ecuador resulted in a willingness of workers to renounce their labour rights.

Conclusion

Structural adjustment has had an impact on workers in the countries studied on two levels. On the first level there is the general impact of policy packages – including stabilization policies and the reduction of public spending, privatization, deregulation and trade liberalization – on employment. At a second level, specific labour market reforms have had a direct impact on wages, job security and protection, working conditions and the strength of labour organizing through the flexibilization of the labour market. These sector reforms often concretize already existing governmental permissiveness allowing practices that violate labour rights. Furthermore, and contrary to what their proponents had claimed, they have not been shown to have had a positive net impact on overall employment generation. While the extent to which the countries studied have implemented and been affected by these policies is not identical, in all cases the trend has been towards exacerbating, rather than correcting, imbalances existing before adjustment programmes were introduced.

In summary, the country assessments have revealed the following:

- *Employment levels have worsened.* New jobs have not been generated to keep pace with new job seekers, and there has been a critical loss of employment in economic sectors on which low- and middle-income groups depend. The concentration of growth in export-oriented production – such as assembly-plant industrialization via *maquiladoras* or export processing zones – has contributed to the low levels of net job creation, as this sector tends to have weak links with the domestic economy, and to keeping wages down.

- *Real wages have deteriorated and income distribution is less equitable today than before adjustment policies were implemented.* The investigations show that the share of wages in gross domestic income has declined, while the share of profits has increased markedly during the reform period. More workers have been employed without job security or benefits, and under-employment has increased. The lowest-income groups have tended to experience the largest increase in unemployment and the greatest deterioration in their wages. A reduction in purchasing power and the further concentration of income is evident in all the countries studied.

- *Employment has become more precarious.* Flexibilization has been applied on a non-level playing field in the labour market. Employers have been given the means to hire and fire workers at the least possible cost and with minimal social responsibility. Workers, particularly in low-skilled and labour-intensive sectors, are in oversupply, face depressed wages, and are in a weak position in salary and contract negotiations. There were no cases observed in which steps have been taken to improve working conditions, include workers in decision-making processes, or link the purchasing power of wages to increases in productivity. Thus, workers worry increasingly about losing their jobs and, as a consequence, are now more likely to renounce their labour rights or refrain from joining unions.

- *Reforms have also allowed employers greater flexibility in establishing employment conditions and have eroded workers' rights.* This greater employer flexibility has been reflected, for example, in the increased use of hourly labour and temporary and part-time contracts, as well as in contracts permitting numerous worker functions. At the same time, workers' rights have been weakened because there are fewer protections of their right to organize and bargain collectively. Lower direct labour costs have also been achieved through reduced wages and benefits.

- *Women have suffered the most as a result of labour market reforms.* Women tend to be the majority of those employed in low-skilled jobs and have been disproportionately affected by job insecurity and policies that have made employment conditions more flexible. In some cases, reforms have eliminated special protections for women, such as protection against lay-offs due to pregnancy, and such benefits as maternity leave.

- *There has been an increase in work by children and senior citizens as a response to the decline in household income by primary wage earners.* An increase in the number of hours worked per week has also been documented, for example, in Ecuador. These family survival strategies have had negative impacts on levels of education and health and have led to deterioration in the quality of life.

- *Productivity and competitiveness, sought through labour market flexibility and related adjustment policies, have not been achieved overall.* Although export sectors may have experienced growth through the use of new technology or lower-cost labour, any such productivity increases have tended to be confined to specific economic sectors or regions. Any benefits of growth in these limited areas have been offset by deteriorating labour conditions associated with an expansion of the informal economy, underemployment, and the shift of labour to low-productivity sectors.

Labour market reforms have had a direct impact on wages, job security and protection, working conditions and labour organizing.

In order to address these problems, an employment-intensive growth strategy should be pursued that stimulates job creation by supporting those labour-intensive productive sectors, particularly small and medium-scale enterprises, that serve the domestic market and fuel the local economy. Tripartite commissions involving workers, employers and government can be established to seek consensus on an adequate regulatory framework for labour and employment practices, as well as wage policies. Reforms should protect and enhance labour rights, including the right to unionize, and ban discrimination against women and minority groups, as well as strengthening protections for workers with regard to job security and employment conditions.

An employment-intensive growth strategy should be pursued, and reforms should protect and enhance labour rights.

CHAPTER 5

The Economic and Social Impact of Privatization Programmes

Privatization has been one of the most important components of the structural adjustment programmes implemented in developing and transition countries. Loan agreements with the IMF and the World Bank have very often involved conditions requiring the privatization of state property regardless of the extent or effectiveness of public ownership. State enterprises and services were taken to be inherently inefficient undertakings that, in order to improve performance, should be privatized.

Privatization as a condition for loans has been part of the Bretton Woods institutions' policy prescriptions since the second half of the 1980s. In Hungary, for example, an adjustment loan signed with the Bank in 1988 included an expectation that legislation would be enacted to enable state enterprises to be converted into joint-venture companies. Similarly, in Bangladesh a three-year arrangement with the IMF's Structural Adjustment Facility in 1987 included a policy prescription for privatization, while privatization also became a precondition for World Bank loans. These are two of the countries that, within the framework of the SAPRI exercise, opted to review the outcome of privatization measures, the others being El Salvador and Uganda.

> **Privatization as a condition for loans has been part of the Bretton Woods institutions' policy prescriptions since the second half of the 1980s.**

In most of the country assessments, surveys of privatized firms were carried out through personal interviews and questionnaires. In Uganda, for example, a structured questionnaire was given to 150 heads of household, identified using a purposive and random-sampling method, that included workers in various firms, in both the public and private sectors, as well as

NGOs and academics. In addition, 20 focus-group discussions were held with workers retrenched as a result of the ongoing privatization process and with those employed by the new owners. In Hungary, representatives of trade unions and other civil society organizations, using 26 case studies, examined the concrete conditions in individual enterprises following privatization. The investigation in Bangladesh relied on more limited surveys carried out previously in the jute sector. In El Salvador, the study focused on one public utility sector and relied on interviews and focus-group discussions for primary data collection.

Reasons for Privatization

In the 1950s and 1960s, governments all over the world played an important role in directing and exercising control over their economies. This involved the establishment and administration of large enterprises – particularly in the areas of energy supply, transport, communications, basic metal industries, and so forth. The most important factors in the genesis and development of state-owned enterprises included:

- the need to maintain control over strategic sectors and to ensure the delivery of essential services;

- the inability of the private sector to undertake certain large investments that were essential to the economy; and

- the need for the promotion and development of indigenous entre-preneurs to strengthen domestic growth and diversification.

It was natural during this period for governments and state entities to play a significant role in fostering economic growth and assuming social responsi-bility to moderate inequalities. In the case of transition countries such as Hungary, the public sector developed and grew with the process of nationalization at the beginning of the socialist era following the Second World War and from the investments made by the socialist states.

When the oil-price shock triggered economic problems of high inflation and economic stagnation that were not resolved by conventional Keynesian policies, the neoliberal paradigm – supported earlier by only a limited group of economists and politicians – became more and more dominant. A number of studies were published criticizing the state's role in the economy, some of which pointed to the supposedly inherent non-viability of state-owned industrial firms on the premise that state ownership inhibited the efficient functioning of any such enterprise. Initially, emphasis was placed on the distortion in prices and quantities derived from state action, but the critique later centred on the supposed 'inefficiencies' in the public allocation of resources compared with the 'always efficient private allocation'. Privatization was advocated as the answer to improve both microeconomic (the individual enterprise) and macroeconomic performance. Given the deficiencies of public enterprises, the difficulties they seemed to be causing the economy and a desire to increase access to assets by private interests, privatization of these enterprises was seen by international financial institutions as the ideal choice for governments.

Privatization aimed to promote the private sector as an engine of growth and to increase efficiency and productivity.

The primary stated goals of all privatization efforts were to promote the private sector as an engine of growth and to increase efficiency and productivity in the economy. In general, it was claimed that privatization policies would improve efficiency of resource use, foster competition, enhance the role of the private sector, obtain higher rates of domestic savings and investment and, last but not least, attract and provide opportunities for foreign investors. In addition, privatization would, it was said, reduce the size of the state, shrink the fiscal deficit, provide better services and give the state immediate resources that would be used to reduce short-term debt and to invest in social infrastructure.

The stated objectives of the privatization process can be broadly categorized in three main groups:

- Economic objectives:

  1   improve the overall efficiency of the economy;
  2   improve the efficiency, productivity and profitability of firms;
  3   improve the quality of products and services; and
  4   attract foreign investment.

- Fiscal objectives:

  1   reduce government subsidies to public enterprises;
  2   raise money from the sale of public enterprises; and
  3   increase tax revenue from private enterprises.

- Social and political objectives:

  1   improve the welfare of society;
  2   promote the ownership of private enterprises by nationals;
  3   create a property-owning middle class;
  4   increase total employment in the economy; and
  5   reduce corruption and the abuse of public office.

Privatization Programmes and Processes

Although sporadic privatization activities could be seen in some countries in the late 1970s, the process has accelerated since the second half of the 1980s. In Bangladesh, while the government began to denationalize the state-owned enterprises following independence and a large number of units were divested during 1975–81, the average size and value of divested units was much greater during 1983–90. In Uganda, following the launching of the Economic Recovery Programme (ERP) in 1987, the government published a policy statement on Public Enterprise Reform and Divestiture (PERD) in November 1991 that outlined its privatization strategy. In Hungary, the privatization process began during the years of systemic change (1989–90) and continued in several waves over nearly a decade.

Privatization programmes and processes, as well as their economic and social impacts, have varied according to the specific features of the given sector of the economy. In the SAPRI exercise, studies exploring the effects of privatization in the public utility, manufacturing and banking sectors were carried out. The performance of privatized and deregulated banking systems is addressed in Chapter 3. This chapter focuses on the privatization of public utilities (El Salvador and Hungary) and industrial enterprises (Bangladesh, Hungary and Uganda), while also assessing the privatization of small businesses and the national pension system in Hungary.

Privatization has usually been carried out in several phases. In Hungary, for example, where almost 90 per cent of production and the service sectors was under state ownership, privatization began with small-scale, state-owned firms, followed by larger companies. Some 10,000 retail shops and restaurants were auctioned off and bought mainly by their former managers, and approximately 500 enterprises – whose assets were valued at less than US$4 million and whose receipts from annual sales totalled less than US$1 million – were sold to the private sector. Following the privatization of the productive sectors, public utilities and the banking sector were privatized and purchased mainly by foreign investors.

The third generation of reforms in El Salvador aimed at privatizing electricity distribution, water utilities, tele-communications and the pension system.

In El Salvador, on the other hand, the process was initiated with the privatization of the banks. The second generation of reforms followed, beginning with the sale of state enterprises that did not provide strictly public services, such as cement factories, sugar refineries and hotels. Steps were then taken to prepare the legal framework for the implementation of the third generation of reforms, which aimed at privatizing services such as electricity distribution, water utilities, telecommunications and the pension system.

Various methods of privatization have also been used in the countries reviewed. Among the primary means have been the sale of assets, the sale of government shares, auctions, management contracts and repossession. In some countries, there has been some attempt to use various employment-preference schemes. In no case, however, did employment-preference schemes result in a wider stratum of small owners.

In Hungary, there was a period (1993–4) in the course of privatization in which would-be Hungarian owners were given priority in the purchase of assets, and preference schemes, such as concessional loans, special guarantees and pre-emptive rights were introduced. During a subsequent period, a new government placed emphasis on obtaining higher revenue from privat-ization and, as a result, the preference schemes faded. In this period, the role of the stock market in the privatization process increased substantially. In general, the Hungarian privatization process was built on cash transfers, and the voucher form used in neighbouring transition countries was not applied.

In El Salvador, in the course of an open bidding process, 20 per cent of each of the electricity distribution companies was reserved for purchase by the workers or for 'priority investors'. In Uganda, one third of the enterprises were privatized through the sale of assets and another third through the sale of government shares. The methods of auction and repossession were used to some extent. While there were no employee-preference schemes, workers did participate in the process in the case of three companies and eventually purchased those formerly public enterprises.

Economic Results of Privatization

The effects of privatization vary, depending on the type of enterprise. Furthermore, there are differences when assessing impacts from a micro-economic or macroeconomic perspective.

Experience of small businesses
Probably the most positive experience can be found in the privatization of small businesses. This phase of the privatization process in Hungary created a rather viable entrepreneur stratum, and these firms are very important in local employment generation and in meeting local needs. The efficiency of these small shops has increased because management has been transferred from a remote central office to the local level, where all the necessary information is available for decision making. However, these small businesses

have had to compete on an uneven playing field with the arrival of large, foreign-owned shopping centres.

Privatization of industrial enterprises

The privatization of industrial enterprises was the backbone of the process of dismantling state ownership in a number of countries. Both micro- and macroeconomic impacts, as well as the social effects, of privatization are well illustrated by the results of the SAPRI exercise. One of the most serious arguments in favour of privatization was that it would increase the efficiency, productivity and profitability of firms and that, as a result, it would contribute to the overall efficiency of the economy and accelerate economic growth. At the microeconomic level, several SAPRI studies address the issue of the relative performance of public and private industries, although it is quite difficult to ascertain the exact performance change that could be attributed exclusively to the change in the form of ownership.

In Bangladesh, an earlier World Bank study analyzing the performance before and after privatization of 13 enterprises that were privatized in the first half of the 1990s showed very mixed results. Some firms increased their profits after privatization, others continued to sustain and even increase their losses, and some went out of business or were shut down. When assessing the experience of privatization in the jute sector, it is evident that the main problem lies not in the ownership form but in the policy regime and management. In the case of the jute mills, both the private and the public sectors have sustained losses, generally attributed to the fact that production costs have tended to be higher than the export price of jute because of the outdated equipment in the mills. Industry-wide data show that labour productivity does not depend on ownership; rather, it depends on managerial efficiency.

In the jute sector in Bangladesh, the main problem with enterprise performance lies not in the ownership form but in the policy regime and management.

At the Opening National Forum, before the field research, civil society representatives delivered an analysis similar to the Bank's, attributing the failure to increase efficiency through privatization to inefficient management, the scarcity and misuse of credit, and the virtual absence of technological and marketing support. They had noted that newly privatized firms had experienced an increase in non-performing loans and defaults and that many had closed, were struggling or were grossly exploiting labour. There was also a focused discussion on the failure of the jute sector privatization to stimulate Bangladesh's industry. Indeed, the precipitous decline in jute production following its privatization had negative ramifications throughout the entire economy. Many jute factories closed and, according to Forum participants, as many as 39,000 workers were laid off. Participants blamed the World Bank, in part because of the faulty advice that it provided. They argued that workers should be incorporated in the policy design process so as to enhance its quality.

In Uganda, the past performance of public enterprises had been poor due to the country's violent political history and depressed economic situation. More recently, the reasons for their poor economic performance have been multiple and complex. Key factors have been a scarcity of foreign exchange, preventing importation of raw materials to support production, and a shortage of spare parts, not to mention the need for replacement of obsolete plants and machinery. Another fundamental problem has been political interference that has led to poor management practices.

As for the results of privatization, the findings of the Uganda investigation reveal that capacity utilization, sales revenue, tax contributions to government, profitability, and product quality and diversification have all increased when compared with the period prior to the privatization process. The surveyed firms showed a positive trend in sales revenue over the period 1997–9, when capacity utilization increased from 47 to 57 per cent. All respondents in the field research were of the view that there had been an increased supply of goods and services on the market following privatization, as a number of enterprises had been established to satisfy local demand. Previously, there had been widespread shortages of most goods – including sugar, soap and salt – and much of what was available was imported.

In Hungary, privatization became the engine of modernization because it brought a large wave of foreign direct investment into the country. At the same time, production and employment levels in the privatized Hungarian firms fell to between one third and one half of original levels. While productivity began to increase rapidly at an average annual rate of 10–15 per cent, this improved performance was due to the transnational firms established in the country and not to the Hungarian ones. Furthermore, privatization was accompanied by a substantial reduction in research and development (R & D) activities. A number of research institutes disappeared or shrank significantly. The ratio of R & D to GDP dropped from 1.4 per cent in the 1980s to 0.7 per cent in recent years.

Privatization of public utilities

Public utilities play a special role in a country's economy. They are 'public' in that they serve the common interest of society and provide basic services that are essential to the lives and livelihoods of families and communities.

Energy, water and, to some extent, mass transport and telecommunications are services on which modern societies are built. Because these are basic services, societies have generally assumed the responsibility for providing them, at least at a minimum level, to all of its members regardless of their income or geographical location. And, because public utilities are largely natural monopolies, the questions of availability, access and affordability are of even greater importance. For these reasons public services have been – with occasional exceptions – under public ownership. With the emergence and predominance of neoliberalism, however, the supposed inherently greater efficiency of private property has been used as a justification for privatizing public utilities.

Rural areas in El Salvador were seriously affected by electricity privatization, and low-level consumers have been the hardest hit by rate increases.

In SAPRI there were two countries – El Salvador and Hungary – in which assessments were carried out of the privatization of public utilities. In El Salvador, the privatization of public services, such as electricity distribution, was part of the third generation of reforms that began in 1996. By privatizing electricity services, the state intended to increase its savings by reducing public spending that had previously been directed towards maintaining certain low rates and providing subsidies for low-income users. It was argued that privatization would increase economic efficiency, as measured by the lowering of costs and the generation of higher revenue. As a result of the privatization process, the four regional electricity distribution companies that had been under state ownership were acquired by firms from Venezuela, Chile and the United States.

Two years after the sale of these electricity distribution companies, and in spite of the gradual upgrading of technology and equipment by the four foreign firms, there were no significant improvements in terms of service quality or coverage. Furthermore, rural areas were seriously affected, both directly, by increases in electricity rates, and indirectly, by price increases in other services that depend on electricity, such as deep-well pumps for potable water that are used in many communities. In addition, users with low levels of consumption, who constitute the majority of the population, have been the most affected by the increases in electricity rates. Low-end users saw their rates increase by 47 per cent on the average, while users with the highest consumption levels experienced an average 24 per cent increase in rates. Participants at the Opening National Forum also explained that higher electricity bills have contributed to the closing of many micro and small enterprises.

The public savings that were supposed to have been achieved by privatizing electricity services in El Salvador are questionable. Subsidies continued to be necessary, through the use of social investment funds, to ensure that services were provided to rural communities and other areas not deemed profitable by the private companies. The creation of a new regulatory entity to cover privatized services also generated new costs. Furthermore, the process of privatization did not succeed in opening the market to free competition and full consumer choice. The four privatized distribution companies now compete for only a 20 per cent share of consumers in the market – mostly large industrial, commercial and service companies. The remaining 80 per cent of consumers have no possibility of switching providers, even though they may be dissatisfied with the service they receive. This reality undermines the system of free competition, which has been said to be a central purpose of privatization.

In Hungary, most of the process of privatization of public utilities was prepared and executed in the early to mid-1990s. By the end of 1995, around 42 per cent of the property of the public utility sector was under foreign ownership. Hungary is now second only to the United Kingdom in Europe in terms of the proportion of private ownership in the utility sector, but it is unique in that the country's basic utilities have become the property of state utility companies of foreign countries. As a consequence of privatization, the quality of services – except telecommunications – barely changed at all, while prices increased at a much higher rate than did wages. Large segments of society now have severe difficulties in paying their electricity, gas and water bills.

Hungary's basic utilities have become the property of state utility companies of foreign countries.

Privatization of the energy sector and of the gas and oil industry was put on the country's agenda in 1990. The Hungarian Electric Works and the National Oil and Gas Industry Trust were each divided into separate companies, which were then sold off in 1994–5. Foreign investors were permitted to purchase up to 50 per cent of company shares while, at the same time and in accordance with the privatization contracts, they received the majority of voting shares in the principal organs of the companies. Therefore, the control over these privatized companies was put directly into the hands of foreign investors, mostly European, who subsequently used their positions to gain majority ownership. Electricity rates for households rose precipitously and were ten times greater in 1998 than in 1989, causing serious difficulties for low-income groups. Public water-supply and sewage-disposal enterprises were also transformed in the 1990s. Only in the larger cities and municipalities were these utility companies privatized, and they are now mostly under foreign ownership; companies serving other regions remained as autonomous institutions under municipal ownership.

The communications sector was reorganized and partially privatized at the beginning of the 1990s and is one of the real success stories of the Hungarian transition. Telecommunications were separated from postal services, and shares in the new telecommunications company were sold on the New York Stock Exchange, with majority ownership under a consortium of European and American telecom firms. Although the company holds a monopoly position, it invested in and carried out a comprehensive modernization of the country's telecommunications system during the 1990s.

The overall impact of the privatization of public utilities has been an exacerbation of inequality and a failure to contribute to macroeconomic efficiency.

The results of the research in El Salvador and Hungary illustrate that – with rare exceptions, as in the case of telecommunications in Hungary – privatization of public utilities has not achieved its original goals. In most cases, the increase in efficiency (the ratio of revenue to expenses) resulted only from the increase in prices following privatization. State subsidies were maintained in order to ensure supply to the poor and to those living in remote areas. With the market opening and the reform in rate structures, large consumers benefited most, while rate increases for those who consume the least were much higher than the average. For these reasons, the overall impact of the privatization of public utilities has been an exacerbation of inequality and a failure to contribute to macroeconomic efficiency.

Privatization of pension systems
The investigation in Hungary reviewed the experience with the privatization of the nation's pension. A three-pillar pension scheme that was proposed by the World Bank was pushed through the Hungarian parliament in 1997. The first pillar of this scheme consisted of a pay-as-you-go, compulsory public pension, financed with contributions paid by employees. The second pillar was a compulsory private pension collected in individual capital accounts. The third pillar consisted of voluntary insurance and could be contracted through private insurance companies.

According to the law, every person entering the labour market for the first time had to join this three-pillar system, while those already employed had the right to choose within a certain period. The law provided substantial benefits to those who were already employed and opted to change to the private pillar. As a result, more than half of the country's employees changed to the private pension system, which led to an increase in the budget deficit of 1 per cent of GDP.

From the perspective of civil society organizations, the new pension system primarily benefited higher-income groups. The minimum benefit in the first pillar was so low that it was, for many, more like a small grant than a basic pension benefit. In the second pillar, future pensioners would pay a higher percentage of their income as a pension premium but, except in the case of those in high-income groups, might well receive lower benefits than before. And the voluntary insurance in the third pillar was, for all practical purposes, available only to those with high and stable incomes. Aware of these problems, the new government that took office in 1998 changed the system, giving much more emphasis to the compulsory public pillar.

Efficiency, ownership and macroeconomic considerations
Summing up the experiences of individual countries, at the microeconomic level there is no evidence that the form of ownership determines the level of efficiency or that privatization itself leads to greater efficiency. In some cases, increases in productivity after privatization can be attributed to the perform- ance of transnational firms that have located in a country as a consequence of the privatization process and the liberalization of capital flows.

At the macroeconomic level, at which the rate of economic growth can be taken as an indicator of efficiency, a review of the real rate of GDP growth in the countries studied shows no sign of any general acceleration of growth following the period of privatization that began in the 1980s. The experience of individual countries may differ, indeed, depending on their particular political or economic circumstances. For example, privatization in Hungary was accompanied by a steep drop in production, although this can be attributed not so much to privatization as to the impact of the collapse of COMECON cooperation. Furthermore, the upturn in subsequent years was due to the activity of transnational firms rather than to the privatized Hungarian ones. Yet, only a limited group of people benefited from this accelerated economic growth, while income and living conditions remained unchanged and even deteriorated for many sectors of society. The con- clusion can thus be drawn that efficiency, even in cases where economic growth has accelerated, does not necessarily lead to an improvement in the well-being of the whole of society.

In terms of the fiscal objectives of privatization, in some cases there is evidence that privatization reduced government subsidies to public enter- prises, although this did not occur in the case of privatization of certain utilities. At the same time, in several cases it appears that governments did not realize their objective of raising funds from the sale of public enterprises because a number of these companies were undervalued when sold. In Uganda, the majority (83 per cent) of those consulted noted such under-valuation in declaring that the government did not meet its financial objectives in the sale of public companies. In fact, the government had also injected substantial capital into these enterprises prior to their privatization. In Hungary, a total of US$9 billion was generated in revenue from the US$17 billion of assets (in 1990 prices) that were privatized. The remainder, approximately half of the original amount, disappeared or was wiped out during the privatization process, or was lost because assets were undervalued when sold. In El Salvador, the sale of public assets, together with the income from the reprivatization of the banks, only generated two million colons (less than US$230,000) or .002 per cent of the country's GDP.

Privatization involves the reallocation of property and property rights in a country. Local populations, however, often possess only limited capital that can be invested in newly privatized firms. Where there are not realistic possibilities to establish broad-based national ownership, or perhaps a lack of political interest in doing so, there is a danger of 'selling off' the entire economy and polarizing the country between powerful capital holders – often foreigners or ethnic minorities – and destitute wage earners.

In Uganda and many other countries, the principal beneficiaries of privatization have been foreigners.

In Uganda, as in many other countries, the principal beneficiaries of the privatization programme have been foreigners, who obtained 75 per cent of the total divestiture proceeds, while the local population gained only a 16-per cent share. This point was driven home at the Opening National Forum in Kampala. Participants reported that privatization has enriched a few transnationals and other large companies at the expense of the Ugandan people and is seen by many as 'legalized robbery', portending major problems down the road. In El Salvador, the privatized electricity distribution com-panies were acquired by foreign firms. In Hungary, privatization – together with new plants built by foreigners – resulted in a level of foreign ownership that is exceptionally high by international standards. According to a study published by the United Nations Conference on Trade and Development (UNCTAD) in 1999, the nation with the largest share of its exports produced by transnational firms is Hungary, at 65 per cent. In countries of similar size that are much more integrated in the European Union (like Sweden and Finland), the share is only in the 10–20 per cent range. The share of foreign capital exceeds 50 per cent in almost all branches of industry in Hungary, and foreign owners dominate the banking sector, as well. As a result, a dual economy has emerged in which all the important branches of industry are in foreign hands. While the short-term goals of privatization in Hungary included the rapid liquidation of state property and an increase in government revenue from its sale, there was no long-range concept of a need to ensure transparent regulation and maintain control over national economic management.

While a certain amount of foreign ownership in the industrial and service sectors may be advantageous for a developing or transition country because it might bring in advanced technology, knowledge and new products, the overwhelming effects of foreign influence may cause much uncertainty and difficulties. The dominance of foreign capital often obstructs the development of local industries or crowds out existing ones. Foreign firms are volatile, seeking higher profits from lower labour costs, and might decide to relocate, laying off employees and causing serious problems at the local level. At the macroeconomic level, the repatriation of profits or the withdrawal of capital can cause current-account problems and, in the worst of cases, destabilize the local currency. The general problem with the dominance of foreign ownership is that decisions affecting the lives of local populations are taken out of the control of local societies and are made by those who are not responsible for the well-being and security of local people.

Social Impact of Privatization

While the record of privatization is mixed in regard to achieving its economic objectives, its consequences are quite disappointing in social terms.

Employment effects
One of the major stated objectives of privatization was to increase employment, but in most cases the privatization of public enterprises has failed to meet the anticipated goal of creating more jobs. In nearly all the public enterprises that have been privatized, the laying off of employees has been a major aspect of the reform. Privatization has led to an increase in the demand for specialized skills but has lowered employment levels for the unskilled. In particular, privatization has worsened the employment situation of women who have lacked specialized skills.

The privatization of public enterprises has lowered employment levels for the unskilled.

In Bangladesh, about 89,000 workers were retrenched during the period 1995–7, and another sizable number of employees were awaiting dismissal as a result of further privatizations. Studies of the employment situation based on a survey of 205 privatized enterprises indicate that, among the firms still in operation, their workforces have been reduced by about a quarter. When taking into account those privatized firms that folded, nearly 40 per cent of workers employed in the previously state-owned enterprises lost their jobs. Furthermore, there has been a tendency to replace permanent workers with temporary labour, thereby reducing the overall job security of the employees who remain. Many of the latter, SAPRI Forum participants reported, are not receiving benefits.

In Hungary, privatization, as a rule, reduced the number of employees in the affected firms. Foreign direct investment, being capital-intensive, barely contributed to employment generation, creating jobs for only 2–3 per cent of the labour force. Thus, privatization did not result in higher employment levels nationally. In the public utility sector, National Forum participants charged, the national government failed to live up to its commitments to the labour unions, and extensive lay-offs ensued. Maintenance people were particularly hard hit, and this has led to declining services. Furthermore, the Forum participants said, the very real threat of unemployment has led workers to compromise their rights. It has become common practice, they reported, for newly privatized companies to contract employees for between one and three months at a time, leaving workers in a highly vulnerable situation. In this environment, employers have proceeded to ignore safety regulations, as well as to sweep aside or obstruct the formation of trade unions. This practice has been facilitated by the country's Employment Code, which came into effect in 1992.

Only in Uganda did a survey (of 39 privatized enterprises) show an overall average increase in employment, although the study concluded that the employment level was increasing at a decreasing rate. A breakdown of the firms surveyed showed, however, that approximately one third actually expanded employment levels, while a similar number experienced no change in employment and nearly as many firms actually saw declining employment levels. Indeed, those attending the Opening National Forum reported that the inadequate expansion of the private sector has enabled a sharp increase in unemployment. Those who have been retrenched by privatization have received little or no severance pay or training, leaving them to seek survival in the informal sector. The Forum participants added that the newly privatized enterprises have not provided job security or followed labour regulations. They have defied the constitution by not recognizing trade unions and by firing union organizers. Government regulatory mechanisms and laws have been weakened.

In general, while neoliberal theory predicted an increase in national employment after privatization as a consequence of attracting foreign direct investment and improvement in overall efficiency, SAPRI evidence shows no such tendency. While there might have been a positive employment impact in particular enterprises, there has been no such impact at the macro level. Privatization has only reallocated income at the national level, failing to contribute to macroeconomic efficiency.

At the enterprise level, while privatization has often increased the wages of some of those who were able to keep their jobs, not all employees have benefited. In Uganda, for example, employees who retained jobs in privatized firms received improved earnings, better benefits (such as medical insurance coverage and loan facilities) and greater opportunities for career enhancement. These improvements have been due primarily to increased productivity and output, as well as to the growing number of foreign-owned companies, which tend to pay higher salaries than do local ones. SAPRI Forum participants noted, however, that expatriates have received the higher-level jobs, leaving Ugandans with the low-level posts. Indeed, they complained of new private owners underpaying their Ugandan employees. At the same time, the move towards rationalization of privatized firms worsened income distribution, since the most vulnerable groups (those with low levels of education and low wages, most of whom are women) were in fact retrenched in the process of privatization. Furthermore, privatization has significantly increased discontent among workers in the sense that improved pay has come with increased workloads and other performance criteria that can be detrimental to the workers.

Impact on women
In most cases, privatization was costly for women, as they tended to be the ones with few specialized skills or none at all and thus formed the highest percentage of those laid off by the new owners. In Bangladesh, for example, privatization policies have led to widespread labour retrenchment, and the women who lost their jobs in this process were likely to be unskilled. Very few training programmes for alternative employment opportunities have been arranged for retrenched workers, and women found even fewer alternative job opportunities after losing their formal-sector jobs in mills and factories. Women have also been indirectly affected by the loss of jobs by male household members and the consequent reduction in family earnings.

Privatization has been costly for women, as they tend to be the ones with few specialized skills, or none at all.

In Hungary, women have often had to face discrimination by the new owners of privatized firms, who tended to rid their workforces of pregnant women and mothers with small children. In the case of privatization of public utilities, as was seen in El Salvador, women have tended to bear the brunt of rate increases following the privatization of electricity distribution. They have been forced to increase their domestic workload in order to compensate for reduced family consumption of electricity.

Family welfare

While those who have retained their jobs and maintained an adequate income stream were provided with a wider range of consumer choice as a result of privatization, a broad range of households were adversely affected by this process due to lay-offs and higher utility rates and service fees.

In Bangladesh, many jute mill employees who had enjoyed reasonably good living conditions lost their jobs and have suffered hardships as a result of privatization. They have been unable to feed their children properly, let alone send them to school and attend to their other necessities. Some former jute mill workers resorted to selling their personal assets, including land passed down through their families for generations and whatever they accumulated over their years working at the mills.

Meanwhile, the privatization of public utilities and services very often increased the prices of these services at an exceptional rate. In Hungary, where the prices for privatized services have risen twice as much as wages, paying for electricity, water, remote-heating service and gas caused often insoluble problems for poor families and especially for pensioners. According to National Forum participants, the rates have been increased to guarantee returns to private investors. In addition, the privatization of the public dental service in 1995 resulted in dentists without patients, on the one hand, and patients without good teeth, on the other, obligating the following government to re-establish the original state of dental care.

In Hungary, prices for privatized services have risen twice as much as wages, creating insoluble problems for poor families.

In El Salvador, as mentioned earlier, electricity rates increased by 47 per cent for low-end consumers in the two years following the privatization of distribution services, twice as much as the rate increase for high-end consumers. In some cases, in fact, rates for the highest levels of consumption, primarily the industrial sectors, dropped slightly during this period. Thus, privatization has both increased hardships for the poor and exacerbated inequalities. Those attending the SAPRI Opening National Forum from around the country explained that the higher rates have forced poor families to ration electricity use or resort to traditional energy sources, such as firewood, significantly increasing the demands of housework, as well as environmental damage. These demands, and the need to reduce family costs while adding to family income, have forced many children to leave school in order to work. The United Nations Children's Fund (UNICEF) calculated that the number of working children in El Salvador doubled during a recent three-year period. At the same time, Forum participants reported, access to electricity and the quality of service have declined. Low-income communities in rural areas, they said, have been hardest hit. The newly privatized electricity distribution companies do not see most rural areas as sufficiently profitable and therefore prefer to export power to neighbouring countries. There are regular and prolonged blackouts in some areas, overcharging is common and customer complaints are rarely addressed.

Distribution of wealth

The objective of creating a strong property-owning middle class through the privatization process was not achieved in the countries examined. Programmes that were intended to support the purchase of state property by employees and small businesses were weak, and governments, seemingly uncommitted to this goal, did little more than pay lip service to it in order to weaken the opposition to privatization from these social groups. There were also technical problems, such as the lack of viable capital markets.

In Uganda, the majority of respondents (82 per cent) in the survey carried out as part of the SAPRI research believed that the objective of creating a property-owning middle class had not been achieved. Very few Ugandans participated in the privatization of public enterprises, and the process has had a negligible impact on the well-being of most of the population. In Hungary, the situation is similar. Only very limited segments of society were able to participate in the privatization process and acquire state property. The heads of state-owned enterprises frequently became owners, National Forum participants pointed out, when these firms were converted into private partnerships. The relatively large middle class that developed during the period of rapid growth under socialism in the 1960s and 1970s has not been strengthened but has, rather, been eroded. The preference given to foreign investors diminished opportunities for local entrepreneurs to acquire privatized firms.

Transparency

It was a general perception of civil society organizations consulted during the SAPRI investigations that privatization had been accompanied by corruption and a lack of transparency. In Uganda, the majority (93 per cent) of those interviewed were of the view that the privatization programme was generally poorly managed and lacked transparency. There was also a widespread belief that privatization processes had not been free from political interference, corruption and underhand dealings in which foreigners and state officials were the only beneficiaries. Public demonstrations have ensued. The bidding process was revealed, in fact, to have been unfair and biased in favour of certain entities. Although the government documented the way in which the divestiture proceeds were utilized, there remains suspicion that the proceeds have been mismanaged.

In Bangladesh, the process of privatization also showed signs of corruption. There was no open tender, and valuation of the jute mills that were privatized was not done in a transparent manner. Just prior to privatization, profitable state-owned enterprises became losing concerns, and mills were sold at a very low price through an unholy alliance between the owner and policy makers. Furthermore, corruption took place in managing the mills even after they had been privatized. It very often happened that the owner himself overvalued the price of the purchased jute or other raw materials, as well as the machinery, and showed a loss on the balance sheet.

Civil society representatives at the Opening National Forum in Hungary complained of the corruption and cronyism that plagued that country's privatization process. They pointed to the insider dealing that enabled the transfer of public assets to the hands of a few influential individuals and to the decline in the value of affected firms.

In El Salvador, where there was a two-phased privatization process, the first generation of reforms was widely criticized for the lack of transparency in its management and implementation. While there was more public debate during the second phase, the general perception of the consulted population is that the programme implemented – including the regulatory framework, the functioning of the privatization agency, the criteria for supervision and the regulation of tariffs – was neither informed by nor sufficiently known to the public. According to Opening National Forum participants, the lack of transparency has led to a low level of public confidence in the supervision of the programme and in the allocation of the revenues generated by the privatization sales, especially in the case of electricity distribution.

Conclusion

The SAPRI investigations found that the effects of privatization varied, depending on the type of enterprise and the management of the process. Yet, overall, economies did not benefit as a whole, while significant sectors of country populations were adversely affected.

In some cases, limited economic benefits were found at the enterprise level, although not all privatized companies have increased productivity. For those that did, the gains did not translate into improvements at the macroeconomic level. Governments were found to have managed the privatization processes poorly; transparency was lacking, and the methods adopted for privatizing firms typically involved a top-down approach to setting the rules. Not surprisingly, the benefits of privatization have tended to flow almost entirely to those managing the process, thereby worsening the distribution of wealth. Retrenchments, which usually accompany the privatization process, exacerbated national employment levels, inequalities increased and the poor were left generally worse off. The process has also led to the displacement of domestic owners by foreigners.

With the privatization of public utilities, rates have generally increased without improvement in service or coverage.

When assessing the impact of privatization, a distinction must be made between the privatization of industrial enterprises involved in production and those enterprises that deliver basic services, such as water and electricity. In the country reviews of the privatization of public utilities, it was found that rates tended to increase without any improvement in service quality or coverage, thereby worsening access to essential services, with serious consequences for poor communities and families. The specific findings regarding privatization of public utilities can be summarized as follows:

- *Utility rate increases following privatization created further hardships for the poor and low-income segments of society.* In some cases, this led to an increase in the burden on women and to further environmental degradation.

- *Fiscal benefits from privatization have been at least in part derived from eliminating subsidies that allowed the poor to access services.* In fact, where state subsidies remained in place to ensure the supply of services to the poor and those living in remote areas, the presumed fiscal benefits from privatizing government ownership and management functions were eliminated.

- *The anticipated increase in efficiency of utility companies, when it did occur, in most cases did not result from improved operations.* Rather, the ratio of revenue to expenses rose as a result of price increases facilitated by virtual monopoly situations and weak government regulatory mechanisms.

- *Privatization has placed strategic services under foreign control.* Most of the privatized assets in the countries studied have been purchased by foreign companies, some of them public enterprises. As a result, the provision of services such as electricity, water and telecommunications in these countries now responds to the interests of foreign capital rather than to local needs.

The privatization of industrial enterprises was found to have had mixed results, depending on a range of pre-existing conditions. Some firms saw a growth in profits, others sustained or even increased losses, and some have gone out of business or have been shut down following privatization. Conclusions from the review of the privatization of industrial enterprises in the countries studied can be summarized as follows:

- *There is no evidence that the form of ownership determines the level of efficiency of a particular enterprise.* Overall, the increased profitability of privatized enterprises observed is due to circumstances that can exist under either private or public ownership. In some cases, increases in productivity at the microeconomic level can be attributed to the liberalization of capital flows and to the fact that transnational firms with ready access to capital had become the new private owners.

- *At the macroeconomic level, the real rate of growth in gross domestic product in the countries studied has revealed no trend towards acceleration resulting from privatization.* Even though the experience of individual countries varies depending on political or economic circumstances, privatization in itself has shown no sign of leading to an increase in overall macroeconomic efficiency.

- *Foreign ownership has increased as a result of privatization, potentially threatening national economic sovereignty.* While foreign ownership may bring advanced technology and new knowledge and products, the dominance of foreign capital tends to obstruct the development of local industries or crowd out existing ones. At the macroeconomic level, the repatriation of profits and the withdrawal of capital have caused current-account problems and, in the worst of cases, destabilized the local currency. Furthermore, foreign firms, seeking higher profits from lower labour costs, have in some cases suddenly decided to relocate and lay off employees, causing serious problems locally and illustrating the dangers of allowing decisions affecting the lives of local populations to be made by those who are not responsible for local well-being and security.

The effects of privatization programmes on the distribution of wealth are a central concern raised in the country studies. Privatization has not improved the socioeconomic welfare of the majority population in these societies, as the main benefits have flowed instead to a small group of the already privileged. In the privatization of both utilities and industrial enterprises, the following problems were observed at the national level:

- *Unemployment and job insecurity have increased overall.* Lay-offs accompanied privatization across the board, and new employment generation did not always compensate for jobs lost. Privatization has fostered discontent among those workers who did not lose their jobs, because workloads have increased, employment has become less secure and the power to organize and negotiate with employers has been weakened.

- *Privatization has contributed to increasing inequality and has been particularly detrimental to minority groups and women, who tend to lack specialized skills.* Income distribution has worsened as large numbers of low-skilled, low-wage workers have been the first to be laid off. Job training or other similar programmes, where they have existed, have been either ineffective or insufficient to address the problems of the newly unemployed. While new employment generated in privatized firms has tended to be better paid, these jobs have required higher skill levels. Furthermore, the anticipated creation of a strong property-owning middle class through privatization has not occurred. Overall, wealth has become more concentrated.

- *Privatization processes have lacked transparency.* Governments have often managed privatization programmes poorly and failed to involve workers and citizens' groups in these processes, while regulatory mechanisms have proven ineffective in ensuring adequate oversight. In SAPRI countries, taxpayers have felt robbed of their public assets, and governments have been unable to raise the levels of revenue anticipated from enterprise sales because many were undervalued when sold.

Privatization has not improved the socioeconomic welfare of the majority population in these societies.

State enterprises often serve important social or national objectives, so the utility of a given public company cannot be measured solely by the profitability of the firm itself. While the privatization of such enterprises may increase their profitability in a narrow economic sense, it may destroy important social and national benefits, thereby reducing efficiency in the broader sense. Furthermore, the desired role of state-owned firms should depend on the development level of the particular country. In capital-poor developing countries, state-owned enterprises may help technological development, strengthen local industries and improve employment levels.

Given these considerations, the following basic recommendations emanate from the SAPRI studies. A decision on privatization should involve considerations of the strategic social and national functions that the enterprise serves; it should not be based solely on narrowly defined measures of efficiency or profitability. A mix of different ownership forms, based on each country's unique set of social, economic, political and cultural circumstances, can best serve the development needs of that country. Experience with the privatization of essential public services in the countries SAPRI studied – and others, too – suggests, however, that these concerns should remain under state or local government control in order to best ensure the provision of affordable quality services to all segments of the population. In any event, decisions regarding ownership structure should be made locally, and foreign loans and aid should not be tied to any pre-conditions in this regard.

A decision on privatization should involve consideration of the strategic social and national functions of the enterprise.

Although the benefits of foreign investment and ownership are recognized, measures should be taken so that transnational companies do not displace local firms through privatization processes. Priority should be given to support the development of domestic industries to meet local needs. Finally, mechanisms of citizen participation should be developed and supported in order to facilitate a transparent flow of information, which would in turn diminish corruption and give citizens greater influence over decision-making processes.

CHAPTER 6

The Impact of Agricultural Sector Adjustment Policies on Small Farmers and Food Security

This chapter summarizes the social and economic impacts of agricultural reform policies drawn from three SAPRI assessments carried out in Bangladesh, Uganda and Zimbabwe, as well as from CASA exercises in the Philippines and Mexico. There were some differences in the focus of each of these investigations. The research in Uganda and Zimbabwe looked at the effects of a series of policies in the agricultural sector, while the Philippines study adopted an approach that analyzed the impact of a particular policy on a specific agricultural subsector. In Bangladesh two separate studies were carried out, one focusing on the impact of the reforms on crop sector profitability and the other addressing the issue of food security.

The agricultural sector is regarded as the backbone of the Zimbabwean and Ugandan economies, providing employment for about 70 per cent of their respective populations. It contributes about 40 per cent of total export earnings in the case of Zimbabwe and 43 per cent of GDP in the case of Uganda. In Bangladesh, the sector represents one third of GDP. In the Philippines, rice is the main source of income in the rural economy and constitutes the staple food for about 85 per cent of the population.

The performance of the sector prior to the reforms in these countries had been deemed inadequate by the international financial institutions for a number of reasons. In Uganda, agriculture was said to have stagnated because of an overvalued exchange rate and the inefficient operations of the parastatal agricultural marketing boards, which had discouraged production. In Bangladesh, production inefficiency, inequity in foodgrain distribution and inadequate foreign exchange for the importation of farming supplies were seen to be undermining the potential of the agricultural sector. In Zimbabwe, the government's direct involvement in production, distribution and marketing of agricultural inputs and commodities was considered an obstacle to the development of the sector.

Objectives, Policies, Strategies and Design of Agricultural Reform

The agricultural reform policies in the various countries studied were implemented within the framework of structural adjustment programmes supported by the World Bank and IMF. The principal stated objectives of the reforms in the various countries were to increase agricultural productivity and production, boost agricultural exports as a basis for national economic growth, improve farmers' incomes and ensure food security.

The policies pursued reflected the development strategy favoured by the Bank and Fund. At the macro level, the strategy includes a reduction in the role of the state in order to reduce government expenditure; restrictive monetary as well as fiscal policies; an expansion of the role of the private sector to promote economic growth; and liberalized internal and external trade intended to allow the market, rather than the government, to direct resource allocation and determine prices of inputs and outputs. While countries implemented similar restrictive macroeconomic programmes that had their own impact on the agricultural sector, there were differences in emphasis when it came to the specific sector policies pursued in each nation. These depended in large part on the diagnosis of the principal reasons deemed to have been holding back the respective agricultural sectors.

The objectives of the reforms were to increase agricultural productivity, boost exports, improve farmers' incomes and ensure food security.

Below is a summary of specific policies aimed at reforming the agricultural sector in the countries studied.

In Zimbabwe, the main policies were:

- reduction of direct state involvement in the production, distribution and marketing of agricultural inputs and commodities;
- removal of subsidies on agricultural inputs and credit;
- liberalization of export and import trade; and
- privatization of agricultural marketing.

In Uganda, the reforms emphasized:

- liberalization of the exchange rate (to eliminate currency overvaluation);
- control of inflation;
- liberalization of trade in agricultural inputs and outputs;

- provision of export incentives to the private sector (removal of export tax); and
- removal of government subsidies in the agricultural sector.

In the Philippines, the principal policies were:

- foreign exchange liberalization and currency devaluation;
- price and market liberalization;
- parastatal reform and privatization;
- export promotion; and
- removal of subsidies.

In Mexico, the measures adopted included:

- constitutional reforms facilitating the privatization and concentration of land and natural resources;
- reduction of state participation in agricultural production;
- privatization of the production and distribution of agricultural inputs and services; and
- liberalization of trade in agricultural commodities.

In Bangladesh, emphasis was placed on:

- increased private sector involvement in irrigation and fertilizer distribution;
- reduction in subsidies on agricultural inputs;
- introduction of floor prices for some agricultural products; and
- liberalization of foodgrain exports and imports.

The lack of participation in the design of these policies by the people most affected by them was an issue of concern from the outset of SAPRI. Policy design has been the preserve of technical experts in the ministries of planning, finance and agriculture, the World Bank and the IMF. In Zimbabwe, interviews with stakeholders in the agricultural sector revealed that there had been no consultation with farmers' groups representing either large-scale producers or smallholders. In Bangladesh, consistent with the criticism of all adjustment programmes, agricultural policies were seen as 'coming from above' from the powerful donors, with inadequate consultation and no effort to take into consideration the concerns of the poor. In Uganda, interviews carried out under the SAPRI study, as well as earlier studies, indicate that, while the rural poor are able to articulate the impacts of economic policies that they experience in their daily lives, they have been given little information about the specific policies negotiated with the Bank.

Civil society representatives attending the Opening National Forum in Kampala stressed that the government had not consulted local producers in the process of policy formulation and had instead imposed policies that did not take into account micro-level dynamics.

The lack of participation in the design of agricultural policies was an issue of concern from the outset of SAPRI.

Economic Impact of the Reform Policies

Production

One of the basic principles behind market liberalization is that the removal of distortions in the market will eventually increase the real producer prices for specific commodities, benefiting individual farmers and giving them a direct incentive to increase production of those goods. According to the country assessments, however, instead of benefiting farmers across the board, the impact of the reform policies on agricultural production has been mixed. These results are not surprising in that they reflect differences in the structure of the economies in the different countries, as well as their internal inequalities. In Uganda, for instance, agriculture is dominated by small-scale producers, while in Zimbabwe, a small group of commercial farmers dominates agricultural production. In some countries – such as Uganda, Bangladesh and Zimbabwe – studies indicated that overall agricultural production increased, while in others it declined. Just as importantly, within individual countries the production of some crops increased while that of others fell.

Export promotion has led to heightened inequalities, as many farmers have lacked an equal opportunity to enter and benefit within a liberalized market.

Export promotion has been an important element of the agricultural reform programmes designed to stimulate agriculture-led growth in all of these countries. Yet, in several cases this emphasis has led to heightened inequalities, as many farmers have lacked an equal opportunity to enter and benefit within a liberalized market. In addition, constraints such as lack of rural infrastructure were inadequately addressed, and export earnings were subject to world price fluctuations. In some countries, such as Zimbabwe, the expected market diversification did not occur, while in others, like the Philippines, an increase in agricultural export earnings in one subsector occurred at the expense of others. Furthermore, production for export has often occurred at the expense of production for the local market, as has been the case in Mexico.

In Zimbabwe, the production of maize increased marginally from 1.42 million tons in 1997/8 to 1.54 million tons in 1998/9 – a level of production that remained below the approximately 2.5 million tons required for human consumption and livestock feed, representing a change from the persistent surplus in production experienced years earlier. This shortfall in production is attributed to liberalization, which has resulted in a shift to tradables, such as horticultural products. Furthermore, the rising cost of inputs, such as seeds and fertilizer, reached such heights that the communities were forced to drastically reduce acreage under cultivation. Following the removal of subsidies on fertilizers and other agro-chemicals, their prices shot up by over 300 per cent in five years. In addition, the more stringent repayment procedures of the Agricultural Finance Corporation that were established under the adjustment programme made this traditional source of assistance to small farmers inaccessible.

Rural sector representatives at the Opening National Forum in Harare explained that farmers' competitiveness had been hurt by cuts in government spending on roads and transport systems, as well as processing, storage and distribution systems. Farmers were also negatively affected by the loss of information once provided by state marketing boards, by an insufficiency of technical services and by high interest rates, as well as by a lack of access to land.

The case of cotton in Zimbabwe illustrates the problem of market monopolization by large companies after liberalization. Prior to reforms, a number of firms competed to purchase farmers' produce. However, deregulation of the cotton industry in 1993 created the context for the Cotton Company of Zimbabwe (Cottco) to dominate the industry and thereby to establish monopolistic control of cotton prices, set quality standards that small farmers are unable to meet and, at the same time, cut back its input credit scheme from which many small farmers had benefited. As a result, most small farmers were no longer able to sell their produce at prices that cover their costs and still meet the quality requirements demanded by Cottco.

The reduced production of maize in Zimbabwe is attributed to liberalization, which forced communities drastically to reduce acreage under cultivation.

In the livestock sector of Zimbabwe, the significant decline in the cattle population was attributed to several economic and environmental problems.

Currency devaluation that was intended to promote exports served to increase the price of imported feed, significantly raising costs to farmers. Market liberalization of the beef sector induced private sector involvement in livestock purchases and in the slaughtering and marketing of beef. It also removed government price supports, which led to a drop in commodity prices to farmers, as the state-run Cold Storage Commission of Zimbabwe was no longer able to compete.

In Uganda, the area under cultivation of coffee, the country's main crop, increased from 250,000 hectares in 1992/3 to 300,000 hectares in 1999/ 2000, while production rose from 2.8 million (60-kilogram) bags to 3.2 million bags. This increase resulted from a government programme to expand coffee plantations through an export-promotion drive that included the removal of export constraints and the improvement of physical infrastructure. However, this occurred as world coffee prices plummeted during the second half of the 1990s, so that the value of coffee exports fell from a peak of US$432.5 million in 1994 to US$164.8 million at the end of the decade.

Fish production in Uganda also increased with the advent of export trade in the subsector, but it later started to decline as a result of liberalization. Overexploitation of lakes by fishermen seeking to take advantage of market opportunities and make quick profits led to environmental problems, depleting fish stocks and endangering future production. Furthermore, prices on the local market increased and rendered fish unaffordable to local communities that had previously relied on this inexpensive and nutritious food product.

The decline of production in the livestock sector in Uganda resulted from a number of factors, some of which are a result of liberalization, such as the increase in the price of veterinary inputs. In addition, demand for meat has decreased as a result of increased poverty due to retrenchments and the restructuring of the labour market, as well as of currency devaluation that reduced the real value of the shilling. There has been a dramatic shift towards poultry rearing and consumption, as both fish and meat are no longer affordable for many households.

In the Philippines, government support for rice production has not kept pace with the rising needs of the growing population. This has been due in part to the quantitative ceilings on budget deficits imposed by the IMF that have prevented adequate and necessary investments in the rice industry, thus leading to a decline in production of rice.

On the other hand, in the case of shrimp farming in the Philippines, the policy reforms led to a conducive environment that stimulated investment in shrimp production for export. This resulted in the adoption of intensive shrimp-farming methods that were intended to shorten the loan repayment period and increase profits. A direct socioeconomic impact of this experience, however, has been the loss of common property rights in favour of private ownership of land and water resources through permits or titles. Furthermore, this intensive production has had quite negative environmental consequences.

In Bangladesh, policy reforms that dramatically lowered input costs, together with the spread of irrigation, fertilizer use and adoption of improved seeds, led to an increase of about 40 per cent in foodgrain production in the 1980s. With the deepening of adjustment reforms in the 1990s, however, agricultural growth was driven by production in the non-crop sectors – forestry, fisheries and livestock – as a result of growing demand constraint, lack of export markets and declining real prices.

Farmers' incomes
Again, one of the important principles of liberalization is that when prices are determined by the market there will be a more efficient allocation of resources within the productive sector. Farmers are expected to respond rationally by allocating more of their productive resources to those commodities that fetch higher prices and hence increase their household incomes. Although this was one of the major objectives of agricultural reforms, it did not occur in practice in the countries studied. Contrary to the assumptions underlying the reforms, production in the sector is not homogeneous and farmers do not have equal opportunities to enter and gain in an open market system.

> **Smallholders in Zimbabwe were most affected by the removal of subsidies on agricultural inputs, a reduction of public expenditure on extension services and the high cost of credit.**

In Zimbabwe, the study found that liberalization did not necessarily result in higher prices to farmers overall. Large-scale farmers who enjoyed economies of scale, as well as export producers who benefited from currency devaluation, may have enjoyed increased incomes. Smallholders and communal farmers and those who produce for the domestic market, however, have not. The situation of smallholders was most affected by the removal of subsidies on agricultural inputs, a reduction of public expenditure on extension services and the high cost of credit, which increased the cost of production and also reduced the returns on most farming activities. Furthermore, as a result of liberalization, private middlemen replaced the state in the marketing of farm inputs and produce for the smallholder sector. This placed these farmers at a disadvantage as far as determining the price of their produce was concerned. Ill-informed about market conditions and facing transportation and infrastructure constraints, they were forced to sell at low prices, sometimes even below market prices, as they did during the 1995/6 season.

In participatory surveys carried out as part of the SAPRI research, Zimbabwean farmers complained that, prior to the reforms, they were buying agricultural inputs such as seeds, fertilizer and farming equipment at relatively cheap prices, but the liberalization of trade introduced by the adjustment programme had allowed traders to charge exorbitant prices for these inputs. Farmers further argued that, forced to reduce their purchases of inputs, they suffered low yields, particularly in areas with low rainfall or characterized by poor soils. They said the phase-out of subsidies on agricultural inputs should have been more gradual. High interest rates and the difficulty of obtaining loans due to the banks' demand for substantial property as collateral security were also general complaints. Lack of an adequate land redistribution programme was another reason cited by communal farmers for their plight.

In Uganda, the picture was quite similar. The assessment there concluded that agricultural reform and liberalization had not improved the real incomes of farmers, particularly the small-scale ones. Although producer prices for some crops rose, there was also a general rise in the cost of production, and only those farmers who already had the resources were able to benefit.

As a result of inadequate investment in the rice industry in the Philippines, productivity has remained low, and this has translated into low levels of income for rice farmers. In the case of shrimp farming, export-oriented production fostered by the policy reforms led to the application of commercial methods of intensive shrimp production. The resulting overexploitation of natural resources in the search for quick profits generated both environmental deterioration and a reduction in areas for cultivation of traditional crops; in turn, this limited the capacity of local communities to engage in traditional economic activities, leading to increased income erosion and growing inequality.

In Bangladesh, findings on crop sector profitability indicate a decline in the 1990s. Liberalization measures, it was agreed at the Opening National Forum, have resulted in a disproportionately large increase in the price of productive inputs, including import-dependent fertilizers, seeds and irrigation equipment. The withdrawal of subsidies for the poor, the privatization of the agricultural input distribution system, the oligopolistic behaviour of private input traders, the inadequate provision of food-purchase and storage facilities by the government, the decline in the regulation of fertilizer, seed and pesticide standards, and reduced access to formal credit institutions and affordable micro-credit have hurt small farmers in particular. At the same time, the prices of most crop sector produce have only marginally increased. With cost increases outweighing the impact of price rises, farmers overall failed to benefit from the reforms.

With cost increases outweighing the impact of price rises in Bangladesh, farmers overall failed to benefit from the reforms.

In Mexico, a series of participatory workshops in four different regions of the country revealed a significant deterioration in conditions for small-scale producers and peasants in rural areas. Participants indicated that the dismantling of state services and the withdrawal of subsidies for rural production created an unequal playing field in which large-scale producers and foreign companies gained at the expense of small farmers, who could not afford the increasing costs of production and did not have access to affordable credit. Under the adjustment programme, placing priority on modernized and large-scale agriculture has created new problems, such as contraction and segmentation of the domestic market, dependency on imports and reduction in consumption. The result has been a growing number of people living in extreme poverty.

Food security

In most of the sample countries, ensuring food security was a specific objective of the reform policies. In this context, food security has been understood to mean access to adequate and nutritious food by all people at all times. Adjustment measures have been designed based on the assumption that local supply is not important, as access to food could be obtained through the market.

All the country studies, with the exception of the one in Bangladesh, concluded that there had been a worsening food security situation as a result of the agricultural reforms. In the light of the level of vulnerability of the rural poor and the decline in the income levels of farmers, as evidenced above, agricultural reform policies should have been oriented to address both overall food supply as well as access to adequate, quality food by all population groups.

In Zimbabwe, where food production during the 1990s did not keep up with population growth, the food security situation worsened at the end of the decade, with 30 per cent of children under age five chronically malnourished. The SAPRI investigation found that the reform policies led to a reduction in the capacity of rural communities to produce their own food due to the rising cost of agricultural inputs. Policy interventions promoted the commercialization of smallholder agriculture, emphasizing production for cash rather than for home consumption. Small-scale farmers were unable, however, to afford expensive hybrid seeds and fertilizers. Farmers were forced to reduce acreage under cultivation, while land fertility dropped owing to limited use of fertilizers and inadequate extension services, and yields decreased.

A policy focus on shifting national production towards horticulture, which became the second largest agricultural foreign exchange earner after tobacco, also did not benefit small-scale farmers. Zimbabwe's export push, SAPRI Forum participants said, also shifted land from the cultivation of maize and other food crops to that of other high-revenue-generating export crops such as paprika and cotton. This created shortages of basic staple foods and further raised consumer prices. Hence, in order to meet household needs, such as school fees for children, poor farmers resorted to the sale of stored grain, which caused families to suffer shortages before their next harvest, or of other assets, such as livestock, which embodied any limited savings they might have had. The increase in basic food prices further exacerbated household food insecurity of the poor. At the national level, Zimbabwe, since the privatization of its marketing boards and the liberalization and deregulation of the agricultural sector, has been transformed, Forum participants said, from a country that met all its domestic food needs and still had enough maize and wheat to export, to one that had to import food from South Africa, Kenya and Mozambique.

The emphasis on exports in Uganda led to higher food insecurity and reduced food reserves among poor households.

In the case of Uganda, the study concluded that the emphasis on exports, including non-traditional exports, when food production was not keeping up with population growth, had led to higher food insecurity and, in particular, to reduced food reserves among poor households. Increases in coffee production, a major Ugandan export, appear to have been achieved at the expense of food crop production in some regions. In Masaka district, for instance, an expansion of coffee production was paralleled by a decline in the production of maize and beans. Furthermore, while the liberalization of agricultural markets resulted in higher prices for agricultural produce, only the better-off farmers were able to respond and increase their production. The situation of poor households was further worsened by the pressing need to meet the higher cost of social services, such as healthcare and education, under the adjustment programme. Participants at the SAPRI Opening National Forum reported an increase in malnutrition in the country.

In the Philippines, food security has suffered because, under IMF-imposed conditions, the production of rice has not been able to keep pace with increasing demand resulting from population growth. As a result of this growing food deficit, there has been a growing dependency on rice imports that have been subject to the volatility of world prices. At the same time, the stimulation of intensive export-oriented shrimp farming was accompanied not only by negative environmental effects but also by the displacement of cultivation of food staples by local communities.

Mexico's *per capita* production of basic grains fell as a result of adjustment policies that liberalized imports and reduced government support for small-scale farmers.

The investigation in Mexico pointed to the growing deficit in the nation's food supply, the increase in the amount of grain imports, and rising malnutrition indices under the country's adjustment programme. The country's *per capita* production of basic grains fell by nearly 10 per cent from 1980 to 2000 as a result of adjustment policies that liberalized imports and reduced government support for small-scale farmers. Food dependence went from an average of 18 per cent in the early 1980s to 43 per cent at the end of the 1990s. In 1996 alone, nearly half of domestic consumption of basic grains was met through imports, at a cost that surpassed by 50 per cent the government's entire budget for the rural sector. At the same time, poverty levels increased, as reform policies served to benefit a small group of large-scale enterprises engaged in production for export markets rather than to stimulate investment in domestic food production that would benefit small-scale producers, generate employment in rural areas and thereby improve food security. In fact, the further concentration of land brought about by the reforms, together with the promotion of large-scale production for export, left many rural communities unable to produce their own food and forced them to buy their required foodstuffs on the market at prices they could not afford. Compensatory programmes proved insufficient to address the problems of much of the rural population and, at best, only resolved issues of immediate survival.

In the case of Bangladesh, the study's conclusion was that the consumption of cereals had reached a level higher than the minimum requirement for achieving balanced nutrition. There was, however, a marginal deficit for tubers and vegetables and substantial deficits for livestock products, pulses and oilseeds. Overall, the observed trend towards improved food security was attributed to the results of Green Revolution technology that, it was pointed out, did not take into account the substantial negative impacts on the environment, especially on soil and surface and ground water.

Social and Environmental Impacts

Socioeconomic differentiation

A major concern of civil society has been the fact that adjustment policies have not taken into account existing socioeconomic differentiation in each nation. Consequently, little or no consideration has been given to how policy impacts might reinforce differentiated access to economic opportunities and exacerbate inequalities. The studies indicate that the reforms did, in fact, generate differentiated impacts on a range of socioeconomic groups. For example, the effects of adjustment policies often differed for large-scale as opposed to small-scale farmers, rich farmers and poor farmers, export crop producers versus those producing primarily for the domestic market.

> **The effects of adjustment policies often differed among farmers, depending on their size, income level and market destination.**

In Zimbabwe, the overall impact of the reform measures proved rather negative for small-scale farmers, in particular, as they were more affected by marketing constraints than were large-scale producers, who enjoyed economies of scale. Poorly developed market information systems to link farmers and buyers, the inaccessibility of some marketing channels, and a lack of guaranteed markets for their produce made smallholders more beholden to middlemen once the government's role was reduced under liberalization. In practice, this resulted in higher input costs and lower produce prices for small-scale farmers. As a result, total acreage under crop production declined in the communal and resettlement areas. Yet, more and more people in these areas became dependent on agriculture owing to the natural growth of the population and adjustment-induced retrenchments in other sectors of the economy. Under these circumstances, the lack of land redistribution proved to be a major constraint on smallholder production. Other constraints on agricultural production, such as the high cost and reduced availability of credit and declining public investment in research and extension services, also bore more heavily on small-scale farmers.

In Uganda, SAPRI Forum participants reported, reduced profitability for small producers is contributing in large part to the very high poverty level in villages. In the absence of government programmes and adequate infrastructure, petty traders and transport owners are profiting from a retail price mark-up in Kampala that can reach ten times the farmgate price.

Differential access to productive resources, roads and markets for different groups of Ugandan farmers conditioned their response to the price incentives created by agricultural liberalization. For instance, increased producer prices for coffee benefited only those farmers with the land and other resources to expand coffee production. Small farmers with limited land were unable to take advantage of such opportunities, and they fared worse since they faced the same increases as large-scale farmers in the cost of inputs. Differences in regional development within the country were another important factor that led to differentiated impacts and tended to exacerbate existing inequalities. World Bank and Finance Ministry representatives at the Opening National Forum acknowledged that poor rural physical and financial infrastructure has contributed to the negative effects of liberalization at the local, or household, level.

Access to productive resources, roads and markets for different groups of Ugandan farmers conditioned their response to the price incentives created by agricultural liberalization.

The participatory survey in Uganda revealed that citizens' views on the agricultural reforms differed from one community to another and according to the socioeconomic position of the respondents. In Kabarole district, for instance, people were of the view that liberalization of trade in agricultural products had produced positive results, since farmers were now free to sell to any buyer of their choice instead of having prices dictated to them by the marketing boards, as was the case in the past. This same sentiment was expressed by the wealthy farmers in Kalangala district, who were impressed with the prompt payment for their produce that the new system had introduced. In the same district, however, the poor farmers complained that farming was not remunerative enough. Only traders and not farmers could afford to buy cars, for example. In other districts across the country, farmers associated liberalization with exploitative traders. Poor roads and the high cost of transportation made it difficult to explore markets outside their immediate locality, putting farmers at the mercy of the middlemen. The barrier that poor infrastructure posed to effective marketing of farm produce was a recurrent theme in many of the responses given by farmers.

The study in Mexico shows that existing economic and social inequalities in rural areas were also exacerbated in that country as a result of the reforms. In the rural economy, a very small percentage of producers have access to good quality land, infrastructure and modern technology, with which they have developed production for export. At the same time, several million small-scale producers, with few resources and little access to infrastructure and technology, are engaged in small-scale production for subsistence and for the domestic market. This dual nature of the economy has created a situation in which only large-scale producers with access to resources have been able to take advantage of agricultural policy shifts and increase production of exports. Withdrawal of government support for production and credit provision particularly hurt small and medium-scale producers who cultivate basic grains. Funds channelled to the rural sector by the state-run development bank fell precipitously in the 1990s, Opening Forum participants reported, and financing generally for any farmers producing for the domestic market became difficult to find. Public programmes that were later instituted to compensate for such negative effects were too limited in scope, were not sustained, and ultimately benefited large-scale producers most. The study concluded that the reforms had increased economic concentration and social exclusion.

Only large-scale producers with access to resources have been able to take advantage of agricultural policy shifts in Mexico.

The displacement of rural communities and the consequent massive urban migration that has resulted from the further impoverishment and marginalization of small-scale farmers in the Philippines, as well as the disproportionate burden on women of a loss of food security, were important social impacts emphasized at the Opening National Forum in Manila. Insufficient state support for infrastructure services, such as irrigation, post-harvest facilities and farm-to-market roads, has meant that small-scale farmers are unable to improve productivity levels or get their products to market at prices that cover their costs. Liberalization of prices following privatization of the marketing board also had a negative impact on farmers. Cultivation of rice and other staples was said to be on the decline, and small-scale farmers who cultivate food crops have found themselves further marginalized. Participants also spoke of the lack of access to formal credit as a key problem for farmers, whose only option is the informal market, which offers short-term loans at exorbitant rates.

In Bangladesh, a participatory well-being analysis was carried out in three villages with different levels of irrigation to assess the impact on poverty of agricultural policies that liberalized provision of irrigation systems. It showed that poverty declined over time in all the villages studied regardless of the intensity of irrigation coverage, but the rate of reduction had been lowest in the village where irrigation development had been the highest. Furthermore, the condition of the very poor worsened over time in all three villages, while those who were already better off gained the most from the irrigation services. Thus, inequality worsened in all three villages over time, although at varying rates.

Gender-differentiated impact

The design of reforms did not take gender issues into consideration, and this was a particular concern of civil society. The country studies indicate that the policy reforms had a substantial difference in impact on men and women that depended on a number of factors. The existing gender-based division of labour, relative access to and control of resources (such as land and credit) by women, and the position of women in various cultures were important factors determining the degree of difference women experienced under the agricultural policy reforms.

> **The design of reforms did not take into consideration the existing gender-based division of labour, relative access to resources by women, and the position of women in different cultures.**

In Zimbabwe, women (and children) do most of the farming work, particularly in the communal areas. Yet, the particular conditions faced by women in the sector were not taken into account in the design of reforms. Women's participation in agricultural activity in Zimbabwe is handicapped by their limited access to land and credit. Land ownership rights are vested in heads of households, who are usually men, and female heads of household have difficulty acquiring land. The constitution of Zimbabwe reinforces this traditional pattern of land ownership and does not guarantee the rights of women to own land or acquire property. As land usually serves as collateral for access to agricultural credit, women have very limited access to bank loans; less than 10 per cent of credit for smallholder farmers was granted to women, who received an even smaller share of extension services. There are only a few programmes specifically aimed at female farmers.

In Uganda, men generally cultivate cash or export crops while women grow food for home consumption. Intensification of production for cash or export as part of the adjustment programme has tended to increase the responsibilities of women, who are often required to contribute to the cultivation of cash crops in addition to their food crops, which are not consistently the focus of adjustment policies. This is particularly true in cases where the families are unable to hire labour.

The investigation also found regional variations in the power relations between men and women that tend to be reinforced by the reforms. Thus, in some places when the agricultural reforms are accompanied by higher incomes, men acquire more wives, who then have to compete more intensely for the favours of the men. In such circumstances, women may even hand over the money they earn for the men to spend. In other places, such as Kabale, women carry out agricultural production without the help of men and even take responsibility for paying taxes. In such cases, women make the decisions as to how to spend their money, and the reforms generally tend to strengthen their position. Women in Bushenyi district, for instance, welcomed the commercialization of traditional food crops, which enabled them to get and control some monetary income. In districts ravaged by HIV/AIDS, women's involvement in cultivation for cash or export tends to be higher, as widows have to take responsibility for activities previously undertaken by their husbands.

In Mexico, the participation of women in agricultural production grew in the course of the reforms – from 12 per cent of the workforce in 1991 to 17 per cent in 1997. The increased female involvement in the sector was due to two main factors. First, some women took the place of their husbands who migrated abroad to find work. The absentee husbands, however, still remained the legal owners of the land, and much of the women's work was regarded as unpaid family labour. The proportion of women in agriculture who received no remuneration increased from 51 per cent in 1991 to 64 per cent in 1997. There was also an increase in paid female labour in the agricultural sector, however, due to the relative increase in agro-export production that is labour-intensive. Yet these jobs tended to be low-paying with poor working conditions, and women employed in them often carry the additional burdens of domestic work and unpaid family labour.

Environmental impact

Agricultural production often has considerable environmental effects, yet these, too, are not taken into account in the design of reform policies.

The reform policies in the Philippines encouraged intensive shrimp farming for export, which produced substantial negative environmental effects.

As noted earlier, the reform policies in the Philippines encouraged intensive shrimp farming for export, which produced substantial negative environmental effects such as the degradation and pollution of the mangrove and coastal ecosystem, as well as the adjacent land and water resources. This was confirmed by case studies conducted in a number of municipalities, including Hinatuan and Mindanao, on intensive and semi-intensive shrimp farms. The study documented negative effects that included the destruction of mangroves through their conversion into fishponds; the pollution of water systems through the use of chemicals, pesticides and antibiotics; the accumulation and discharge of untreated residues (such as prawn wastes and uneaten feeds); and salinization and depletion of local water resources.

Agricultural reforms have also caused considerable soil degradation and loss of biodiversity in the Philippines. As was related at the Opening National Forum in Manila, the expanded allocation of public resources and services, such as irrigation, to the production of bananas and other export crops has engendered a large increase in their cultivation, large-scale mono-cropping and the extensive use of chemicals.

In Bangladesh, there has been concern about environmental degradation resulting from fertilizer use without proper controls and compliance with standards, a product of market liberalization and deregulation. In addition, intensive irrigation schemes also fostered by market liberalization have caused excessive extraction of ground water that is believed to have led to the drying up of aquifers during the dry season, as well as to arsenic poisoning of the water.

The elimination of government extension programmes in Uganda, it was explained at the country's Opening National Forum, has left private traders to advise on farming methods, such as the use of chemicals, and this has had disastrous consequences. There is evidence, as well, that although liberaliza-tion has helped expand production in the fish sector, it has also caused various environmental problems. The European Union, for example, placed a ban on fish from Uganda in response to poor sanitary conditions in the sector. The study also indicates that commercialization has led to depletion of fish stocks in most of the country's water bodies due to overexploitation resulting from unregulated competition between traditional artisan fishing and sophisticated commercial fishing trawlers.

The assessment in Mexico indicates that the reform policies that have favoured large-scale monoculture and have led to a further concentration of resources have also served to accentuate the loss of biodiversity and to promote the overuse of poor-quality land, which is accelerating the process of soil erosion. In the southwestern states of Michoacan and Guerrero, for example, large-scale horticulture, with its indiscriminate use of agro-chemicals, has accelerated soil degradation. In the more arid northern and central regions, the diversion of scarce water resources to large-scale producers – made possible by legislative changes that have served to privatize certain aspects of water distribution – is accelerating deterioration of water tables, with potentially catastrophic social and environmental consequences. At the same time, small-scale farmers and the poor have been pushed onto more marginal quality land, which they use more intensively as they are faced with a lack of alternatives for employment and income, causing further soil erosion and other environmental degradation.

> **The reform policies have favoured large-scale monoculture in Mexico and promoted the overuse of poor-quality land by small-scale farmers and the poor.**

Conclusion

The investigations show that the agricultural sector reforms have not, on the whole, improved the well-being of those living in the rural sector in the SAPRI and CASA countries. Agricultural production has increased in some countries but not in others, while some crops have gained as the production of others declined. Where exports have expanded, often this has occurred at the expense of production for the domestic market. Furthermore, these adjustment policies have had differentiated impacts along socioeconomic lines, and, as a result, rural inequality has worsened. Those who previously had access to productive resources have tended to be those who benefited, while the poor have often been further marginalized.

The real incomes of farmers, particularly small-scale ones, have not improved, principally because the prices of agricultural inputs have risen everywhere. Even where there were increases in produce prices, the rise in the cost of production has generally been higher. With reduced or inadequate cultivation of food crops for the domestic market, along with a lack of improvement in earnings by many low-income sectors and a rise in the cost of living, there has been a general deterioration in food security nearly everywhere. In several areas, the new patterns of agricultural production resulting from the reforms have led to negative environmental impacts. At the same time, women have tended to bear a greater burden under the reform process.

> **The incomes of farmers, particularly small-scale ones, have not improved, principally because the prices of agricultural inputs have risen.**

More specifically, the following findings emerged from the exercises in Bangladesh, Uganda, Zimbabwe, the Philippines and Mexico.

- *Agricultural reforms have exacerbated inequalities.* Export promotion, import liberalization and the withdrawal of government support in the agricultural sector have served to reinforce differentiated access to resources for production. Where exports have expanded and earnings increased despite being subject to world price fluctuations, much of the economic benefit has accrued only to large-scale producers, as small farmers have lacked equal opportunities to enter and gain within a liberalized market. Constraints such as lack of rural infrastructure, particularly in more remote areas where the poor are concentrated, were inadequately addressed in the reform process. In addition, the concentration of land use for large-scale production of export crops has replaced cultivation of food crops for local consumption and has tended to push small farmers to overexploit marginal-quality land.

• *The income of farmers overall has not improved as a result of reforms.* This has primarily been due to cost increases associated with agricultural production (seeds, fertilizer, irrigation and equipment), as production costs tended to increase more than any growth in income from sales. Small-scale farmers have been particularly affected because, as a result of the reforms, production subsidies were removed, public expenditure on extension services declined, and obtaining credit became more costly. In addition, liberalization has increased the reliance of these producers on middlemen who market both farming supplies and produce. This has increased the costs and lowered the income of these farmers, whose marketing options have become more limited as a result of the withdrawal of the state from this function.

• *Food security has declined in most countries.* The impact of adjustment policies on food supply and accessibility has varied depending on socioeconomic conditions, with the rural poor tending to be the most affected. Reforms were undertaken with the assumption that local supply is not important, as access to food can be obtained through the market. However, the reduction of local food supplies has not been paralleled by increased market access by the rural poor, who lack the means to purchase food, with the result that many rural residents have suffered from inadequate food intake and increasing malnourishment. In some countries, a major cause of food insecurity has been low yields, which have been linked to reform policies that have reduced state support for extension services and production inputs.

• *Agricultural adjustment policies have led to further environmental problems.* Sector reform policies have favoured large-scale monoculture and led to a further concentration of resources. These new patterns of agricultural production have polluted land and water with chemicals from intensive and uncontrolled fertilizer use, depleted water tables through irrational use of irrigation, caused soil erosion and exhausted vital natural resources. They have also served to accentuate the loss of biodiversity. At the same time, small-scale farmers and the poor have been pushed onto more marginal-quality land, which they use more intensively as they are faced with a lack of alternatives for employment and income. This has caused further soil erosion and other forms of environmental degradation.

- *With policy design failing to take gender issues into consideration, agricultural adjustment measures have had substantial differentiated impacts on men and women, with women tending to bear the greater burden.* The existing gender-based division of labour, the level of women's access to and control of resources (such as land and credit), and the position of women in different cultures were found to be important factors determining the differential impact of agricultural policy reforms on women. The problems faced by smallholders due to these reforms, especially those measures that have promoted production for export, have placed particularly heavy burdens on women in countries in which they are primary producers.

In the light of these findings, some initial recommendations can be made. The policy approach in countries in which agriculture is an important sector should be reoriented to give priority to production geared towards supplying the domestic market and ensuring food security. While agricultural exports are an important element of most countries' development strategies, policy choices and investment decisions must take into account the differentiated ability of certain groups – particularly women and smallholders – to access new market opportunities and improve their access to land and other critical resources. Likewise, trade policy in the sector should be nuanced, allowing countries to pursue some degree of self-reliance while stimulating production by marginalized farmers, including women, in order to support the rural poor in accessing affordable food.

The implementation of effective steps to support small producers and achieve food security should precede, and then be integrated with, the opening of the sector and the promotion of exports. As part of such a rural development policy, the state should provide the support needed to ensure these farmers' access to affordable agricultural supplies and extension services, improvements in rural roads and transportation, further development and regulation of irrigation systems, and promotion of land tenure reforms. Furthermore, formal institutions should be in place, with state support, to provide equal access for all producers to information and markets, as well as to ensure environmental oversight and address negative impacts.

Steps to support small producers and achieve food security should precede the opening of the sector and the promotion of exports.

In general terms, agricultural policies should be designed to reduce existing inequalities by boosting the capacity of small and medium-scale producers and helping subsistence farmers to build sustainable livelihoods in the rural sector. To this end, policies should emerge from a participatory process involving all stakeholders, and environmental and socioeconomic factors, including gender considerations, should be integrated into policy design.

CHAPTER 7

The Socioeconomic and Environmental Impact of Mining Sector Reform

The principal objective of this chapter is to assess the socioeconomic and environmental effects of the mining sector reforms implemented under structural adjustment programmes, with particular reference to affected mining communities in Ghana and the Philippines. It considers whether the World Bank's economic adjustment and investment strategy for countries with a significant resource extraction sector has been successful from an overall economic, social and environmental perspective. Both countries have a history of implementing adjustment policies dating back to the early 1980s and have received numerous loans in support of their respective mining sectors. They are currently in what could be called a 'third phase' of adjustment, focusing on deregulation, privatization and investment liberalization. It is in this context that the resurgence in mining and resource extraction, not only in the Philippines and Ghana, but globally, should be situated.

This analysis is based on SAPRI research undertaken in Ghana and information gleaned from a CASA study in the Philippines. Both studies were conducted at the community level, but were also scaled up with secondary information from the district, regional and national levels to address micro and macro aspects of the assessment. Primary data collection involved visits to selected communities and the use of focus-group discussions and interviews with stakeholders, including communities affected by mining operations, mining companies, government-support agencies, and non-governmental and community-based organizations. The desk studies consisted of literature reviews of existing reports and previous field investigations.

Background

With its emphasis on private-sector-led development as the engine of growth, the structural adjustment paradigm was vigorously applied to the

153

resource extraction sector in a number of Southern economies. Countries with important mining sectors were obliged to shift their policy emphasis towards maximizing tax revenue and away from such previous goals as employment and control of national resources. This shift was to be achieved through a new division of labour in which governments restricted their role in the industrial and mining sectors to regulation and promotion, leaving the ownership, operation and management of enterprises to the private sector.

Table 7.1 • International Institution Credit Provided to the Resource Extractive Sector, 1995–99

Institution Estimated fossil fuel & mining totals	
World Bank Group[1] total	US$ 5,950,000,000
World Bank (IBRD and IDA)[2]	3,681,500,000
International Finance Corporation (IFC)[3]	1,458,300,000
Multilateral Investment Guarantee Agency (MIGA)[4]	807,200,000
European Bank for Reconstruction & Development[5]	946,000,000[6]
Asian Development Bank (ADB)[7]	2,025,000,000
Inter-American Development Bank (IDB)[8]	1,073,000,000
Export credit agency financing of upstream oil and gas development (not mining)[9] 1994–9[10]	40,500,000,000

1 It is estimated that US$1 of World Bank financing leverages US$5 of additional capital from other sources.
2 See *World Bank Annual Reports* (1995–9), Washington, DC: World Bank.
3 See 'Lending By Sector FY95–FY99', IFC *Annual Report* (1999), Annex. Based on year of commitment by IFC. Loans and equity only are not the total commitment. If commitments were made in multiple years, including years prior to 1995, so long as a FY95–FY99 commitment is made, the entire loan or equity issued to date is included. This includes projects involving oil refineries.
4 See 'Guarantees By Sector FY95–FY99', MIGA *Annual Reports* (1995–9). Includes loans to oil, mining and gas (OMG) initiatives and on-lending activities to banks where the annual report description notes that money from the loan is expected to go toward OMG projects in that particular country (of course it could be less than the total amount of the on-lend guarantee that goes to OMG, but there is no transparency, so the burden should be on MIGA to prove otherwise), and privatization of OMG services.
5 The US$–euro ratio fluctuated between 1995 and 1999; therefore, we assume a 1:1 ratio.
6 This figure includes gas distribution and power market assistance projects.
7 See ADB *Annual Reports* (1995–9). This includes loans and technical grant assistance. Power distribution and transmission is included in countries that rely heavily on fossil fuels but not in countries that have a hydropower focus. In many cases, the ADB does not distinguish whether these services are provided for various fuel sources, so Friends of the Earth took a rather conservative approach in this respect.
8 See IDB *Annual Report* (1995–9). Includes electricity sector 'reform' programmes.
9 Owing to the lack of transparency of export credit agencies, the authors do not have complete ECA mining figures.
10 Crescencia Maurer with Ruchi Bhandari, 'The Climate of Export Credit Agencies', *Climate Notes* (World Resources Institute), May 2000, p. 4. According to WRI, every dollar of ECA financing leverages and draws in more than 2 dollars of private capital.

Source: 'Phasing Out Public Financing for Fossil Fuel and Mining Projects', Friends of the Earth International Position Paper, 25 September 2000: 2.

Along with their support for adjustment policies, the international financial institutions have also significantly increased their lending, investments and guarantees in support of the resource extraction sector. These institutions allocated around US$51 billion to projects in the oil, mining and gas sectors from 1995 through 1999. In addition, their actions are a significant leverage of other sources of capital, as Table 7.1 illustrates.

Adjustment Policies, Legislation and Actions Affecting the Sector

In response to a global push for national policy changes to attract international mining investment, both Ghana and the Philippines shifted their focus from direct state investment in the mining sector to promotion and regulation of private companies. Within the framework of their structural adjustment programmes, the mining sector was a major target for reforms to address the concerns of investors and financiers, to arrest and reverse the decline of the industry, and to achieve greater growth.

The adjustment policies and initiatives promoted by the World Bank that relate to the mining sector in the countries under consideration include privatization of state mining interests, enactment of laws affecting the mining sector and the environment, and measures that lift almost all fiscal burdens from mining companies. In order to attract exploration and investment in the sector, efforts have been made to create a more favourable investment climate for foreign investors to expand foreign participation. Legislation has aimed to reduce risk for investors, ensure access to mining permits and concessions, and protect investors from government interference.

The first years of Ghana's adjustment programme focused on increasing the worth of existing mines through rehabilitation. Funding was made available from multilateral and bilateral sources and guaranteed by the government. This enabled the move to the next stage, which involved massive privatization of mines either through the selling off of shares or through complete divestiture. The main purposes of the privatization programme have been to reduce the role of the state in the economy and improve business competitiveness and efficiency, to reduce the fiscal deficit by using the proceeds from the sales to retire external and domestic debt, and to generate new cash flows through investment and tax revenues.

There has been a push to privatize and deregulate the mining sector to create a more favourable investment climate for foreign investors.

The push to privatize and deregulate the mining sector and create a more favourable investment climate for foreign investors has often entailed legislation to put both macro-level and sector-specific policy reforms into effect. In both Ghana and the Philippines, this has included changes in fiscal policy to grant concessions to investors in the form of:

• exemptions from duties;

• exemptions from payment of income tax;

• tax-free remittances for employees;

• scaled-down corporate income tax liability;

• increased capital allowance;

• reduced royalty fees;

• scrapping duties; and

• retention of foreign exchange earnings in external accounts.

These changes have been introduced in Ghana through the promulgation of a number of pieces of legislation since 1983. Table 7.2 shows the amount of foreign exchange that foreign mining firms investing in the country have been able to retain off-shore.

Table 7.2 • Ghana: Percentage of Export Value Retained Off-shore

Company	Minimum	Maximum
Ghana Australia Goldfields	55%	80%
Abosso Goldfields Ltd	55%	80%
Associated Goldfields	25%	45%
Takoradi Goldfields	25%	45%
Goldfields (Ghana) Ltd	60%	95%
Ghana Gold Mines Ltd	60%	69%

Source: Thomas Akabzaa (2000), *Boom and Dislocation: Environmental Impacts of Mining in the Wassa West District of Ghana*, Third World Network, June.

In the case of the Philippines, many of the above-mentioned changes were effected through the promulgation of the Philippine Mining Act (RA7942) in 1995. The Act provides a host of incentives through which the government expects to entice foreign investors to infuse capital into, and thus revive, the industry. These include the removal of the restriction on a maximum of 40 per cent foreign equity and a shift from a leasehold system to shared or joint-venture production agreements.

The liberalization of the Philippine mining industry resulted in the opening up of vast tracts of land and the increased vulnerability of local communities.

The liberalization of the Philippine mining industry through these legislative changes has permitted total private ownership of equity and control of mining projects, thus opening up the mining industry to control by foreign companies. As a result, vast tracts of land and other natural resources are being opened up, and communities are made more vulnerable to exploitation. Large foreign mining companies are now allowed to explore and mine a maximum area of 81,000 hectares for a period of 25 to 50 years in exchange for a minimum investment of US$50 million in the country's mining industry.[1] Auxiliary rights and incentives are granted, thus allowing unhampered mining operations and ensuring increased profitability. As a result of the 1995 Mining Act, the number of applications for permits in the mining sector, known as Financial and Technical Assistance Agreements (FTAAs), had grown to 115 by October 1997. By mid-1999, there were 408 pending applications. The FTAA applicants have been predominantly Australian, Canadian and American corporations, and in 1998 approximately 71 of the pending applications, including those that were approved, covered indigenous peoples' ancestral lands and, in some cases, ecologically critical areas.

Economic Impacts: Foreign Exchange, Government Revenue Generation and Employment

In Ghana, the policy changes succeeded both in creating a favourable perception of the investment environment and in raising the volume and value of mineral output. The country fast became a citadel of commerce and mining in West Africa. Internationally, Ghana is now known to be among a few selected African countries with the most attractive geological and investment environments. The renewed investor confidence in Ghana's minerals industry is reflected in the ballooning volume and value of minerals produced (see Table 7.3 and Figure 7.1).

---

[1] In March 1996 the Philippine Congress approved legislation that eliminated the Negative List C and reduced the minimum paid-in capital requirement for foreign companies from US$500,000 to US$200,000.

Table 7.3 • Performance of Ghana's Mineral Industry under the Structural Adjustment Programme (1987–98)

Year	Gold (ounces)	Diamonds (carats)	Bauxite (m/t)	Manganese (m/t)
1987	328 926	440 681	201 483	242 410
1988	373 937	259 358	299 939	284 911
1989	429 476	285 636	374 646	273 993
1990	541 400	636 503	368 659	246 869
1991	845 908	687 736	324 313	311 824
1992	998 195	656 421	399 155	276 019
1993	1 261 424	590 842	364 641	295 296
1994	1 430 845	757 991	451 802	238 429
1995	1 708 531	631 708	530 389	186 901
1996	1 606 880	271 493	383 370	300 000
1997	1 788 961	714 341	504 401	436 903
1998	2 481 635	808 967	442 514	536 871

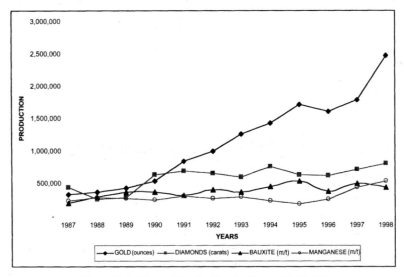

Figure 7.1 • Mineral Production in Ghana (1987–98)

Ghana is now Africa's second most important producer of gold, surpassed only by South Africa, and gold accounts for more than 90 per cent of the total value of minerals output in the country. Gold production, which had followed a downward trend in the post-colonial period after mining was nationalized in 1961 and had dropped to its lowest point in 1984, reached an all-time record high in 1995 and has since exceeded that record by 45 per cent. At the same time, foreign ownership now accounts for 70 to 85 per cent of the large-scale mining industry, a reversal of the situation prior to reforms when the Ghanaian government controlled 55 per cent of all mining companies.

The net foreign exchange contribution of gold mining to Ghana's national economy has been minimal due to generous incentives and tax breaks given to investors.

Among the presumed and most publicized benefits of the increased mining sector investments resulting from Ghana's economic reforms are that mining is the leading earner of foreign exchange in the country; that the industry provides substantial revenue to the government, as well as capital and social infrastructure to the public; that it generates direct and indirect employment; and that it contributes to local community development. Yet, on closer examination, many of these assumed benefits cannot be demonstrated. The SAPRI study puts the issue in perspective by comparing the actual benefits accruing to Ghana and its people with the post-reform level of performance in the sector.

Gold in particular has assumed a leading role in Ghana's foreign exchange earnings. In 1994, gold exports amounted to US$549 million, representing 45 per cent of total export revenue (US$1,215 million), pushing cocoa (25 per cent of total exports) down to second place for the third year running. But, while in gross terms mining is the country's leading foreign exchange earner, its net foreign exchange contribution to Ghana's national economy has been minimal thanks to generous incentives and tax breaks given to investors and the fact that the mining companies retain on average about 75 per cent of their export earnings in off-shore accounts for various purposes.

Similarly, the mining sector's contribution to Ghana's government revenue has been relatively small, given that mining attracted over 70 per cent of total foreign direct investment during the Economic Recovery Programme. While royalties and the income taxes of local employees increased this contribution from 8.4 per cent of total revenue in 1990 to 14.4 per cent in 1995, most of the companies in the study area, and more broadly in the country, do not pay corporate income taxes, but enjoy a virtual tax holiday as a result of the generous capital allowances granted them.

At the same time, the sector today has a relatively limited capacity to generate employment. This is because surface-mining operations are capital-intensive, with relatively low labour requirements, and all post-adjustment mining ventures have been surface operations. With the investment in, and rehabilitation of, the mines in order to get them ready for privatization during the late 1980s and early 1990s, employment in the sector surged. The sector's total, full-time labour force rose from 15,069 in 1987 to 22,500 in 1995. The divestiture of formerly state-owned mines resulted, however, in significant restructuring and cost-cutting by their new private sector owners to ensure efficiency. In addition, the persistent decline in commodity prices – especially gold – has resulted in radical restructuring to reduce costs. Many mines have reduced their labour force substantially, especially between 1997 and 2000. According to those participating in the Opening National Forum in Accra, these same pressures, combined with ineffectual regulatory mechanisms, have also engendered extremely poor working conditions.

The mining industry has been responsible for the high rate of unemployment found in surrounding communities.

In addition, in both Ghana and the Philippines, the mining industry has been responsible for the high rate of unemployment found in surrounding communities in direct and indirect ways. Large-scale surface mining has taken large tracts of land away from farmers, and mining activities do not provide enough jobs to match the total number of people laid off from agriculture. Many families who made their livelihoods in artisan-style mining activities, it was explained at the SAPRI Forum in Ghana, were forced off the land they worked when private mining companies staked their claims to newly privatized, mineral-rich land. In the Philippines, within four years of the passage of the 1995 Mining Act liberalizing the industry, there were applications for mining rights pending for nearly a quarter of the country's total land area. Opening Forum participants reported that 70 per cent of those lands bordered on, or were located within, areas occupied by indigenous peoples, who constituted a significant portion of the small-scale mining population. Their dislocation has led to a serious loss of livelihood and to increased family indebtedness, the Forum participants said.

Social and Community Impacts

The social organization of every community is guided and directed by certain principles. The concentration of mining operations in both the Philippines and Ghana has had a seriously adverse impact on the social organization and cultural values of the people in the affected regions. Concerns have been expressed about housing, unemployment, family disorganization, social dislocation and polarization, school drop-out rates, prostitution and drug abuse. While these problems are not new, they have risen to a level that the population perceives to be particularly threatening, and the main cause has been attributed to the concentration of mining activities in the area.

The concentration of mining operations has had a seriously adverse impact on the social organization and cultural values of the people in the affected regions.

In both Ghana and the Philippines, case studies were undertaken to assess the impact of mining activities on local communities. In Ghana, the study area was Tarkwa and its environs in the Wassa West District of the country's Western Region. In the Philippines, the study focused on two communities: Didipio in Kasibu, a district in Nueva Vizcaya and Quirino provinces, and Manicani Island, Eastern Samar.

Background

Tarkwa, Ghana

Tarkwa has nearly a century of gold-mining history and the largest concentration of mines in a single district on the continent of Africa. Half of Ghana's 16 large-scale mines, including the six new surface-mining operations, are located in the Tarkwa area and produce a significant proportion of the country's gold output. The only manganese mine in the country is also located there. In addition, there are over 100 registered, small-scale gold- and diamond-mining companies in the area and more than 600 unregistered miners popularly known as *galamsey* operators. The area contains a significant proportion of the last vestiges of the country's tropical rain forest, which declined in area from 8.2 million hectares in 1992 to 750,000 hectares in 1997.

All eight companies operating in Tarkwa employ the open-pit method of mining and use cyanide heap leach operations, as shown in Table 7.4. These methods have far-reaching consequences for human health and environmental safety. The use of heavy machinery to exploit low-grade ore has a destructive effect on the vegetation of the area and generates both dust and noise pollution. These environmental issues are considered later in this chapter.

The heavy concentration of mining activities has generated environmental problems, social difficulties related to resettlement and relocation, and negotiation and compensation questions. The persistence of these problems accounts for frequent resistance by the affected communities and clashes between them and the mining companies. The destruction of sources of livelihood and the spate of conflicts have given rise to an environmentally conscious population from which local social movements are emerging.

Table 7.4 Mining Companies Operating in Tarkwa Mining District, Ghana

Company	Location	Start	Processing method
GFL	Tarkwa	1993	Underground/open cast/heap leach
TGL	Teberebie (Tarkwa)	1990	Open cast/heap leach
BGL	Tarkwa	1990	Open cast/CIL
GAG	Iduapriem (Tarkwa)	1992	Open cast/CIL/heap leach
Barnex (Prestea) Ltd	Prestea	1997	Underground/open pit/CIL
Sankofa Gold Ltd	Prestea	1995	Tailings treatment/CIL
Abosso Goldfields	Abosso	1997	Open pit/CIL
SGL	Tarkwa	1999	Open pit/CIL

Notes: GFL – Gold Fields Ltd; TGL: – Teberebie Goldfields Limited; BGL – Bogosco Gold Limited; GAG – Ghana Australian Goldfields; SGL – Satellite Goldfields Ltd; CIL – Coal India Ltd
Source: Thomas Akabzaa (2000), *Boom and Dislocation: Environmental Impacts of Mining in the Wassa West District of Ghana*, Third World Network, June.

Didipio and Manicani Island, the Philippines

Climax-Arimco Mining Corporation (CAMC) is fully owned by an Australian company that obtained a permit in the Philippines in 1994 to build an open-pit mine and related infrastructure for gold and copper mining in Didipio. The permit covers about 37,000 hectares located in Kasibu in Nueva Vizcaya and Quirino provinces, part of which is home to the Ifugaos and Bugkalots, the indigenous peoples in the area, and to others considered part of the Ilocano, Tagalog and Visaya ethnic groups.

Hinatuan Mining Corporation (HMC) operates on Manicani Island and is owned by the Zamora brothers, who have maintained significant political and economic influence since their ascendance in the Marcos years. They are widely believed to exercise control over the Philippine nickel industry. The company stopped operations in 1994 when the price of nickel fell on the international market, but resumed again two years later despite major concerns expressed by local communities regarding negative social, economic and ecological impacts of the mining operations. After succeeding in sidestepping environmental protection measures and social accountability mechanisms, HMC again restarted its mining operation in March 2001 amidst popular opposition and despite not having settled questions related to social acceptability, prior informed consent, and other matters.

Displacement and relocation

Between 1990 and 1998, mining investment in Tarkwa, Ghana, led to the displacement of a total of 14 communities with a population of over 30,000.

Some people had to migrate in search of farmland, while others were relocated or resettled by the mining companies. The growing displacement of communities and people has also resulted in increased migration of young people – who were not considered for compensation – to the towns, especially Tarkwa, in search of jobs.

The relocation and compensation measures of the various mining companies in the Tarkwa area have had serious consequences for the family as a close-knit social unit. The compensation schemes, in particular, have contributed to the break-up of families. In the Tarkwa area, male family heads have opted for cash compensation instead of resettlement and have subsequently abandoned their families. This has deepened the plight of affected rural women and children.

Impact on women

Mining generally tends to offer women fewer job opportunities. In both Ghana and the Philippines, the direct involvement of women in formal, large-scale mining is generally limited to support activities, such as administrative, clerical, catering and related jobs. In the case of small-scale mining and quarrying, women usually play subsidiary roles, such as selling cooked food and assorted goods to male miners. At the same time, on Manicani Island in the Philippines, the bulldozing and burning of the mountains related to open-pit mining deprived the residents, especially women, of their sources of raw materials – *tikog* and *bariw* – used for weaving mats and hence of a source of supplemental income.

The loss of nearby sources of potable water and firewood has also made the lives of community residents more difficult. Women now spend more time fetching water and gathering firewood, time which could have been devoted to other important livelihood activities. As they tend to be the primary caregivers, responsible for household and child-rearing activities, women are also the ones who carry the burden of caring for the sick. This was the case observed in Manicani in the Philippines during the outbreak of respiratory diseases which is attributed to the mining operation of Hinatuan Mining Corporation. On the other hand, women have also tended to take on more leadership roles in community organizing around the problems related to mining.

> **The loss of nearby sources of potable water and firewood due to open-pit mining has made women's lives more difficult.**

As men have lost sources of income, however, due to transformations in the mining industry, an increased production burden has fallen on women,

Opening Forum participants in the Philippines said. Furthermore, the differentiated gender impact of mining was observed at the community level, where women complained of unfair treatment when it came to compensation for people to be resettled or relocated. Compensation was given to heads of household, who were traditionally men, with subsequent cases of family abandonment.

Prostitution and drug abuse

One of the major social problems that has emerged from the concentration of mining activities in Tarkwa, Ghana, is prostitution. Some women who had migrated into Tarkwa with the intention of trading or finding other jobs were compelled to resort to prostitution as a survival option when they failed to attain their original objectives. Over 70 per cent of the communities contacted complained of the increase in prostitution and cited it as one of the factors responsible for the erosion of social values in the area. Reported cases of HIV in the Wassa West district have also been on the increase since 1992, growing incrementally from six cases in 1992 to 100 in 1996.

Similarly, frustrations associated with unemployment have pushed some of the youth in Tarkwa towards drug abuse, and an addictive drug subculture was found to be taking root. In addition, drug use is rampant among illegal small-scale miners, who believe that drugs stimulate miners to work harder.

High cost of living

One of the well-known negative effects of mining is the high cost of living within communities near mine locations. All the basic needs – food, accommodation, health, water – required for a dignified standard of living gain a price tag beyond the reach of the average person.

The Ghanaian mining industry has pushed people out of agriculture by eliminating farmland.

Two main factors are responsible for the high cost of living in Tarkwa, Ghana. First, there is the disparity in incomes in favour of mining company staff, whose salaries are indexed to the dollar and drive up prices. Second, the mining industry has both pushed and pulled a significant percentage of the labour force out of agriculture and other income-generating activities by eliminating farmland and holding out the often false promise of gainful employment. The consequent fall in food production in an area that is already densely populated accounts for high food prices. The harsh economic conditions faced by many families have pushed school-age children into menial jobs at the expense of their education. Child labour and rising school drop-out rates are notable in communities in the study area.

Environmental Impacts

The structural adjustment policies pursued by the government had a significant influence on the mining boom in Ghana and within the Tarkwa area, in particular. Transnational companies operating in Tarkwa and its environs, taking advantage of these policies, gained greater control over resources and people's livelihoods. In this context, national environmental policies have been inadequately applied and have thus failed to protect local communities from the adverse impact of mining operations. This has led not only to environmental degradation, but to a deepening of poverty levels among the local population.

The ascendancy of adjustment policies and foreign mining companies in Ghana has contributed to environmental degradation and deepening poverty.

While the mining sector reforms were under way, very little was done to reform existing environmental laws to deal with the destruction that was certain to arise from accelerated growth in the sector. Even before the boom, in 1988, a conservative estimate of the anticipated ecological damage that would be caused by the mining industry each year was about 4 per cent of GDP. As a result of this growth and lack of regulatory action, the environment in most parts of Tarkwa has been undergoing further rapid degradation, and its immense economic value has been diminishing from year to year. Not only has the heavy concentration of mining activities in the area generally degraded farmland, but the decrease in land available for agricultural production has also led to a shortening of the fallow period from 10–15 years to 2–3 years. The traditional bush fallow system, which recycled substantial amounts of nutrients and made the next cycle productive, can no longer be utilized in the absence of sufficient land. Large-scale mining activities have continued to reduce the vegetation of the area to levels that are destructive to biological diversity.

National environmental policies in Ghana have not been able to protect local communities from the adverse impact of mining operations.

Similarly, in the Philippines, the entry of large-scale corporate mining activity in the areas studied has destroyed or altered the traditional and often ecologically compatible systems of shifting cultivation. Those utilizing these systems have been confined to small areas, and the fallow periods have been reduced or even eliminated, leading to soil exhaustion, accelerated erosion, food insecurity and worsening poverty. On the island of Manicani, mining activities, which have entailed bulldozing mountains, have resulted in the loss of topsoil and have thus affected the fertility of agricultural land. The farmers on Manicani say that agricultural work is useless and a waste of their time, since they have seen that their fields will be bulldozed anyway. Moreover, residents fear that the mining operations have contributed to the island's vulnerability to landslides, flash floods and other accidents, a particularly serious problem given that the area is in the typhoon belt.

Furthermore, the principal elements of the environment – land, water and air – have been severely damaged by operations that employ methods, such as open-pit mining, banned in countries like the United States and Canada. Consequently, the continued ability of the environment to support the well-being and development of the rural populations in the case study areas in both Ghana and the Philippines is currently in doubt.

In the Tarkwa area in Ghana, for example, the tailings dam, plant site and feed stockpile of Ghana Australia Goldfields Ltd alone will affect a total of about 315 farmers currently cultivating around the area. This has significant implications for the farmers' incomes and the food security of their families. In both countries, deforestation that has resulted from surface mining has long-term effects even when the soil is replaced and trees are planted after mine decommissioning. The new species that might be introduced have the potential to influence the composition of the topsoil and subsequently determine soil fertility and fallow duration for certain crops. In addition to erosion when surface vegetation is destroyed, there is deterioration in the viability of the land for agricultural purposes and loss of habitat for birds and other animals. This has culminated in the destruction of the luxuriant vegetation, biodiversity, cultural sites and water bodies.

Deforestation resulting from surface mining has long-term effects on the environment.

In the case of Manicani Island in the Philippines, the nickel mining operation of HMC is believed to have caused environmental problems such as adverse effects on the soil geochemistry and the flora and fauna in the area. Residents on the island, considered one of the main breeding grounds in the region for numerous varieties of fish, noticed a tremendous decrease in the volume and varieties of marine life in the area after HMC operations began.

Environmental impact assessments
In both Ghana and the Philippines, environmental impact assessment (EIA) mechanisms have been put in place. Proponents of mining view this as a

positive step that guarantees local community input into the decision-making process while helping to ensure adherence to environmental sustainability principles. In Ghana, a major requirement of the EIA process, which was introduced in 1989 as an environmental management tool and a prerequisite for all development projects, is that the project proponent must give notice and advertise the proposal in the national press to enable the public to express its interest or concerns, or in other ways comment on the project. Similarly, the new Philippines Mining Act (RA 7942) is considered by some to be a step forward because of its provisions requiring social acceptability and prior informed consent by the affected communities as part of the EIA process.

In practice, however, there are many shortcomings in the process, as the case studies illustrate. The following weaknesses of the EIA process were identified in both countries:

- EIA reports are presented in technical language, and the affected communities do not have the capacity to study and understand the issues they raise. Other sources of information, which are primarily the national press and the District Assemblies, are inaccessible to these communities.

- Environmental audit reports are treated as confidential documents, thus limiting public access to the information required to promote and ensure environmental compliance by mining companies, which can refuse to accept a report's recommendations to minimize the negative impact of mining activities on the environment.

- Prior-consent rules mandating community consultations have been routinely flouted by restricting attendance at meetings – a divide-and-conquer strategy by the mining companies that favours their supporters – as well as through bribery.

- The promise of social service provision by mining companies in return for a community's consent in support of mining operations has led to the polarization of communities between pro- and anti-mining groups.

- The mining companies have been weak on the delivery of their promises, but have rewarded the residents who have demonstrated pro-mining sympathies by dispensing benefits such as employment, skills training and livelihood projects.

- The social impact of mining projects has been inadequately addressed; action is usually limited, at best, to payment of compensation and royalties.

- There are no provisions by which communities can reject or terminate a mining permit; this limits their ability to stop an invasionary project that would be seriously detrimental to their land and livelihood.

- Affected communities have had little or no say in determining basic issues, such as the location of the various components of the mining project.

- There has been little or no follow-up in cases in which hearings have raised serious objections to an EIA.

In addition, at least in the case of Ghana, local authorities have lacked the necessary legal backing to enforce the requirement that an EIA be completed for all industrial and other development projects, as well as the personnel and financial capacity to ensure compliance with environmental quality standards. These weaknesses in the EIA process have provided the leeway for mining operations to take actions that have a severe impact on the environment, deepening the plight and poverty of local populations and affecting their overall livelihoods. Mining companies and their sympathizers argue that community concerns are addressed adequately during environmental impact hearings, which are supposed to be organized to hear the views of the community regarding the project in question. Experience has shown, however, that such public hearings are nothing more than public relations forums in which companies largely dwell on the expected positive economic benefits of the project to both the state and the local population, while downplaying the project's negative impacts.

Water and chemical pollution
The concentration of mining operations in Ghana has been a major source of both surface and groundwater pollution. Four significant water pollution problems have been noticed in Tarkwa mining areas. These are chemical pollution of groundwater and streams, siltation through increased sediment load, increased presence of fecal matter and dewatering effects.

Various chemicals, such as cyanide and mercury, are used during ore processing. These chemicals constitute the major pollutants of surface and groundwater. In addition to chemical pollution, heavy metals from mining operations contribute to water pollution. The presence of such heavy metals above a certain threshold can be injurious to human health and the environment, particularly aquatic life. The main concern of the communities has been potential cyanide pollution of surface and groundwater resources by large-scale, surface-mining operations, and mercury contamination from small-scale and illegal *galamsey* mining activities.

Mining in Ghana also has active dewatering effects that lower the water table or divert major watercourses away from the mines, with damaging consequences for the quality and availability of surface and groundwater. Apart from consuming a huge amount of water, the extensive excavation of large tracts of land and the piling of large mounds of earth along watercourses remove the source of water recharge for groundwater and ultimately reverse the direction of flow of groundwater, causing active dewatering. A number of boreholes, hand-dug wells and streams in the area have either become unproductive or now provide less water.

On the Philippine island of Manicani, farmers complained that their fields have been exposed to laterite, thereby limiting crop growth. At the same time, the dwindling fish catch resulting from overfishing and laterite pollution has further pushed people to engage in ecologically destructive fishing methods, such as dynamite and cyanide fishing. Finally, water pollution has deprived residents of bodies of water that were the sites for their leisure and recreation activities.

Air and noise pollution and health effects

Mining activities and mining-support companies release particulate matter into the ambient air. Airborne particulates of major concern within the Tarkwa area in Ghana include respirable dust, sulphur dioxide, nitrogen dioxide, carbon monoxide and black smoke. The concerns of the affected communities also include noise and vibration, the sources of which in the area include mobile equipment, air blasts and vibration from blasting and other machinery. The effect of high-pitched and other noises is known to include damage to the auditory system, cracks in buildings, stress and discomfort.

Adverse impacts of mining operations have included the generation of diseases due to pollutants.

Adverse environmental and health impacts of mining operations have also included the generation of diseases due to pollutants. The effects of some of these pollutants manifest themselves immediately (cyanide, for example), but others (such as mercury) take a long time to appear. In Ghana, the extraction and processing of gold have given rise to various environmentally related diseases and accidents. According to Tarkwa's District Medical Officer, the common, mining-related diseases observed in the area over the years include, but are not limited to:

- vector-borne diseases, such as malaria, schistomiasis and onchocerciasis;

- respiratory tract diseases, especially pulmonary tuberculosis and silicosis;

- skin diseases;

- eye diseases, especially acute conjunctivitis;

- accidents resulting from *galamsey* activities; and

- mental illness.

National Forum participants in the Philippines testified to similar health problems in areas of open-pit mining, especially among women and children. There has been a significant increase in the incidence of skin disorders, for example, and deaths from poisoning have been reported. On the island of Manicani, the mining operations and the attendant pollution were perceived as causing the sudden rise in the incidence of coughs and colds, as well as other respiratory diseases, especially among the young population. At the height of the mining operations, which involved massive earth movement – open pit diggings, hauling and shipment of soil, and the traffic of truck and heavy-equipment vehicles – almost all the children in the communities suffered from respiratory ailments.

Conclusion

The investigations in Ghana and the Philippines found that the restructuring exercise in those countries' respective mining sectors and the accompanying mining policy reforms provided investors with generous incentive packages. These incentives have contributed to an enormous increase in mining investment, significant expansion of the sector, a great increase in mineral production and the generation of significant foreign exchange earnings. The wealth produced, however, has brought few benefits to national economies and has been generated by draining resources from communities located near the mines. With these operations destroying both the local environment and sources of livelihood, the consequences have been a deepened crisis of health and environmental sustainability, social upheavals and economic deprivation. In net terms, the expected economic benefits have accrued largely to the mining companies, which are mostly foreign-owned and which have taken advantage of these attractive investment and profit repatriation policies and of the effective weakening of environmental regulations.

Mining operations have drained resources from communities while delivering few benefits to national economies.

The findings point to the following conclusions, which indicate the overall detrimental impact of the World Bank's support for large-scale mining through the application of economic adjustment measures:

• *Liberalization, deregulation and privatization of the mining sector have enabled transnational corporations to remove resources and profits from countries while failing to generate sustainable economic growth that is of net benefit to national or local economies*. These reforms and the legislative changes through which they have been put into effect have granted generous incentives and tax breaks to investors and allowed them to retain the bulk of their export earnings in foreign accounts. Therefore, growth in the mining sector has contributed very little to national economies in terms of government revenue and net foreign exchange earnings. Nor have the privatization, deregulation and liberalization of the mining sector generated significant new employment, because surface-mining operations have relatively low labour requirements. At the same time, the privatization of formerly state-owned mines and the persistent decline of commodity prices have resulted in cost cutting, which has often meant massive lay-offs. In addition, mining has taken away large tracts of land from farmers but has not provided enough jobs to offset subsequent employment losses in agriculture.

- *Sector reforms have allowed large-scale mining to expand without effective environmental controls, thereby polluting local and regional environments and degrading sensitive, biologically rich zones.* Mechanisms to conduct environmental impact assessments exist in both Ghana and the Philippines, but adjustment measures have left the governments of those countries with little capacity to enforce this requirement effectively or to ensure compliance with environmental quality standards. As a result, mines have often lowered water tables, diverted watercourses and caused water pollution through the use of chemicals and the unleashing of heavy metals. The widespread removal of trees and vegetation has also resulted in soil erosion and decreased soil fertility, which have made land unsuitable for agricultural purposes. In addition, mining operations have destroyed traditional, ecologically sound systems of shifting cultivation by reducing fallow periods as a result of the reduction in land available for cultivation. Furthermore, mining and related activities have contributed to air pollution through the release of particulate matter and emissions of black smoke.

- *Reforms have allowed the expansion of large-scale mining without safeguards, causing adverse effects on the health of local populations.* Vector-borne diseases, such as malaria, and respiratory-tract illnesses, such as tuberculosis, as well as skin and eye diseases, have been documented over the years as common mining-related problems in Ghana. Mercury and cyanide poisoning have also been observed. Constant high-pitched noise and vibration from mining machinery and air blasts have damaged hearing and caused stress and discomfort. In addition, accidents and injuries have frequently occurred in mining areas without safeguards.

• *The unregulated expansion of large-scale mining has also had negative social impacts.* Such mining operations have forced many local residents to migrate in search of new farmland or be resettled by the mining companies, both of which outcomes have weakened the family as a social unit. The growing displacement of communities has pushed youth into towns, where frustration over unemployment has often resulted in problems such as drug abuse and prostitution. When male heads of households have opted for cash compensation instead of resettlement, they have sometimes abandoned their families, deepening the plight of rural women and children. Another problem has been the increased cost of living in communities near mines, which has compounded the loss of traditional sources of livelihood. Harsh economic conditions have pushed school-age children into menial jobs, with the result that child labour and school drop-out rates are notably high in mining communities.

• *The structural adjustment policy framework has allowed large-scale mining to expand unabated, threatening the traditional land rights of indigenous peoples and weakening community control over land and resources.* Marginalized from the decision-making processes that determine the location and operation of mines, local populations have been displaced from their traditional lands and communities. Information on environmental and social impacts has been largely inaccessible to them because of a lack of effective dissemination in rural areas, the compilation of impact assessment reports in technical language, and the confidentiality of audit reports that measure a company's compliance with established standards. Mining companies have often promised social services in return for a community's consent to locate, pitting pro- and anti-mining groups against one another, and they have tended to dispense favours to their supporters while leaving general promises unfulfilled.

In the light of this evidence, it is recommended that the World Bank cease lending for large-scale mining activities and end its support for the wholesale deregulation, privatization and liberalization of the mining sector pending a comprehensive review of the impact of these policies and a full consideration of alternative development strategies for national and local economies, in general, and the mining sector, in particular. A thorough cost–benefit analysis of the mining sector and the role of the Bank and sister institutions in promoting it should take into account the net effect of these policies on the national and local economy, factoring in the environmental and health damage, as well as the social crises, arising from mining activities.

Furthermore, the national institutions and regulatory mechanisms, weakened under adjustment, that serve to limit or reduce the negative impacts of large-scale mining must be refortified. Legal and policy frameworks, for example, should be overhauled so that mining companies have greater responsibility and accountability with regard to environmental and social issues. Environmental legislation should be strengthened and appropriate penalties applied for violations, and environmental impact assessments should be fully implemented and their results made public. Clear and fair guidelines should be established for obtaining community consent prior to undertaking mining activities, and communities should be empowered to recommend the rejection or termination of mining agreements where negative impacts have been ascertained. Finally, internationally accepted 'best practices' should be applied in the mining industry in developing countries, including an end to open-pit mining practices in populated areas.

National institutions and regulatory mechanisms, weakened under adjustment, must be refortified in the mining sector.

CHAPTER 8

The Effects of Public Expenditure Policies on Education and Healthcare under Structural Adjustment

Structural adjustment policies have had a profound effect on all aspects of political, social and economic life in developing and transition countries. That impact has been felt quite deeply in the social sector. Civil society organizations, often joined by United Nations agencies like UNICEF, have been particularly critical of the impact on the poor of large budgetary cuts in such areas as healthcare and education, carried out under adjustment programmes over the past two decades. The social sector is also one of the areas in which the World Bank has found itself vulnerable to the charge that its policies are disproportionately hurting the poor.

In response, measures have been taken by the Bank in the second generation of adjustment to address what the institution has called the Social Dimensions of Adjustment (SDA). The Bank programmes have been designed to ameliorate the social costs of what the Bank has regarded as painful but necessary macroeconomic measures. More recently, through the Heavily Indebted Poor Country (HIPC) initiative and Poverty Reduction Strategy Paper (PRSP) process, the Bank has been involved in efforts with the international donor community to see that government spending in the critical areas of healthcare and education is protected and enhanced. The Uganda experience is pointed to by the Bank as a successful example of its learning from mistakes and correcting them.

Yet, as this chapter demonstrates, the Bank's prescriptions for the social sector have gone far beyond what were said to be regrettable but necessary cutbacks in healthcare and education spending. Such cuts have in many respects been a vehicle for a comprehensive transformation in most of the countries undergoing adjustment, whereby the social sector has also been subjected in significant ways to free market forces. These changes have entailed a redefinition of the problem of poverty and of the state's redistributive role. According to the Bank, poverty is no longer to be addressed through state intervention in the social sector but by eliminating what are considered to be the constraints to wealth generation by the private sector.

The social sector has also been subjected in significant ways to free market forces.

Education and healthcare have been areas of particular concern in the seven SAPRI/CASA countries that carried out studies on the impact of public expenditure reform under adjustment programmes implemented in the 1980s and 1990s. Investigations in Ghana, Zimbabwe, Mexico and Hungary focused primarily on the impact of reforms on access to, and the quality of, education and healthcare, while the Uganda and Philippines assessments looked at the impact on spending for these services. The review in Ecuador focused on social subsidies, addressing the more overarching issue of the role of the state in the social sector and the question of state support for universal *vis-à-vis* targeted coverage. This last issue was also addressed in the study in Hungary, which made the 'transition' from a socialist to capitalist economy. Both Hungary and Zimbabwe are interesting examples of nations in which adjustment programmes were implemented following a long period of extensive state involvement in the economy that included the provision of state-subsidized and/or state-owned and state-managed public services.

Table 8.1 • Timeline of Structural Adjustment Programmes in SAPRI/CASA Countries

Country	'82	'83	'84	'85	'86	'87	'88	'89	'90	'91	'92	'93	'94	'95	'96	'97	'98	'99
Uganda						X	X	X	X	X	X	X	X	X	X	X	X	X
Zimbabwe										X	X	X	X	X	X	X	X	X
Ghana		X	X	X	X	X	X	X	X	X	X	X	X	X	X	X	X	X
Ecuador	X	X	X	X	X	X	X	X	X	X	X	X	X	X	X	X	X	X
Mexico	X	X	X	X	X	X	X	X	X	X	X	X	X	X	X	X	X	X
Philippines						X	X	X	X	X	X	X	X	X	X	X	X	X
Hungary							X	X	X	X	X	X	X	X	X	X	X	X

This chapter presents a cross-country synthesis of the major results of these related studies. By no means, however, does it cover all the critical information, knowledge and learning that the studies generated. The following section considers adjustment policies as they relate to the public sector and reviews some of the assumptions behind these Bank policies.

Next, the chapter assesses the impact the policies have had on public spending for education and healthcare. It then considers the effects of the policies – including gender-differentiated effects – on access to and the quality of these services. The impact on the poor of the elimination of basic subsidies receives special attention before the chapter draws its conclusion regarding the impact of public expenditure reforms under adjustment, and puts forward a set of basic recommendations.

Adjustment Policies Addressed

The structural adjustment policies addressed in the country studies were in part an outgrowth of IMF-supported stabilization programmes implemented to put the economy on track towards recovery from severe balance-of-payments deficits, inflation and related problems. Fiscal, as well as monetary, policies were central to these stabilization packages. They emphasized revenue increases and expenditure controls in the following forms:

- a ceiling on budget deficits;

- a freeze on, or reduction in, spending levels;

- the removal of subsidies;

- a rationalization/streamlining of government bureaucracy;

- an increase in certain types of taxes and/or introduction of new taxes; and

- currency devaluation.

In some cases, IMF and World Bank conditionalities did not explicitly specify measures to control spending on social services. But in the interest of achieving the bottom-line objectives of curbing deficits and reining in inflation, reductions in spending on public services were considered inevitable, acceptable and even necessary consequences of adjustment. The maintenance of debt servicing and stabilization were non-negotiable elements of all the adjustment programmes studied.

The fiscal and public sector reforms that were designed and implemented as part of adjustment programmes, while an extension of those carried out under stabilization programmes, were of a more comprehensive nature, as they were pursued in combination with privatization, liberalization and deregulation policies. The structural reforms in the social sector were not only geared to the immediate objectives of curbing deficits and increasing revenues; they also aimed at achieving large-scale changes in the role of the state in the economy. At their core they involved a radical shift away from the role of the state as one of provider and guarantor of universally accessible social services to one of providing essential services in a targeted manner only to those on the margins whom the market has failed to reach.

The structural reforms in the social sector were aimed at achieving large-scale changes in the role of the state.

This shift in concept is rooted in the belief that all forms of government spending, including social spending, constitute subsidies, with the assumption that subsidies represent state intervention that interferes in market functioning and leads to economic inefficiency. Such economic arguments have marked the rationale for a complete transformation of the social sector that has included the following elements in most of the countries implementing adjustment programmes:

- the drastic reduction of government spending, with a focus on basic functions that include only essential aspects of social service provision, as governments are required to streamline their role in the provision and financing of these services;

- the implementation of cost-recovery and cost-sharing measures; and

- the ceding of control and management of social services to the private sector wherever possible.

But civil society groups consulted in the countries studied rejected the notion that market forces, rather than the state, should determine the nature and extent of service provision and asserted that education and healthcare have important social value that is left out of the economic efficiency equation. They argue that the long-term cost to society of the state failing to provide universal access to quality education and healthcare services is greater than any short-term fiscal savings achieved through social spending cuts or cost-recovery schemes.

The Impact of Adjustment Reforms on Public Spending for Education and Healthcare

The implementation of spending controls and cost-sharing schemes was undertaken in the SAPRI/CASA countries during periods of economic decline and growing poverty, when social assistance and social services for the poor were in greatest demand. While the reduction in government revenues during periods of economic deterioration served as justification for controls on public expenditure, the logical and expected response in these situations, from a human development perspective, would be to seek and implement alternatives to cuts in social spending and social assistance, and to give high priority to these items in government budgets. This was not the case, however, for the countries covered by the studies.

Spending controls and cost sharing were undertaken during periods of economic decline when the needs of the poor were greatest.

This section looks at how adjustment policies have affected public spending on education and healthcare services. The analysis addresses:

- trends in the allocation of public spending for education and healthcare;
- the priority given to debt servicing compared with social sector spending;
- the effects of devaluation on the cost of service delivery;
- the introduction of cost-recovery and revenue-generating schemes; and
- the effects of decentralization.

Trends in allocation of public spending

All but one of the studies conducted in the seven countries show that stabilization and structural adjustment programmes have led, at best, to a lack of improvement and, at worst, a sharp decline in public spending for social services, specifically education and healthcare. Both general expenditure controls and other non-budgetary policies were responsible for this situation. In several instances, adjustment programmes directly and explicitly called for a freeze or cutbacks in social spending.

Box 8.1 Indicators of Trends in Budget Allocation and Spending

The indicators used in the country studies to determine and demonstrate the patterns of social-sector budget allocations and spending are the following:

- Allocation and spending as a percentage of GDP
- Allocation and spending as a percentage of total expenditures
- Rate of increase in spending compared to the rate of increase in the total budget
- Comparative spending in nominal and real terms
- Allocation and spending in the social sector compared to other items in the budget.

**Table 8.2 Annual Earnings per Employee (in US$)
in Healthcare and Education in Zimbabwe**

	1990	1991	1992	1993	1994	1995	1996
Healthcare	4,321	3,641	2,742	2,330	2,183	2,546	2,408
Education	4,934	4,415	3,259	2,725	2,386	2,516	2,249

Source: Central Statistical Office, *National Accounts*, 1985–96.

During the periods covered by the studies, a decline in both education and healthcare spending occurred in Zimbabwe, Hungary and Mexico. In Zimbabwe, public expenditures on health and education fell in the 1990s. Healthcare spending dropped to 2.1 per cent of GDP in 1996 from 3.1 per cent in 1990. Government allocations to the Ministry of Health decreased from 6 per cent of total government expenditure to about 4 per cent. The *per capita* budget for healthcare fell from US$22 in 1990 to US$11 in 1996. As the Zimbabwe report notes, 'The public health budget is not enough to meet health needs. The *per capita* budget has fallen since 1991 to a level where it does not even pay for prevention, clinics and district hospital costs *per capita*'.

Similarly, total education spending in Zimbabwe declined from 6.29 per cent of GDP in 1986–7 to 4.82 per cent in 1999. Allocations to education as a percentage of total recurrent expenditure fell from 39 per cent in 1999 to 21 per cent in 2000. *Per capita* spending for education also declined in real terms from Z$37.83 in 1990 to Z$30.44 in 2000.

In Hungary, state expenditures on education, healthcare and social provisions diminished by 25 per cent in real terms in the seven years following 1989. Healthcare expenditure fell from 5.5 per cent of GDP in 1991 to 4.3 per cent in 1999, and budget estimates have projected a further decline in subsequent years. Spending on education fell from 5.6 per cent of GDP in 1991 to 4.4 per cent in 1999, with primary and secondary education experiencing the most precipitous declines. Overall, the real value of education expenditure dropped by one third between 1990 and 1998.

Adjustment programmes have led, at best, to a lack of improvement and, at worst, to a sharp decline in public spending for social services.

In Mexico, social spending fell drastically during the 1980s, both in proportion to GDP and in real terms, and did not regain its pre-adjustment levels until ten years later. In 1983, federal spending on education was

Table 8.3 • Hungary: Spending on Education as a Percentage of GDP (1991–2002)

	1991	1993	1995	1998	1999 modified target	2000 proposal	2002 prognosis
Total welfare[†] expenditures	38.2	37.1	31.2	28.1	27.0	27.5	25.8
Education	5.6	5.7	5.2	4.8	4.4	4.8	4.5

† Includes spending for education, healthcare, social insurance and welfare services, housing, cultural activities and environmental protection.
Source: Ministry of Finance, ÁHIR Database, consolidated data.

reduced in real terms by 40.8 per cent with respect to the previous year, and the budgets for healthcare and education in the late 1980s were the lowest in 20 years. Social spending fell again by 13.5 per cent in the period following the economic crisis in 1994 and did not regain previous levels until 1998. In 2000, public resources devoted to reducing poverty were equivalent to one quarter of the annual cost to the Treasury of bailing out the private banks following the 1994 financial crisis and less than one third of military spending.

In Ecuador and Ghana, stagnation and a decline in spending for education were observed. Increases in spending for healthcare were noted, but these increases were at times only nominal, while at other times they were at very low rates or not proportional to the rates of increase in overall spending.

Education spending in Ecuador fell from 4.3 per cent of GDP in 1980 to 2.1 per cent in 1983 after adjustment policies were first introduced and then gradually increased to 3.8 per cent in 1999. Health sector expenditure fell to its lowest levels, in both absolute and relative terms, in 1983 when spending represented 0.6 per cent of GDP. It then increased slightly, averaging just over one per cent of GDP throughout the 1980s and 1990s, and reached 1.2 per cent in 1999. Much of this public expenditure on healthcare services has benefited urban residents, as nearly 46 per cent of spending is directed towards 32 large hospitals in urban areas.

In Ghana, government expenditure on tertiary education declined drastically from the mid-1980s through the 1990s, dropping from 15 per cent of the education budget to 12 per cent during the period 1988–98 despite an 80 per cent increase in student enrolment. Spending on healthcare in real terms has remained relatively unchanged since 1987.

In the Philippines, there have been reductions in healthcare spending and low net increases in education spending, with the education sector also suffering cutbacks in certain years. Spending for the health sector increased slightly from 1986 to 1991, but declined in succeeding years, particularly in 1993, 1995 and 1998–2000. The percentage share of spending on health care in the Philippine government's annual appropriations declined from 3.71 per cent in 1991 to 1.78 per cent in 2000. The biggest cut was made in 1993 when the health budget dropped from P11.3 billion in 1992 to P6.2 billion the following year.

As a percentage of the Philippine national budget, education spending ranged from 9 per cent to 12 per cent in the 1970s, then from 11 to 15 per cent in the 1980s and the early 1990s. The lowest budget share was registered in 1987 at only 10.7 per cent. With the partial recovery of the economy after 1986, increases were registered, reaching 15.4 per cent in 1989. A reversal of this trend was again observed in the 1990s, however, when the budget share dropped to an average of 12 per cent. The share of education expenditure in GDP was limited to a range of 2.4 to 3.7 per cent.

Table 8.4 • Uganda: Share of Total Government Expenditures Allocated to Healthcare and Education (1988–98)

	1988/ 89	1989/ 90	1990/ 91	1991/ 92	1992/ 93	1993/ 94	1994/ 95	1995/ 96	1996/ 97	1997/ 98
Education expenditures	10.0	8.4	8.0	2.3	6.4	5.8	12.0	11.5	14.6	16.6
Healthcare expenditures	2.6	2.6	2.6	0.8	2.3	2.3	4.7	5.7	4.2	4.3

It was only in Uganda that increases were observed in both healthcare and education spending during the period that adjustment policies have been in place, although healthcare spending experienced a decline at the end of the last decade. In fact, spending on healthcare has fluctuated considerably under structural adjustment in Uganda, at first declining from 2.6 per cent of government expenditures in 1987/8 to 0.8 per cent in 1992/3, then increasing to 5.7 per cent in 1995/6, only to fall again to 4.3 per cent in 1997/8. The share of education spending in total expenditure declined sharply from 10 per cent to 2.3 per cent between 1988/9 and 1992/3 and then increased to 16.6 per cent by 1997/8. Most of the spending increases in the education sector have been directed at the primary level, which began receiving 70 per cent of recurrent expenditure for education following implementation of the Universal Primary Education programme in 1997. However, as the Uganda study notes, 'this [increase] was possible following increase in resources made available by the concerted efforts of donors and increase in domestic revenue' as a result of the debt relief conceded through the HIPC initiative.

Spending priorities

One of the strongest criticisms by civil society groups of public expenditure policies under adjustment is that foreign debt servicing takes priority over all other areas of spending, especially in the social sector. In the Philippines, for instance, the largest single item in the government's national budget continues to be interest payments on public sector debt, which participants at the Opening National Forum pointed to as an obstacle to increasing budget allocations for health and education.

The Ecuador study notes that the Ecuadorean government's 'budget and its components are permanently constrained by the ever-increasing amounts devoted to payment of the public external and internal debts. The implementation of structural adjustment policies, which was supposedly aimed at improving the balance of payments, has only reinforced this trend'. Instead of decreasing over time, public external debt rose from 49 per cent of GDP in 1982 to 115 per cent of GDP in 1999, tripling in absolute terms to US$16.4 billion. Debt service in Ecuador reached 52 per cent of government expenditure in 2000, decreasing to 43 per cent in 2001 as a result of debt restructuring, while the budget dedicated to all social spending remained at 20 per cent of total expenditures. Furthermore, in the view of those attending the Opening National Forum in Quito, the foreign debt has provided a mechanism by which the international financial institutions can apply external pressure for the adoption of their policy prescriptions.

Effects of devaluation

Public expenditure reform has taken place in the context of massive devaluations in most of the countries studied that further increased the cost of social services. And a continued growth in the cost of service delivery further reduced that which could be provided within declining budgets for healthcare and education.

The devaluation of local currencies against the dollar had a particularly strong impact on healthcare, as most medicines and medical equipment must be imported by these countries. In the Philippines, for example, a major devaluation of the peso intensified the economic hardship resulting from the Asian financial crisis that erupted in 1997, itself caused in large part by capital account and financial sector liberalization under adjustment. According to the Pharmaceuticals and Health Care Association of the Philippines, this devaluation resulted in a 25–30 per cent increase in the price of drugs and a 40–60 per cent increase in the cost of small medical equipment.

From 1991 to 2000 in Zimbabwe, the medicare price index rose by 2106.3 per cent and the education price index by 857.2 per cent as a result of extensive devaluations and inflation. Even in Uganda, where there have been increases in spending for education and healthcare, the negative effect of the rise in relative prices in these sectors has outweighed the positive effect of the spending increases. This observation was validated by numerous complaints reported during the fieldwork regarding the excessive cost of education and healthcare services at all levels.

Cost-recovery and revenue-generation schemes

Controls on spending were accompanied in most cases by revenue-generating schemes that required the users to share in the cost of services. In Zimbabwe, for example, the government began systematically to enforce a system of user fees for healthcare services in 1991. Those earning more than Z$150 per month were made to pay for services rendered for healthcare, while the unemployed and those earning less than Z$150 were entitled to free treatment. This cost-recovery measure was put in place just as the worst drought of the century hit the country in 1991–2. After a brief respite in the application of fees the following year, the system of user fees for healthcare services was revised in 1994, and substantial fee increases were established for all services. In the education sector, although primary school fees had been abolished at independence in 1980, fees were reintroduced in urban primary schools and all secondary schools in 1992, with exemptions for children from households earning less than Z$400 per month. While the Z$400 limit corresponded to the threshold for payment of personal income tax, it was far below the poverty line of Z$593 for a family of six in 1991.

Controls on spending were accompanied in most cases by revenue-generating schemes that required users to share in the cost of services.

In certain cases, the application of user fees offset possible gains to the population from increased spending for healthcare services. In Ghana, the Economic Recovery Programme of 1983–6 initiated the removal of general subsidies, which led in the health sector to an intensification of fee collection for services and enforcement of the Hospital Fees Act. From a system of charging token fees for consultations under this Act, the user-fee regime changed in 1985 to one in which fixed fees were charged for consultations, examinations and laboratory and related diagnostic procedures, and drugs were priced at full cost. Separate charges were established for outpatients, medical and surgical treatment, hospital accommodation and catering. The price schedule moved from lesser charges at lower levels of service (clinics and health centres) to higher charges at hospitals, with the highest fees charged at the teaching hospitals.

Revenue-generating programmes also included the transformation of service institutions into public corporations mandated to ensure cost recovery and even profit generation. In the Philippines, there has been an ongoing process of transforming public health institutions – regional and national hospitals – into public corporations. The 'corporatization' of these public service institutions involves fiscal and management autonomy to achieve financial stability and viability. They are allowed to collect, retain and allocate revenues from the user fees they generate. At the same time, direct subsidies from both the national and local governments for hospitals have been reduced.

Effects of decentralization

Many of the country assessments indicate that a key feature of reforms in the social sector has been the decentralization of services and their administration to the regional and local levels. While this goal has had some merit, it has proved to be disastrous in practice in many contexts because it has often been little more than a downloading exercise without adequate funding to support it. The Mexico study indicates that decentralization has involved a deconcentration of administration, with greater responsibilities and fewer resources at the local level. State governments were assigned the administration of health services – previously the responsibility of the Department of Health and the Mexican Institute of Social Security – and basic education programmes. Yet, in the context of a fiscal crisis in which states were receiving less income from the federal government, decentralization left insufficient resources to adequately fulfil the new responsibilities for service delivery at the local level.

> **The decentralization of services has proved to be disastrous in many contexts because of inadequate funding.**

In the Philippines, the decentralization of healthcare services has been beset with economic and administrative problems. The investigation there found that local governments have lacked the knowledge and skills needed to assume their additional functions. They have also lacked the necessary resources to be able to deliver basic healthcare services effectively and expand the coverage of these services because of the mismatch between the cost of devolved functions and the corresponding revenues allocated. A key problem resides in the regressive nature of the distribution formula by which central government funds are allocated to the local level for these purposes.

The formula assigns more financing to localities with higher *per capita* income and does not take into account the burden imposed on the local governments to support the devolved functions, particularly hospital operations. Consequently many municipalities and provinces have experienced financing shortfalls aggravated by the fact that some towns have diverted funds from healthcare to other priorities.

According to the Philippines study, provincial and district hospitals that were performing poorly prior to decentralization have in fact deteriorated owing to the inability of local governments to maintain previous expenditure levels. This has exacerbated the lack of supplies, drugs and allowances for repairs and maintenance of the medical equipment of these hospitals, most of which are already in a deplorable state. As a result, health services have become more inadequate and inaccessible to many, particularly the poor. Participants at the first National Forum testified that this reality has forced NGOs increasingly to carry the burden of service provision that should be the responsibility of the state.

In Hungary, poor municipalities now have more difficulty maintaining and developing schools.

In Hungary, the transformation of the educational system in the 1990s devolved the responsibility for education to the local level, with basic *per capita* funding provided by the state while financing for school development was left to the municipality. Although this has had some positive impacts in terms of the relationship between schools and communities, it has meant that poor municipalities have more difficulty maintaining and developing schools. This situation has also led to the appearance of private schools, which has segmented the education system and increased inequalities of opportunity. National Forum participants reported that children from poorer regions of the country and from unskilled, unemployed, poor or Romany (gypsy) families, were less likely to be able to continue their education in order to acquire a skill, a problem compounded by the fact that a higher local drop-out rate induces a decrease in funding from the central government. This situation will only perpetuate the cycle of poverty from generation to generation.

The Impact of Reforms on Access to, and Quality of, Education and Healthcare Services

The previous section highlighted the effects of adjustment measures on the allocation of public spending towards education and healthcare in the countries studied. This section considers the consequences of these trends for service access and quality, particularly for the low-income and poor segments of society. The analysis addresses the following issues:

- the impact of user fees on access to services by the poor and low-income segments of society;

- the impact of user fees on the quality of education and healthcare services; and

- gender-differentiated impacts.

Impact of user fees on access to services by the poor and low-income groups

The introduction of user fees under cost-recovery and revenue-generation schemes has imposed serious constraints on access by the poor to education and healthcare services. This was found to be true in all the countries studied, although the impacts varied according to the way the policies were applied and the extent of the spending cuts made.

Access to education

After a decade of free education following independence in Zimbabwe, school fees were reintroduced and led to a dramatic increase in drop-out rates. Primary school drop-out rates continued to be significantly higher throughout the 1990s, particularly in the first grade; in the grades with the greatest drop-out rates, the numbers were higher for girls than for boys. Furthermore, by the end of the decade, only 70 per cent of the children finishing primary school were continuing on to secondary school, while in the fourth and final year of lower secondary school there was an average drop-out rate of 92 per cent for males and 93.4 per cent for females over the period 1990–7.

In Zimbabwe, the introduction of fees led to a dramatic increase in school drop-out rates and a serious impact on the utilization of healthcare services.

The imposition of user fees has led to reduced enrolment rates in Ghana, particularly in rural areas, said Opening National Forum participants. With children being pulled out of school to help support their families, they added, the primary school drop-out rate had reached 40 per cent. Fees rise sharply at the secondary level and yet again at the tertiary level, where now only one out of every 400 Ghanaians is enrolled. User fees have led to increasing inequalities, both between and within communities, as the poor are left behind. Indeed, the Ghana study found, income levels are the most important determinant of enrolment at institutions of higher education.

The same was found to be true in Mexico: there, for every 100 children who enter primary school, 64 graduate, only 40 go on to complete the secondary level, 14 finish the equivalent of high school and seven graduate from university. Primary education was said by National Forum participants to be free only in theory owing to expenses – that families often cannot afford – for uniforms, books and transportation. Secondary education was cited as being even more restricted, in large part by the common need for children to help increase family income. Overall, funding cutbacks have adversely affected a range of educational services, Forum participants said, leading to high repetition and drop-out rates.

In Uganda, where a Universal Primary Education programme was introduced in 1997 and funded through a debt reduction agreement under the HIPC initiative, access to primary education improved. Access to secondary and tertiary education, however, was found to be skewed against the poor, as the burden of school costs at these levels must now be borne primarily by parents. There has also been a marked drop in the number of girls finishing primary school who are enrolling in secondary school.

Increased school costs were cited in other countries, as well, as a reason for declining school attendance. Book fees, in particular, were emphasized at the first National Forum in Hungary, while forum participants in the Philippines said that charges for materials, vaccinations and meals amount to user fees that the poor cannot afford.

Access to healthcare

Various country studies found that the establishment of user fees for healthcare services had led an increasing number of people and families to resort to self-medication and home care instead of visiting clinics and hospitals. This has been the case especially for women. There has been an increase in the number of persons reducing their length of stay in hospitals, as well as of those who cannot complete the full course of their treatment because they cannot afford to buy medication. More people now seek medical attention only when their illness is already severe, causing an increase in the number of people who die in their homes from curable diseases and often creating public health hazards by spreading disease in their communities. The persistence of such infectious but preventable and curable diseases as bronchitis, pneumonia and tuberculosis has been observed in most countries.

With the establishment of user fees for healthcare in Zimbabwe, cost increases for patients were dramatic, in some cases exceeding 1,000 per cent. This has had a serious negative impact on the utilization of healthcare services in both rural and urban areas, particularly for the poor. According to the Zimbabwe study, 'immediately after fees were raised in 1991 and again in 1993/94, declines were noted in outpatient and prenatal care sought, prescriptions dispensed, admissions, and X ray, lab and dental services. Most people sought early discharge or absconded to save money'.

High hospital fees in Ghana, coupled with increasing poverty, prevented patients from using healthcare facilities.

In Ghana, the introduction of user fees against a backdrop of continuous decline in the real wages or earnings of many workers, coupled with increasing poverty, has been largely responsible for poor access to health services. It was found that high hospital fees prevented patients from using healthcare facilities and forced them to resort to self-medication. It was noted at the first National Forum that user fees had reduced out-patient attendance by as much as a third, particularly in rural areas. Many poor people, the Forum participants said, are turned away for lack of funds. Furthermore, the payment arrangements are cumbersome and too much staff time is devoted to collecting fees. The poor are simply being priced out of hospital care, they added, and a *de facto* two-tiered health system for rich and poor has been created.

According to the SAPRI/Ghana study, proximity and cost of services are key determinants in the utilization of health facilities. The study found that the dispersed location of health facilities and their distance from settlements, particularly in the northern region of the country, imposed additional costs on those seeking treatment, most of whom are poor. Furthermore, long-distance travel was found to involve risks and inconveniences that can often result in health complications and sometimes even death. Analysis of household expenditure for health services during a family illness showed that some spent more on healthcare than on all other items combined. Studies have shown that the contribution of households to the financing of health is almost three times that of government funding in *per capita* terms.

The user fee system established in Ghana provides for differential charges for adults and children, as well as exemptions for various categories of patients, such as those unable to pay and, more recently, children under five. Some services have also been made free of charge, including immunization, pre- and post-natal services and treatment at child-welfare clinics. One of the objectives of the Ghana study was to determine the extent to which people at the community level were aware of the exemption policy. The field study revealed in the main that

> the exemption policy has not been as effective as it was meant to be. There seemed to be some ignorance about the exemption policy among women with children under five years in the rural communities, who eventually paid for everything anytime they visited the health facility. Only a few people therefore enjoy free medical care.

Only 65 per cent of the population has access to the modern health system, although this figure disguises gross geographical inequality. Health status indicators show little change in the marked inequalities in the mortality rates between different regions of the country and between rural and urban areas.

Cost sharing has made hospital care too costly for the poor in Uganda, as well. People at the Opening National Forum testified that those who cannot pay for critical healthcare simply die. Hospitals, they said, have administered the programme poorly and have been closed down in areas where too many people have been unable to pay.

In the Philippines, profit-generation schemes of 'corporatized' health institutions have particularly affected access by the poor to curative health-care services. Measures adopted under such schemes include: stricter screening of indigent patients; imposing a ceiling on the amount of assistance for indigent or charity patients; requiring a deposit from indigent patients before treatment is administered; and requiring all types of patients to buy all the medical supplies needed for their treatment or operation, such as cotton, bandages, sutures, plaster, intravenous fluids, syringes and needles. Further measures include increasing the caseloads of hospital personnel and the elimination of some of their economic benefits, such as hazard pay. The overall rise in the cost of healthcare services and medicines is the primary reason that most poor households engage in self-medication and delay seeking appropriate medical treatment. This situation has aggravated the spread of communicable diseases, such as tuberculosis.

The overall rise in the cost of healthcare services and medicines in the Philippines has aggravated the spread of communicable diseases.

In the absence of consensus on healthcare reform in Hungary, only partial reforms were implemented in the public health system in the 1990s. 'The public health strategy of the World Bank,' the country study explained, 'was built around three elements: cost efficiency; access; and quality. Yet in practice, the first element proved much weightier than the other two'. The report goes on to note that

> the requirement of universal access to healthcare is mentioned as a priority but is regarded as feasible only if the realization of this aim does not exceed the limits of economic performance or collide with the interests of economic sustainability and the labour market. These conditions could be met if the state were to provide only a 'basic package' of healthcare, meaning that health services would fall victim to the reduction of the redistributive role of the state.

In spite of reductions in resources for healthcare throughout the 1990s, the system has continued to function and provide universal access to nearly all, a reality attributed in large part to the sense of vocation in the medical and nursing profession. Still, the poor have been the primary victims of the liberalized pharmaceutical market, reduced subsidies on therapeutic equipment, and the growing costs of medical care, as they can ill afford to pay the higher cost of medicine and specialized care.

Impact on the quality of education and healthcare services

The poor and, in many cases, deteriorating quality of education and healthcare services is a central finding of the country investigations. The combination of cuts in education and healthcare spending and reforms to rationalize resource use and reduce the role of the state in service provision has had a negative impact on the quality of these services available to the majority of the population, particularly the poor.

Education quality

In every country studied, inadequate infrastructure and the lack of educational materials and supplies, as well as declining salaries and insufficient training for teachers, have negatively affected the quality of education provided. This was found to be true of the different levels of education that were the focus of the various country studies.

Inadequate infrastructure, the lack of educational materials, and declining teacher salaries have negatively affected the quality of education.

In Hungary, low teacher salaries and high student–teacher ratios were found to have placed obstacles to the improvement of the quality of education following the reforms of the 1990s. In 1998, the real value of net wages in education was 20 per cent lower than it had been five years earlier. Salaries of primary school teachers were 68 per cent of *per capita* GDP in 1993, while that of secondary school teachers was 72 per cent. The situation worsened as GDP increased while the real value of teachers' salaries declined. It is estimated that teachers earn less than half of other professionals with similar educational levels. In addition, lay-offs of teachers increased the student–teacher ratio and created higher unemployment in the early part of the decade, although an increase in enrolment led to new hiring of teachers in later years.

In Zimbabwe, the decrease in real, *per capita* spending on education under adjustment in the 1990s led to a fall in the real wages of teachers. Yet 90 per cent of public spending on primary education went to salaries, leaving only 10 per cent for maintenance and repair of school infrastructure, the acquisition of furniture, textbooks and didactic materials, and ongoing teacher training. This situation adversely affected the quality of education in the country.

Even where public spending has increased, as in the case of Uganda, where the Universal Primary Education programme was implemented in 1997, the quality of education has suffered. Although resources have been provided to increase the numbers of teachers, textbooks and classrooms in the country, these increases have been overwhelmed by the dramatic upsurge in enrolment, which doubled at the primary level to over five million compared with the previous ten years. As a result, the ability to ensure an adequate quality of education has become strained, and there are indications, particularly in rural areas, that the majority of students are unable to read and write even after six years of primary school.

The National Forum participants in Ghana lamented that the quality of their country's education system had declined since the onset of structural adjustment and that the results of more than US$400 million in World Bank lending since the early 1980s have been extremely poor. Civil service lay-offs and a decline in the real wages of teachers have led to higher student–teacher ratios, and the 1991 education reforms failed to address the difficult working conditions that teachers face. Furthermore, there is a widespread shortage of textbooks, despite the imposition of user fees. These factors have led to declining teacher morale, said the Forum participants, as well as an erosion of confidence in public schools.

A general lack of adequate infrastructure and human resources was found to be affecting the quality of Ghanaian tertiary education, in particular, following the reforms. The squeeze in financing has been felt in the area of recruitment and development of personnel, as well as in research. This has occurred at a time in which enrolment has increased tremendously, despite the fact that many more qualified students, numbering in the thousands, have been denied enrolment due to lack of facilities and their inability to pay.

Against a backdrop of growing enrolment in the Philippines (18.8 per cent growth in primary and 15.9 per cent growth in secondary school participation between 1992/3 and 1999/2000), the study found severe and chronic shortages of schools, classrooms, teachers and textbooks, while teacher salaries and benefits fell as class size and workloads increased. The teacher–student ratio was 1 : 44 at the primary school level and 1 : 34 at the secondary school level in 1999, the year in which the government imposed a hiring freeze for teachers (the internationally accepted standard is 1 : 25). At the same time, a survey of primary and secondary school teachers found that one quarter teach in classrooms without roofs, while nearly half their schools lack sufficient furniture and electricity. The textbook–student ratio for the 2000 school year was estimated at 1 : 37, making learning much more difficult.

These problems, which have led to a poor quality of education, were found to be more pronounced in rural areas, particularly in the poorer regions of the country. A secondary school teacher in western Mindanao, for example, testified at the Opening National Forum in Manila to the deplorable conditions in schools: 50 classrooms for a student population of 11,000 and the need for students to share the relatively few textbooks available. Drop-out rates in Mindanao primary schools reach as high as 50 per cent, literacy rates remain low and young people have ever-greater difficulties finding gainful employment.

Healthcare quality

Deteriorating conditions in healthcare facilities, the lack of medicines and inadequate staffing, were consistently found to have resulted from reforms under adjustment, particularly in rural areas and poorer regions in the countries studied. This decline in the quality of healthcare services for large segments of the population was of serious concern to the civil society groups consulted.

Deteriorating conditions in healthcare facilities, the lack of medicines and inadequate staffing have resulted from reforms.

Reductions in public spending on healthcare in the 1990s in Zimbabwe were found to have resulted in reduced maintenance, delayed upgrades of deteriorating health facilities, shortages of equipment and essential drugs, and a high rate of staff attrition and loss to the private sector and abroad. The study reported an estimated 30 per cent drop in the quality of healthcare services in the country in 1993 when compared with the gains in the post-independence period. Twice as many women were found to be dying in childbirth in Harare hospitals in 1993 than before 1990. In 1998, high levels of wasting and stunting in children under five were found, particularly in rural areas, a situation that had worsened since the 1980s. At the same time, infant and child mortality rates increased after having shown a steady improvement prior to the implementation of adjustment policies. Several district hospitals and government clinics were closed after 1995, and there has been a decline in pre-natal services and in immunization coverage. Rural facilities tend to offer poor quality or insufficient care, often forcing the sick to pay the costs of travel and admission to higher-level or urban facilities.

The HIV/AIDS pandemic has added to the health crisis in Zimbabwe, where hospitals have had problems keeping up with the demand for services, as estimates indicate that as many as 3,000 victims of the disease

Table 8.5 • Zimbabwe Infant Mortality Rate and Child Mortality Rate per 1,000 Live Births (1978–97)

	Infant mortality rate			Child mortality rate		
	Rural	Urban	Total	Rural	Urban	Total
1978	88	64	83	40	25	57
1981	85	59	79	38	22	34
1984	77	50	69	33	17	28
1986	72	47	64	30	15	25
1988	69	46	61	28	15	23
1990	71	55	66	30	20	26
1997	89	63	80	N/A	N/A	36

Source: MoHCW, *National Health Strategy for Zimbabwe, 1997–2007.*

may be dying every week. 'Because we operate on a specific budget we can no longer admit more patients than we can afford to,' stated a staff member of the Harare Central Hospital. 'It simply doesn't make economic sense.' The following passage from a Zimbabwean newspaper sums up even more dramatically the condition of the country's healthcare system resulting from the implementation of adjustment policies:

> Not only do these hospitals face critical drug, equipment and staff shortages, they are becoming extremely expensive for the ordinary worker who is battling to make ends meet due to the high cost of basic commodities. Consultation and admission fees are pegged at Z$169 for adults and Z$84 for children and are now demanded upfront. The exemption certificate from the Social Development Office for low-income earners is now only worth the paper it is written on. In the context where the HIV/AIDS pandemic is claiming 1,700 people a week over and above a host of many other fatal diseases, the deplorable state of the health delivery system could be seen as a bombshell of seismic proportions. (*Daily News*, Harare, 8 November 2000, p. 16)

In the Philippines, the study reported on deteriorating conditions in primary healthcare facilities, such as rural health units and *barangay* health stations, due to lack of funds. These basic, non-hospital healthcare facilities are commonly housed in dilapidated and leaking structures and have chronically experienced shortages of medical supplies, medicines and basic medical instruments and equipment, such as stethoscopes, weighing scales and microscopes. Moreover, many of these public health units, particularly those in rural areas, do not have competent medical staff owing to the uneven distribution of healthcare workers and professionals. Nearly two thirds of physicians were found to be concentrated in the country's urban centres, leaving many rural health units 'doctorless'. It was found that large numbers of women and children in the rural areas die without having seen a doctor, with only about 40 per cent of deaths in the country reported as having been medically attended.

Participants in the Opening National Forum in Manila spoke to these issues and to the effects of two decades of structural adjustment. They pointed in particular to the deregulation of pharmaceuticals, the increase in hospital and doctor fees and the contracting out of hospital services as part of the liberalizing reforms of the 1980s, and to the consequently reduced access by the poor to healthcare and drugs. They added that public clinics often lack medicines and that public services provide more curative than preventive care.

Decentralization of health functions to the local level in the Philippines, part of the restructuring of the health sector, was found to have contributed to an exacerbation of the inefficient and inequitable national health delivery system. Many hospital workers and employees have been retrenched or displaced from their jobs. Those who have been transferred to the locally administrated healthcare system have had their labour contracts breached. Their wages have declined, and economic benefits like hazard pay and overtime are no longer paid in cash, but rather transformed into non-monetary compensation. Healthcare personnel have also experienced an increase in the number of working hours and in the volume of caseloads.

Meanwhile, in Ghana, low and unacceptable ratios of healthcare personnel to patients and poor remuneration of staff were found to negatively affect the quality of public health services. Those attending the first National Forum pointed in particular to public sector lay-offs and to poor working conditions for health providers as reasons for the departure overseas of many young doctors once they qualify to practise.

In Mexico, according to the Mexican Foundation for Health, 44 per cent of citizens cite poor quality as the primary problem with healthcare services. General healthcare provision has been restricted to the most basic services, such as vaccinations, it was noted at the Opening National Forum. Minorities and rural populations have even less access to adequate care than do others. Women in rural areas, particularly indigenous women, have, for example, a disproportionately high incidence of problems related to childbirth.

Even in Uganda, where there was an increase in the number of health facilities, the utilization of these units remains limited as a result of a lack of medicine and insufficient staffing. It was found that those facilities serving poor areas of the country, in particular, experience long periods without drugs in stock, which serves as a disincentive to seek treatment. Furthermore, recruitment of specialized health workers, such as laboratory technicians and dental assistants, as required at lower-level health facilities, has proved to be problematic owing to low salary levels. Qualified personnel often opt to work in urban areas where they have access to private clinics in which they can obtain additional income by taking on a second shift. Although there have been minimal wage hikes for health personnel as a result of budget increases in the mid-1990s, salaries continue to fall short of a living wage, leading to low morale and poor quality of services as employees engage in other activities to supplement their low incomes. Thus the study concluded that, despite improvements in social spending, social indicators continue to reflect poorly on the health sector.

Gender-differentiated effects

In many countries implementing adjustment programmes, women and girls, in order to compensate for the lack of access to publicly provided services and the means to acquire these services through the market from the private sector, have had to take on greater responsibility for the education and healthcare needs of the extended family, including caring for the sick and elderly. Care must be provided in the household even for severe illnesses, which translates to a yet greater burden on women in their traditional role as care givers. This reality has compounded the impact of adjustment policies on women. The studies point to two key areas in which girls and women have been the most adversely affected by policy shifts.

Women and girls have had to take on greater responsibility for the education and healthcare needs of the extended family.

Cutbacks in budgetary allocations to the health and education sectors and in public sector management

As the Uganda study points out, there is a lack of a clear understanding of gender issues in the area of public expenditure management. Women have long borne the 'double burden' of production – engaging in income-earning activities to support their families – and reproduction – bearing, nurturing and taking care of children, doing household chores, preparing food and caring for the sick. Many of the country assessments have shown that it is the women at the household level who have had to cope with the need to compensate for the reduction in provision of public services and the inability to access through the market what the government no longer provides.

Drastic government cuts in healthcare spending have affected maternal health services, a factor of pivotal importance for the welfare of children. In 1995 in Mexico, for example, trained personnel attended only 88.5 per cent of births, and the percentage was even lower in rural areas. In that same year, 6.8 per cent of pregnant woman received no pre-natal care, and those that did receive care averaged only 3.9 consultations – below the minimum of five per pregnancy recommended by the World Health Organization. Gender differences in educational achievement are also notable in Mexico. Women who participated in workshops during the study noted that girls are the first to leave school to take care of domestic responsibilities so their mothers can expand their income-earning activities. Data from 1995 show that girls have an average of 6.9 years of education while boys average 7.5 years. Of the population between 6 and 14 years of age, 8.5 per cent of girls do not attend school while 7.1 per cent of boys do not. The literacy rate of males over 15 years is 91.4 per cent, while for women it is 87.2 per cent.

Cost recovery and the imposition of user fees

The Zimbabwe study shows that large increases in school fees resulting from cost-recovery measures in education have had a negative impact on girls. Primary school data demonstrate that, in grades with the highest drop-out rates, these rates are highest among girls. The results of a broad monitoring survey found that, among the reasons given for not being at school, 'because it was too expensive' was more frequently cited in all age groups by girls than boys. This indicates that, although parents prefer to send both male and female children to school, if they are forced to withdraw a child, the girl will usually lose out.

Cost-recovery measures in education had a negative impact on girls in Zimbabwe and Uganda.

Cost-recovery mechanisms were also found to have an inherent gender bias against women and girls in the Uganda study. When a family is faced with financial difficulties, cost sharing tends to affect women to a greater extent than men. In the case of education, it was found that preference is often given to boys when it comes to payment of fees at post-primary levels, with participation rates of girls declining at higher levels of schooling. In the area of health, maternal care services were reported to be inadequate by women in rural areas, and what access there was has been further constrained by cost-sharing measures. Among the poor who are unable to afford healthcare services under the cost-sharing arrangements, it was observed that women are more likely to either forego medical services or resort to home-care treatment. The impact of HIV/AIDS on women as care givers was also noted. Those participating in the first SAPRI National Forum in Ghana pointed to similarly severe impacts of such policies on women and girls in that country, as well.

The Impact on the Poor of the Elimination of Basic Subsidies

The study in Ecuador assessed the impact of a distinct, common and important aspect of public expenditure reforms under adjustment programmes, namely, subsidy policy. The first issue encountered was the different understanding that the parties involved in this investigation had of subsidies. Civil society actors perceived subsidies as a way in which government could help to reduce the gap between the production cost of a good or service and the market price paid by consumers or producers. The World Bank and the government, however, conceived of subsidies as the difference between the national price of a good or service and its opportunity cost, which is implicitly understood as its international price. In addition, they tend to think of public spending on basic education and healthcare as subsidies, while social actors distinguish between subsidies and social spending, believing the latter to be the responsibility of the state. Furthermore, civil society groups were clear that subsidies also include those public transfers made in support of the corporate and financial sectors.

These differences in conceptualization reveal a difference in belief as to what role the state should play in poverty reduction. 'Due to structural adjustment policies,' explained the study's authors, who were selected jointly by SAPRIN and the Bank, 'the meaning of poverty was redefined in Ecuador. Instead of being understood as a problem that requires state intervention, poverty is currently seen as an economic issue that should be resolved by market forces.' This has meant an end to universal subsidies and the introduction of targeting of beneficiaries as the preferred means of allocating government resources to the social sector and compensating the poor for any negative impacts from the new policy regime.

As part of public expenditure reform in Ecuador, the elimination beginning in 1996 of subsidies for cooking gas and electricity dramatically increased their price to consumers. To mitigate the impact of this measure, the government created a targeted social protection programme in 1998 that provided cash transfers to the poor and the elderly through the *Bono Solidario* programme. Yet the cash transfers made through this programme amounted to only US$180 million annually, far below the US$390 million that was saved by eliminating the cooking gas and electricity subsidies. Civil society participants at the Opening National Forum called the targeted subsidies unjust, noting that they were reaching, at best, 17 per cent of the more than seven million Ecuadoreans living in poverty.

The SAPRI assessment found that the *Bono Solidario* programme was not well designed. Initial targeting procedures were conceived of as very short-term measures, and the eligibility criteria for receiving the *Bono* ensured that a significant number of applications made by poor citizens were rejected by the government. While the criteria were later improved, discontent continued about the overall characteristics of the programme. It merely provided for the minimum level of caloric intake necessary for subsistence and allows for no improvement in the conditions of the poor, as the transfer is withdrawn if a person acquires additional income or assets. The *Bono* was also found to be inaccessible to most of the rural poor, as the cost of transportation necessary to collect the subsidy would cancel out most of the benefit. Assessed from the perspective of both beneficiaries and non-beneficiaries, the *Bono Solidario*, as the government's targeted subsidy programme, was ineffective.

Targeting subsidies is not viable when the majority of the population is poor and economic policies fail to generate production, employment and increased incomes.

The results of the Ecuador study indicate that the removal or reduction of universal subsidies for essential services, such as electricity, affects those with the lowest income the most. When this policy was combined with a reduction in government spending for education and healthcare, there was a severe increase in the number of poor, as well as a deepening of poverty in the country. These impacts were found to be more pronounced in rural areas and female-headed households. The subsequent targeting of subsidies through direct transfers was found to be ineffective in reaching many of those most in need, though the transfers did help those able to access them maintain basic nutrition levels. The Ecuador investigation concluded that the policy of targeting is rendered unviable when the majority of the population is poor and becoming poorer, and that it does not compensate for the failure of macroeconomic policies to reactivate national production, generate employment opportunities and increase incomes. Both the research study and National Forum participants also made clear that, while the poor have been increasingly deprived, powerful economic groups have continued to receive *de facto* subsidies in the form of financial bail-outs, currency devaluations, credit guarantees, tax incentives and other such measures.

Meanwhile, according to the participants at the Opening National Forum in Mexico, the targeting of social programmes has served to deny many segments of the population needed benefits. National poverty alleviation programmes, including PRONASOL and PROGRESA, were designed to provide limited support in a targeted manner only to those in extreme conditions of poverty, rather than to improve conditions for the society as a whole. Participants charged that this policy of targeting resources was used for political-electoral ends, created conflicts within communities and even within families, and failed to provide for the most basic needs of large segments of the poor. Furthermore, fiscal policies under adjustment that have included the removal of subsidies on basic food items (such as milk and *tortillas*), as well as price increases for basic goods and services and new taxes on food and medicine, have caused additional hardship for low-income sectors of the population. Participants emphasized that women, children and the indigenous population have been those most negatively affected.

Conclusion

The review of the impact of public expenditure reform under structural adjustment programmes inevitably addressed the issue of the role of the state in the social sector. The policy design of adjustment programmes has had as a clear goal the reduction of the state's role, on the one hand, and, on the other, the strengthening and expansion of the role of the market and the private sector in the provision of education and healthcare. The investigations have shown that, in practice, reforms have usually led to a systematic reduction in the role and capacity of the state to provide social services to the majority of the population, allowing service access to be increasingly subjected to the rules and forces of the market. Education and healthcare have become less service functions of the state and more goods to be bought in the market by those who can afford them.

Civil society organizations have strongly criticized these policy shifts under adjustment for, in effect, transferring resources from the poor to the rich. Low-income groups have been asked to sacrifice and suffer the consequences of cuts in subsidies and social spending and the imposition of cost-sharing and cost-recovery measures. Yet subsidies continue to be extended to private corporations through credit guarantees, tax incentives and even bail-out packages and loans to rescue ailing banks and corporations. At the same time, the persistent external debt problem faced by many countries has been a major factor behind the constraints imposed on public spending. Six of the seven countries reviewed in this chapter are saddled with huge external debt, and interest and principal payments on their public sector debts have received the highest priority in the allocation of government resources.

Reforms have usually led to a systematic reduction in the role and capacity of the state to provide social services to the majority of the population.

In the face of low wages and high unemployment levels, the imposition of user fees and the rising cost of services to local populations have increased hardships on the poor. The targeting of those in extreme poverty as recipients of state subsidies has failed to be an effective policy instrument for addressing poverty and has only perpetuated inequality. The deterioration in health conditions among low-income groups and their inadequate access to quality education translate into an underdeveloped potential and the erosion of the capabilities of individuals and their communities to build sustainable livelihoods. These long-term human costs have been the outcome of policies premised on a distorted calculus that considers investments in the social sector as subsidies that can be eliminated, with the assumption that this will lead to greater economic growth. Yet, as evidenced by the country assessments, the result has been an expansion and deepening of poverty and greater social exclusion.

Specific conclusions drawn from the country investigations are as follows:

- *Structural adjustment programmes have led, in the worst of cases, to a sharp deterioration in public spending for healthcare and education, while, even in the best of cases, there has been inadequate improvement in spending levels.* In Hungary and Zimbabwe, where the state had been extensively involved in the universal provision of social services, public spending for education and healthcare dropped precipitously as a result of expenditure controls under adjustment. Spending for these services in Ghana has stagnated in real terms, although population growth and the nation's demographic structure indicate that higher spending levels are needed to maintain the same level, much less improve the quality, of services. In these and other countries, servicing the foreign debt has been given priority over spending for social service provision. In Uganda, the only sample country that has seen an increase in spending on education and healthcare, in large part due to debt reduction under HIPC, the review showed a lack of improvement in the allocation of resources to ensure service quality. Overall, cutbacks in budgetary allocations to the health and education sectors have limited access by the poor to these public services and imposed on women and girls the added burden of compensating for the reduction of their provision by the state.

- *The imposition of cost-sharing and revenue-generating schemes has created additional constraints to access by the poor to quality services.* As a result of an increase in fees, school drop-out rates have risen in most countries, particularly among girls, exacerbating a disturbing gender gap that increases at higher levels of education. Access to secondary and tertiary education, in particular, was found to be skewed against the poor. Fees for health services were found to limit access by the poor to timely care, particularly in rural areas, and exemptions for certain groups and services have not been effective because information about such programmes has not reached potential beneficiaries. As a result, an increasing number of people, particularly women, have resorted to self-medication and home care. Many seek medical attention only when their possibly infectious illness is already severe, creating a public health hazard in the community.

• *Educational quality has worsened as a result of budget constraints.* In general, the quality of education, particularly in rural areas and poorer regions of the countries studied, was found to be woefully inadequate. In many places, school infrastructure has deteriorated or is entirely lacking due to insufficient investment, while shortages of educational supplies, such as textbooks and didactic materials, are widespread. Although recurrent spending on salaries tends to make up the vast majority of education budgets, real wages for teachers have dropped while student–teacher ratios have increased. Teacher training, important for improving educational quality as well as for keeping experienced teachers, has been inadequate and underfunded.

• *The quality of available healthcare has not improved and has worsened in some regions, and large disparities persist between rural and urban areas.* Deteriorating conditions in healthcare facilities, lack of medicines and inadequate staffing were consistently found to have resulted from reforms. In some countries, physicians tend to be concentrated in urban centres, while many rural health units remain 'doctorless'. In several cases, health facilities serving poor areas, in particular, have experienced long periods without drugs in stock.

• *The elimination of universally provided subsidies for essential goods and services has negatively affected the quality of life of the poorest.* The removal or reduction of subsidies for essential services, such as electricity, was found to affect those with the lowest income the most. The policy of targeting subsidies is rendered unviable when the majority of the population is poor and becoming poorer, and it does not compensate for the failure of macroeconomic policies to reactivate national production, generate employment opportunities or increase incomes.

The country assessments coincide in concluding that there is an important redistributive role for the state, exercised through budgetary formulation and public policy, to provide universal access to affordable quality services. To this end, a series of basic recommendations are suggested.

There is an important redistributive role for the state to provide universal access to affordable quality services.

User fees and other cost-recovery schemes for primary and preventive healthcare and basic education should be abolished. Increases are required, in real terms, in budgets for healthcare and education. An emphasis should be placed on improving allocation to ensure the efficient use of resources, as well as the quality of services and equitable service delivery. Overall, more spending is required for supplies and maintenance, as well as for improvement in infrastructure and personnel salaries and training, that will improve the quality of healthcare and education. An emphasis on primary and preventative healthcare and basic education is key, but this should not occur at the expense of curative health facilities or secondary and tertiary education, which are also of prime importance for human and economic development.

The expansion of social service coverage should not lead to a decline in service quality. When greater access translates into a significant growth in the number of students and/or patients, and that growth threatens a decline in service quality, financing must be found to ensure both quality and expanded coverage. At the same time, where universal subsidies have been in place for essential services, these should not be eliminated and replaced with targeted programmes of direct transfers. Resources can be generated for these purposes in a number of ways, including through reductions in debt payments and military expenditures, the termination of corporate subsidies, and the application of higher taxes or tariffs on luxury and other goods consumed by more well-to-do citizens.

There is also an immediate and massive need for greater investment to deal with the problem of communicable diseases, which requires making available the medicines that exist for their treatment and prevention. In this regard, the HIV/AIDS pandemic must be given utmost and urgent priority, especially in the Africa region. More resources should be channelled towards HIV/AIDS campaigns, and there must be democratic access to drugs and treatment being developed for this disease. Increased attention and importance should also be given to maternal healthcare services.

Finally, social expenditures should be protected from cuts during times of fiscal crisis. Toward this end, the budget formulation process should be democratized to allow for the meaningful participation of civil society. Transparency and accountability should be strictly upheld in the whole process of policy formulation and implementation and in the monitoring of public expenditures. In this regard, a policy of full public disclosure of information, including easy access to all such data, should be observed.

CHAPTER 9

Structural Adjustment, Poverty and Inequality

When Jim Wolfensohn agreed to engage civil society in an on-the-ground analysis of the effects of structural adjustment policies soon after he assumed the presidency of the World Bank, he said that he wanted to find out what the effects of economic reform were on poverty reduction, income differentials and disparate population groups. The preceding seven chapters have in large part focused on that impact. This concluding chapter brings together those findings, summarizes them and reorganizes and presents them in a manner intended to facilitate an understanding of the consequences of the adjustment policies studied in the SAPRI and CASA countries and the dynamics that account for the extensive poverty and inequality that they have generated.

The conclusion of this unprecedented policy review coincided with a renewed focus by the international community on poverty and with the official promotion of poverty assessments as policy tools. What SAPRI/CASA and this book contribute to those endeavours, and what the Bank itself does not address in the assessments that it promotes, is an analysis of the relationship between economic policy reforms and the generation of poverty, without which an understanding of poverty creation and reduction is impossible. Indeed, an understanding of the relationship between trade and financial sector liberalization, labour market reforms, privatization and agricultural and other sectoral reforms, on the one hand, and the productive sectors of the economy, on the other – as well as an appreciation of the significance of productive sector dynamics for the well-being or impoverishment of various population groups, are indispensable to addressing the aforementioned problems constructively.

Adjustment policies have contributed to the further impoverishment and marginalization of local populations, while increasing economic inequality.

The SAPRI/CASA investigations have identified four basic ways in which adjustment policies have contributed to the further impoverishment and marginalization of local populations, while increasing economic inequality. The first is through the demise of domestic manufacturing sectors and the loss of gainful employment by laid-off workers and small producers due to the nature of trade and financial sector reforms. The second relates to the contribution that agricultural, trade and mining reforms have made to the declining viability and incomes of small farms and poor rural communities, as well as to declining food security, particularly in rural areas. Third, the retrenchment of workers through privatizations and budget cuts, in conjunction with labour market flexibilization measures, has resulted in less secure employment, lower wages, fewer benefits and an erosion of workers' rights and bargaining power. Finally, poverty has been increased through privatization programmes, the application of user fees, budget cuts and other adjustment measures that have reduced the role of the state in providing or guaranteeing affordable access to essential quality services. These four issues are reviewed in sequence below.

The Impact of Trade and Financial Sector Reforms on Manufacturing, Employment and Small and Poor Producers

Liberalizing reforms in trade policy and in the financial sector have combined to destroy domestic productive capacity, particularly among the small and medium-sized enterprises that are at the core of national economies and that employ the large majority of their workforces. The orientation in bank lending and government policy has been towards financing and facilitating export production, but there has been limited linkage in much of this production to the local economy and local producers. At the same time, the latter have been by and large unprepared to compete against the influx of imports that has come with the lowering of trade barriers. The result has been a large increase in unemployment and a loss of income, most notably among poor, unskilled workers, particularly women and those living in low-income rural areas.

Trade policy and financial sector reforms have destroyed domestic productive capacity, particularly among small and medium-sized enterprises.

• *Domestic manufacturing sectors and employment have been hit hard by indiscriminate import liberalization and financial sector policies that have attracted investment away from productive activities.*

The removal of import barriers, justified on the basis of enhancing competition and efficiency, has taken place before, and in many cases without, the complementary steps required to help local enterprises become competitive. This has engendered a reduction in output and bankruptcies of a great number of enterprises, leaving workers to search for employment in the informal sector and in other less remunerative activities. The loss of formal sector manufacturing jobs has made a major contribution to the growing gap between national employment opportunities and the volume of new entrants to the labour market.

While the industrialization process has faltered in all the countries studied, nowhere is the phenomenon of deindustrialization and concomitant retrenchment and impoverishment more evident than in Ecuador. Industry's share in the national economy is now approximately half of what it was in the mid-1980s when the liberalization process began, and the jobless rate in urban areas is more than twice what it was at the start of the 1990s, with the greatest increases in unemployment found among lower-income groups. Similarly, in Bangladesh, where the precipitous reduction of tariffs opened a floodgate of imports from well-financed transnational corporations and helped undermine the development of indigenous industries, the number of manufacturing jobs has nearly halved since reforms were instituted. Zimbabwe also experienced a serious contraction in formal sector employment under adjustment, especially among women, to the point where the rate of employment growth in this sector fell to half the rate of growth of the labour force and where, as in many other countries, most new employment has been in the form of low-quality jobs in the informal sector. For its part, Hungary experienced a workforce reduction unmatched in any period of its recorded history.

• *Coupled with trade liberalization measures, financial sector reforms have had a particularly devastating impact on small and medium-sized firms and the large number of jobs they provide.*

High interest rates and other obstacles to borrowing by some sectors have been particularly debilitating for small firms that do not generate sufficient internal savings to satisfy their need for long-term working capital. Most lending has been directed to larger companies in the export sector and to non-productive activities instead of to broad-based production needed to stimulate national economies and especially economic activities in poor rural areas. During the second half of the 1990s, for example, after financial sector reforms had been introduced in Ecuador, average loan size increased nearly five-fold and 95 per cent of the loans had a maturity of less than a year. Long-term, non-export-oriented activities, in Ecuador and elsewhere, have become increasingly unfeasible. Precipitous import liberalization and the failure to sequence trade reforms have also been particularly painful for this subsector. As many as 20,000 Mexican small businesses had been forced into bankruptcy by 1998 as a result of trade and financial sector liberalization. In Hungary, tens of thousands of small shops have lost their viability as suppliers because of the country's rapidly paced open-trade policy. Though this sector has employed some 70 per cent of all Hungarian workers, it has not been given the time or support needed to develop the capacity to compete with the flood of cheap imports. In Bangladesh, too, a sharp reduction in employment in the manufacturing sector has occurred, primarily in small and cottage industries.

• *Women and indigenous producers, especially in rural areas, have had difficulties accessing affordable credit, or credit at any price, from formal lending institutions.*
The high interest rates resulting from liberalization, along with the application of stringent collateral and other loan requirements, have effectively discriminated against poorer and more geographically remote producers in favour of wealthier, urban borrowers. In El Salvador, for example, where women are often not property owners, satisfying the banks' collateral requirements has proved to be impossible for female producers, who have thereby been trapped in a vicious circle of poverty. In Bangladesh – where more than 70 per cent of bank financing in the post-reform period was directed towards 1 per cent of borrowers – women, who contribute more than a quarter of all bank deposits, receive less than 2 per cent of all available credit. They and other small producers are further handicapped in their search for capital by the difficulties faced by smaller and more informal lending institutions in gaining entry to the sector, and by the government's declining support for, and role in, development banking.

• *Increases in exports have failed to generate significant domestic economic activity and employment.*
Whatever employment increases have taken place in the manufacturing sector have occurred largely in the export-oriented industries, particularly in assembly plants in export processing zones. The employment generated by these plants is limited, however, in that they operate in essentially foreign-owned enclaves without forward or backward production linkages, representing a breakdown in the integration of economic sectors. While these factories hire mainly women, they are employed in low-paying, unskilled jobs with poor working conditions and few benefits or job security. In El Salvador, for example, 83 per cent of assembly-plant or *maquiladora* workers

are women, and large percentages of them receive less than the minimum wage, suffer abusive treatment and are denied paid maternity leave and severance pay. Overall the benefits of the increases in export growth have gone primarily to foreign corporations and are not felt significantly in the local economy.

The Impact of Agricultural, Trade and Mining Reforms on Agricultural Production, Small Farms, Food Security and Poor Communities

Trade liberalization, agricultural reforms and other sectoral and structural adjustment measures have served to marginalize the poor in rural areas, to reduce the availability of productive farmland for cultivation for the local market and to undermine food security. The design and implementation of the agricultural sector reforms failed to take into account existing socio-economic differentiations, and, as a result, poverty and rural inequality have worsened. The more well-to-do, large-scale producers with access to productive resources, particularly those producing for export, have generally benefited from the liberalizing reforms. Small farmers, particularly those producing food for the domestic population, have seen their costs skyrocket and their access to credit, land and markets become more problematic. These policy effects have been felt strongly, in particular, by women, who are bearing a heavier burden under the reforms. The cost of living in rural areas has risen while incomes have fallen. These problems have been compounded by the impact that the privatization, liberalization and deregulation of the mining sector and other extractive industries have had on land use and the environment.

> **Trade liberalization and agricultural and other reforms have marginalized the rural poor, reduced cultivation for the local market and undermined food security.**

• *The liberalization of economic activity in rural areas and a reduction of the development role of government, along with trade liberalization and currency devaluations, have favoured exports over production for the domestic market and have increased inequalities.*
The agricultural reform policies implemented in the SAPRI/CASA countries were designed to increase agricultural exports as a principal basis for economic growth and as a means to improve farmers' incomes. At their core is the liberalization of internal and external trade, intended to allow the

market, rather than government, to direct resource allocation and determine the prices of inputs and outputs, enabling the reduction of government expenditures in the process. However, adjustment programmes have provided incentives and attractive policies for investment in foreign-exchange-earning activities, including large-scale mining, thus helping to concentrate the benefits of the reforms in relatively few hands.

Meanwhile, the removal or reduction of barriers to the influx of cheap agricultural goods, of controls on interest rates, of regulations on financial institutions, of subsidies on agricultural inputs, and of government involvement in the production, distribution and marketing of inputs and commodities has greatly increased the costs and accessibility of productive resources for most farmers. This increase in costs of inputs and marketing has outstripped the increase in the prices of the goods produced, causing a decline in incomes. Without government regulation and services, farmers are operating, without adequate information, in a market that is neither competitive nor efficient.

• *Market reforms have deepened the problems faced by small farmers, and women in particular, in accessing resources for production.*
The disappearance of development banks, of subsidized credit and of the regulation of interest rates, along with the difficulty of entry for smaller lending institutions into the deregulated financial sectors, have made it particularly difficult for small producers to obtain credit from formal institutions. Although women in many countries, such as Zimbabwe, do most of the farmwork, they often face the additional problem of lacking collateral for bank loans because land ownership rights are generally vested in male heads of household. Without land as collateral, women receive, for example, less than 10 per cent of credit for smallholder farmers in Zimbabwe. There has thus been a considerable increase in reliance in most countries on informal sources for credit and – for similar reasons – for marketing services, seeds, pesticides and other inputs. The consequences of this dependence are well illustrated by the case of Uganda, where the absence of government programmes and adequate infrastructure has enabled petty traders and transport owners to profit from a retail price mark-up in the capital that can reach ten times the farmgate price. This reduced profitability for small producers is contributing significantly to the very high poverty levels in the villages.

• *Agricultural and mining reforms have affected the ownership, control and use of productive land, further skewing the distribution of wealth and incomes in rural areas.*
The rising cost of inputs following the liberalizing reforms has reached the point in some countries where farmers have been forced either to reduce their application per acre, reduce acreage under cultivation or convert to the

production of non-food crops. Many have left farming altogether, as in Mexico, where reduced government support for small farmers, increased costs, a surge of cheap food imports and a liberalizing of the rural land market through a constitutional reform has made thousand of farmers into day labourers, *maquiladora* workers and migrants. As in Mexico, many small producers have been effectively, or literally, pushed off their land by large-scale export ventures in agriculture, mining and other areas. In Ghana, for example, private mining companies, staking their claims to newly privatized, mineral-rich land, forced farmers and families engaged in artisan-style mining off their land and destroyed farmland with open-pit mining methods. Ghana, like other countries, is seeing community control over land and other resources lost to major mining interests.

Indeed, a great deal of productive, smallholder farmland is also being lost to environmental degradation caused by the intense exploitation of resources for export. In the Philippines, for example, policy reforms have led to the conversion of common property rights into the private ownership of land and water resources, and to the overexploitation of those resources through the application of commercial methods for intensive shrimp production. This has reduced the acreage available for the cultivation of traditional crops and has increased income erosion and inequality. Similarly, the liberalization of the Philippines' mining industry in 1985 led to the opening up of large tracts of land for large-scale corporate surface-mining activity that has destroyed farmlands belonging in large part to indigenous peoples, creating a serious loss of livelihood and increased family indebtedness. Little has been done in the liberalizing climate of adjustment to reform environmental laws to protect local communities from the mining operations.

• **The concentration of landholdings for export production, engendered by economic reforms, and the resulting environmental damage exacerbated by the liberalization of agriculture and mining, have raised the cost of living and reduced food security.**
The necessary cutbacks in production by struggling small food producers and the displacement of many of them by large agricultural and mining interests producing principally for export have seriously affected consumers. Virtually all of the SAPRI/CASA countries have experienced deteriorating food security as a result of similar liberalizing reforms. In Zimbabwe, for example, reform policies led to a reduction in the capacity of rural communities to produce their own food due to the rising cost of agricultural inputs. The country's export push, which shifted land from the cultivation of food crops to the production of paprika and cotton, increased the shortage and prices of staple foods and thus exacerbated the food insecurity of the poor. As a result, 30 per cent of children under the age of five are chronically

malnourished. Zimbabwe was been transformed from a country that produced enough maize and wheat to meet all its food needs to one that must import food – approximately one million tons annually by the late 1990s.

In Mexico, adjustment measures that concentrated land for large-scale export promotion, reduced government and financial support for small farmers, and liberalized imports, have left many rural communities unable to produce their own food and forced them to buy the food they need on the market at prices they cannot afford. A similar pattern has existed in Uganda, where increases in coffee production have been paralleled by a decline in the production of maize and beans, contributing to the failure of food production to keep up with population growth. In the Philippines, the displacement of the cultivation of rice and other staples by shrimp farming and the imposition by the IMF of budget deficit ceilings that have reduced necessary investments in the rice industry have created a growing dependency on rice imports and a vulnerability to the volatility of international prices.

In the Philippines and Ghana, the loss of farmland to mining and the significant environmental impact that mining has had on health, energy sources and other local conditions, have pushed up the cost of living in the communities near the mines, compounding the destruction and loss of traditional sources of livelihood.

Virtually all the principal adjustment measures have had profound effects on small-farm food production and on the cost of food. This includes currency devaluations, which have raised the prices of imported food, on which countries and regions are increasingly dependent, and the cost of imported inputs for production. Rising food prices were very bad news for the poor in Ghana, for example, in an environment marked by increasing lay-offs and stagnating wages. Reforms in the rural sector were promoted on the premise that local food supply was not important, as food access and security, it was claimed, could be attained through the market. The reality is that the poor often lack the means to pay for the imported food, on which of necessity they often now rely, and consequently have suffered from increasing malnourishment.

Beyond the destruction of farmland, livelihoods and food security, open-pit mining has created other serious problems for neighbouring communities. Production and the relaxation of environmental controls have generated extensive health problems, particularly respiratory-tract illnesses, and increased the burdens on women of finding drinkable water and firewood and caring for the ill. The destruction of family incomes, and mining's inability to provide significant gainful and safe employment to compensate, have increased child labour and school drop-out rates, generated increased migration and contributed to family and social disintegration, as marked by increased drug use and prostitution, and to a rising incidence of HIV/AIDS.

The Impact of Labour Market Reform and Privatization on Wages, Employment and Poverty

While employment levels and wages have been affected by a range of adjustment measures, employment has become more precarious and generally less remunerative with the increase of privatization and the introduction of labour market reforms in a growing number of countries. Greater discretion in the determination of wage and job levels has been placed in the hands of private employers with the selling off of state enterprises and public utilities, and with the liberalization of labour laws and regulations. Employees have lost much of their bargaining power and protection. Family incomes have fallen as a result, and more members must work longer hours to sustain the household.

Employment has become more precarious and less remunerative with the increase of privatization and the introduction of labour market reforms.

• *Real wages have deteriorated as a result of labour market reforms and other adjustment measures, particularly among the lowest income groups.*
The SAPRI/CASA investigations found that, since adjustment measures have been implemented, wages have declined, worker purchasing power has been reduced, and income distribution has become less equitable. There has been no effort to link the purchasing power of wages to increases in productivity. The share of wages in gross domestic income has fallen, while the share of profits has risen markedly where adjustment has been implemented. Wage flexibility, in the form, for example, of temporary, individual employment contracts, has helped suppress incomes so that they now frequently do not cover a family's basic needs. This problem is exacerbated by the common absence of benefit packages in these contracts and by a loss, as a result of the reforms, of protection of the right to organize and bargain collectively. The relaxation of hiring and firing constraints and of labour market regulation generally has given employers added leverage in determining wages.

The combined effects of labour market flexibilization and other adjustment policies in the SAPRI/CASA countries is striking. Real wages declined in Zimbabwe, for example, to the point where many workers live below the poverty line and two thirds of the population survive on less than two dollars a day. In Mexico, where the minimum wage has lost close to 70 per cent of its purchasing power since adjustment measures were first introduced in 1982, the number of people living in extreme poverty and unable to purchase the basic food basket rose from six to 30 million between 1994 and 2000. Two thirds of economically active Salvadorans now earn less than the minimum wage, and, after adjustment reduced workers' incomes by more than one half over the past 20 years, the average real income of those employed in urban Ecuador today is less than $200 a month.

• *Unemployment and job insecurity have increased and working conditions have often deteriorated with the increase in privatizations and the introduction of flexibilization measures.*
Lay-offs have accompanied privatization across the board, and there has often been insufficient new employment generated to compensate for jobs lost. While adjustment advocates predicted an increase in national employment from the privatization of state-run enterprises through the attraction of investment and the achievement of greater efficiencies, the evidence from SAPRI/CASA shows no such tendency. From Ecuador to Bangladesh, the formal sector is now generating less employment and producing ever-greater social exclusion. In Bangladesh, where nearly 40 per cent of workers employed in previously state-owned companies have lost their jobs, there has been a tendency to replace permanent workers with temporary labour. Similarly, in Hungary, newly privatized firms commonly contract employees for only one to three months at a time. While privatization has eliminated a massive number of jobs, it has been particularly costly for women. In most countries, women have constituted a large percentage of those workers without specialized skills, and they are thus among the first to be laid off. In countries such as Hungary, this problem has been exacerbated by the tendency of the owners of the privatized businesses to rid their workforces of pregnant women and mothers with small children.

Similar discrimination is often found in export processing zones, which manifest many of the problems created by flexibilization measures. Without effective bargaining power or sufficiently strong laws and regulations to protect them, many workers are exploited through low pay, few benefits and poor working conditions. Women, typically the majority of the workforce, are vulnerable to harassment and unilateral and arbitrary decision making regarding, for example, lay-offs and the granting of leave during pregnancy or sickness, reflecting the pervasive failure of employers to respect basic labour rights. In this case, the increase of women in the labour force reflects not greater gender equity but rather opportunities for employers to hire workers at the least possible cost and with minimal social responsibility.

Flexibilization has been applied on an unlevel playing field in the labour market. Labour laws have been shaped to provide employers with maximum leverage in their relations with workers, as reflected in the increased use of hourly labour and temporary, fixed-term and part-time contracts. Workers, particularly in low-skill and labour-intensive sectors, are in oversupply and in a weak position in salary and contract negotiations. There were no cases observed in the SAPRI/CASA countries in which steps have been taken to improve working conditions or to include workers in decision-making processes. As a result, workers worry increasingly about losing their jobs and thus are now more likely to renounce their labour rights or refrain from forming unions.

• *Labour market reforms and privatization have increased inequality and decreased family incomes, generating an increase in child labour, other survival strategies and social dislocations and problems.*
Income distribution has worsened as large numbers of low-skilled, low-wage workers, especially minorities and women, have been the first to be laid off by privatized firms. Job training has not adequately addressed the problems of the newly unemployed. The new jobs created in the private companies are generally well-paying, but have required higher skill levels. At the family level, the loss of wages and gainful and secure employment has resulted in the modification of survival strategies wherever these reforms and related adjustment measures have been adopted. Many heads of household have had to take second and third jobs, usually in the informal sector, and additional family members have often had to join the workforce. Increasingly, children have had to drop out of school to supplement declining family incomes by taking jobs that pay salaries that are usually far below the minimum wage. A third of Mexico's agricultural day labourers, for example, are below the age of 18. Girls frequently leave school to take on responsibility for household chores in the absence of their mothers. Longer working days for both parents in Mexico and other countries often leave children with inadequate parental guidance. Juvenile delinquency has increased, as has domestic violence, fuelled by household tensions caused by the inability to meet basic needs. Health, nutrition and the ability to find adequate housing have suffered. Migration has increased, and many family structures have fractured as a result.

The Impact of the Privatization of Public Utilities and Public Expenditure Reform on the Availability of Affordable Services and on Poverty

The privatization of public utilities, including such essential services as the provision of water and electricity, has led to significant rate hikes and has increased financial pressure on poor families. Such privatizations also tend to discriminate against the poor with regard to price, access and consumer choice, thus exacerbating existing economic inequalities. Where government public-welfare functions have not been transferred to the private sector, they have undergone a comprehensive transformation that has entailed a redefinition of the problem of poverty and the state's role in addressing it. At its core, it involves a radical shift for government from providing and guaranteeing universally accessible social services, such as education and healthcare, to targeting only those on the margins whom the market has failed to reach with those essential services. Within this context, governments have drastically reduced funding in the social sectors, implemented cost-recovery, cost-sharing and revenue-generating schemes, and often decentralized service provision to local authorities.

• *The privatization of public utilities and services has usually resulted in significant price increases for the general public, paralleled by little improvement or reductions in access and service quality.*
In Hungary, for example, rates for electricity, heat, water and gas increased on average twice as much as wages in order to guarantee returns to private investors. Foreign companies took over the oil and gas industry and raised electricity rates until they were ten times higher in 1998 than in 1989. Poor families, and especially pensioners, now have severe difficulty in paying their utility bills, while the quality of service has barely changed. Indeed, the privatized social security system, according to Hungarians consulted in the SAPRI exercise, provides lower benefits for higher premiums except to high-income groups. In El Salvador, electricity rates increased by nearly 50 per cent for low-end consumers in the two years following the privatization of distribution services, double the rate increase for high-end customers. Furthermore, access to electricity and the quality of service have declined, especially for poor communities in rural areas, which the private companies do not see as sufficiently profitable. Thus privatization has exacerbated inequalities and increased hardships for the poor, leading many families to resort to traditional energy sources, such as firewood, and forcing the closure of many micro-enterprises. As in Hungary, the privatization of public utilities has failed to achieve its efficiency goals. Whatever increases there have been in the ratio between revenues and expenses have been achieved at the expense of the poorer consumers.

• *The elimination of universal subsidies for essential goods and services has negatively affected the poor and their quality of life.*
Lower-income groups are affected most when subsidies on such essentials

as electricity and cooking gas are reduced or eliminated, as they were from 1996 in Ecuador. While this measure conformed with the country's public expenditure reform programme, it dramatically increased prices for consumers. The targeted social protection programme that replaced the universal subsidies has reached less than 20 per cent of those living in poverty. Similarly, in Mexico, the removal of subsidies on basic food items has caused hardship for low-income sectors of the population, especially women, children and indigenous groups. The targeting of the benefits has also failed to assist the many segments of the population in need, reinforcing the contention that the policy of targeting is not viable when the majority of the population is poor. While the poor have been increasingly deprived, subsidies have been extended to private corporations in various forms, including credit guarantees, tax incentives and financial bail-outs.

• *Stabilization and structural adjustment programmes have generally led to a sharp deterioration in public spending on social services, often during economic downturns, while debt obligations continue to be paid.*
In Hungary, for example, state expenditure on healthcare, education and social welfare provisions decreased by 25 per cent in real terms during the first seven years of the 1990s. Along with related policy reforms, these cuts contributed to the expansion and deepening of poverty and to the dramatic increase in social inequality, and served to dismantle, almost irreversibly, the country's integrated social systems. Reductions in public spending have not been applied, however, to debt servicing, which has become an unquestioned and key function of governments. In fact, controls on social spending, related policies and the theoretical framework in which they fit have been implemented precisely so that debt obligations could be met. The experiences of the SAPRI and CASA countries illustrate how the poor pay the external debt several times over despite having had little or no role in creating it, especially private sector debts that have often been assumed by governments. Beyond their tax contributions to debt servicing, the poor pay for it through the sacrifices and suffering they bear as a result of the reduction in public spending and the price they now must pay for basic services and for the now more expensive, privatized public utilities. Furthermore, as civil society participants in Ecuador have emphasized, foreign debt has provided a mechanism by which the international financial institutions have applied external pressure for the adoption of policy prescriptions that so often induce poverty.

In several of the countries studied, public resources have been used not just to service public debt, but also to rescue private corporations and banks that have not been able to meet their obligations. These spending priorities are evident in Mexico, for example, where social expenditures have fallen dramatically since adjustment measures were first applied to the economy in 1983. As of 2000, public resources devoted to reducing poverty were equivalent to just one quarter of the annual cost to the Mexican treasury of rescuing the private banks amidst the financial and economic crisis of 1994. Indeed, spending controls and cost-sharing schemes have been implemented in the SAPRI/CASA and many other countries during periods of economic decline and growing poverty, when social assistance and services for the poor have been in greatest demand.

• *The quality of education and healthcare has generally declined as a result of pressures to reduce public expenditure.*
In most places, particularly in rural areas and poorer regions, educational quality was found to be woefully inadequate by the SAPRI/CASA researchers. The decentralization of services and their management to the regional and local levels, a key feature of reforms in this sector, has proved disastrous because it has often been accompanied by inadequate funding. School infrastructure is often lacking, shortages of educational supplies are widespread and teachers' incomes have declined, as have teacher–student ratios. Reductions in public spending on healthcare have left countries with public health budgets insufficient to meet health needs. A deterioration of conditions in healthcare facilities, inadequate staffing and a lack of medicines, especially in rural and other poor areas, have had serious consequences. Many rural health units are without doctors and adequate staffing and have lacked drugs for long periods. The devaluation of local currencies has contributed to these problems, as most medicines and medical equipment must be imported. Maternal and childcare services are commonly inadequate. The HIV/AIDS crisis has overloaded hospitals in many countries, and many patients have been sent away. In most cases it has been women and girls who out of necessity have had to take on greater responsibility for the education and healthcare needs in poorer families.

• *Cost-sharing schemes have imposed serious constraints on access by poor people to healthcare and education.*
This was found to be true in all the countries studied. School drop-out rates have risen, particularly among girls, in most of the countries where user fees have been charged. Fees have increased inequalities in Ghana, for example, both between and within communities, as income levels are the most important determinant of enrolment at higher education institutions. When school fees were reintroduced in Zimbabwe after a decade of free education, there was a dramatic increase in drop-out rates. Fees for health services were found to limit access by the poor to timely care, particularly in poor, rural

areas. An increasing number of people have been resorting to self-medication and home care. More people seek medical attention only when their illness is already severe, causing an increase in unattended home deaths and creating public health hazards. The introduction of user fees in Zimbabwe raised treatment costs for patients by as much as 1,000 per cent. In Ghana, high hospital fees and a continuous decline in the earnings of many workers have prevented patients from using healthcare facilities.

Weak Macroeconomic Performance under Adjustment

The World Bank and other advocates of adjustment policies have increasingly acknowledged that many of these adjustment measures have generated losses among the poor. In fact, it was concern about the connection between adjustment programmes and growing poverty and inequality that led President Wolfensohn to accept the NGO challenge and undertake the SAPRI investigation. The Bank claims, however, that the macroeconomic gains from the implementation of adjustment policies offset any short-term losses among certain population groups and sectors by setting countries on the path towards sustainable growth. This is part of its implicit argument for its lack of attention to the adjustment–poverty connection in the Poverty Reduction Strategy Papers, and for insisting that the Bank/Fund economic framework provide the parameters of any poverty reduction programme.

Civil society actors have not accepted these arguments for several reasons. First, the losses to the poor and working people around the globe – including those within the SAPRI and CASA countries – have not been short-term. In fact, because of the certain differentiated impact that they would have on disparate population groups and sectors, it was predictable that many of these policies would have an immediate and long-term negative effect, and the predictions based on this analysis turned out to be correct.

Second, after two decades of adjustment, it is clear that there is nothing intrinsic to the policies assessed in the previous chapters that would lead one to believe that they will eventually work their magic in the market and reduce poverty and inequality, rather than continue to increase both of these negative phenomena. Third, the evidence, including that found in the SAPRI/CASA countries, does not indicate that the macroeconomic benefits claimed to be derived from adjustment policies and programmes have been achieved at anywhere close to the levels assumed by their advocates. Thus, the trade-off – short-term pain for long-term gain – has little basis in empirical fact.

Structural adjustment programmes have failed to engender the healthy economies promised by their architects.

More to the point, the economic policies that comprise the core of structural adjustment programmes have failed to engender the healthy economies promised by their architects. To the contrary, as judged by the experience of the countries profiled in this book, the overall impact of adjustment policies has included the generation of increased current-account and trade deficits and debt; disappointing levels of economic growth, efficiency and competitiveness; the misallocation of financial and other productive resources; the 'disarticulation' of national economies; the destruction of national productive capacity; and extensive environmental damage. Poverty and inequality are now far more intense and pervasive than they were 20 years ago, wealth is more highly concentrated, and opportunities are far fewer for the many who have been left behind by adjustment.

Despite extensive export promotion, export revenues have for the most part been outpaced by the rising cost of imports. The large import content of many exports and the increasing importation of consumer goods facilitated by trade liberalization have contributed to this imbalance. Ecuador, for example, experienced, amidst an economic crisis, an explosion in consumer imports in the 1990s that far outstripped export growth. A high dependence on exports has also made economies vulnerable to deteriorating terms of trade, as Uganda discovered during the second half of the past decade. These growing imbalances have created pressures on foreign exchange reserves, leading to more foreign borrowing and increased debt burdens.

Macroeconomic indicators attest to the validity of the SAPRI/CASA participatory studies. As the ratio of foreign trade to GDP in the SAPRI/CASA countries grew on average by two thirds over the past two decades as a consequence of trade liberalization and a growing surplus of imports, negative trade balances also sharply increased. By the end of the century, they had settled at about 5–6 per cent of GDP, more than double the level of the 1960s. As a result, the total external debt of the original ten SAPRI/CASA countries doubled between 1984 and 1999.

Nor has foreign investment proved to be the panacea in this area. In the mining sector, for example, policy and financial support from the IFIs has increased investments by foreign companies and foreign exchange earnings, but the net impact has been small. Most of Ghana's large-scale gold-mining industry, which is now foreign-owned, receive generous incentives and tax breaks and utilize offshore accounts for export earnings, minimizing returns to the government. With foreign firms often the beneficiaries of the privatization of state holdings in this and other sectors, dual economies have emerged or become more pronounced and the development of local industries has been threatened. The increased ease of profit repatriation, capital withdrawal and, in many sectors, plant relocation has had a strong destabilizing effect. At the same time, key economic and social decisions have been removed from national hands.

The privatization of public utilities has also failed to achieve the goals set for it. At the microeconomic level, there is no evidence that privatization itself leads to greater efficiency and productivity. Where there have been higher profit margins, they have usually resulted from price hikes that have made services inaccessible to the poor. At the macro level there has been no sign of any general acceleration of growth in the SAPRI/CASA countries following the period of privatization. The change in ownership has only reallocated income at the national level. Often a public monopoly has been replaced by a private one. In El Salvador, for example, when electricity services were privatized, the market was not opened to free competition, and full choice was not available.

Over two decades of adjustment, growth performance has fallen far short of 1960s levels.

Overall, economic restructuring, after two decades of adjustment, has not led to greater modernization and competitiveness. The growth of GDP has been irregular and insufficient – since the mid-1980s, growth performance in the SAPRI/CASA countries has fallen far short of 1960s levels – and has been concentrated in exports and in other favoured sectors, businesses and regions to the detriment of large, important and increasingly impoverished economic sectors. Production for the domestic market, especially in agriculture, has often suffered, as has food security.

New patterns of agricultural production, particularly for export, have, in an environment of liberalization and deregulation, polluted land and water with chemicals from intensive fertilizer use, depleted water tables through the irrational use of irrigation, caused soil erosion and exhausted vital natural resources. Reforms favouring large-scale monoculture have led to the loss of biodiversity. Small farmers and the poor have been pushed in the process onto marginal lands, which they have had to overexploit in order to survive; they and the local environment have also suffered from the elimination of most government advisory services. Intensive shrimp farming in places like the Philippines has degraded and polluted coastal ecosystems and adjacent land and water resources. The commercialization of fish production in Uganda and the advent of an export trade has, as a result of liberalization and unregulated competition, caused an overexploitation of lakes and depleted fish stock, thereby endangering the future of the sector. And, as the Ghana and Philippines experiences have demonstrated, the chemicals, machinery and methods employed in liberalized open-pit mining have far-reaching and destructive consequences for human health, farmland, vegetation generally, biodiversity and water bodies.

Perhaps the reforms that have had the most damaging and far-reaching impact have been those made in the financial sector. The liberalization of interest rates, credit allocation, capital flows and the entry into, and regulation of, the sector, among other measures, has enabled the consolidation of financial assets in private hands, a surge in financial speculation at the expense of productive investment, the loss of financing for development, capital flight and banking and financial crises. Since the early 1990s, as a consequence of stabilization and adjustment policies, the real interest rate, on average, in the SAPRI/CASA countries has hovered around 10 per cent, which, being considerably higher than the rate of real economic growth, has helped to attract potential production capital to local money markets. The creation of oligopolistic structures and non-competitive practices in the private sector, in the absence of effective public oversight and supervision, has led to inefficiencies, corruption, destabilization and social exclusion.

The Ecuador and El Salvador experiences are instructive. In the latter, the privatization of the banks was manipulated by the country's élite to gain control of the majority of financial assets, while taxpayers were left to foot the bill for all outstanding bad debts. From the beginning of the liberalization process in Ecuador, scarce capital was diverted from agriculture and industry to higher rates of return provided by rising interest rates. Inefficiencies in the form of the increasing spread between these rates and those borrowers were charged have constituted a massive transfer of funds from productive enterprises to the financial system. Irresponsible bank lending and the volatility of foreign and domestic capital under capital account liberalization have contributed to disastrous banking crises that prompted a massive bail-out of the private system with public funds, exacerbating the country's already dire debt situation.

Shaping a Different Future

For the dozens of countries that have travelled down the adjustment road, the problem is not that the reform process has failed to generate economic benefits. It is that these benefits have tended to be concentrated in relatively few hands, both domestic and foreign, while millions of other people have increasingly been deprived of the resources and opportunities they require to move out of poverty. To understand the dynamics that make such results a virtual certainty requires a radical shift in perspective. A major policy change made by a country of the South to meet a World Bank or IMF loan condition may look benign and, in fact, universally beneficial to a banker sitting in London, but to a poor farmer in the South who has come to understand how local, national and even global systems, structures, institutions and markets work to reward the more powerful and influential, expectations may be much lower.

This shift in perspective was at the core of the SAPRI/CASA design and experience. The voices that were sought, and heard, were those of local populations often living and working at the margins of their respective societies. The issues that were selected for investigation were those that they had prioritized. And their analysis was based on an intimate knowledge of their own circumstances and on an understanding of the political economy of their respective communities and countries. Unlike the current PRSP processes, SAPRI/CASA encouraged and supported the broad-based mobilization of civil society and people's efforts to explain the connection between economic policies and their own respective economic and social situations. Their assessments constitute the body of this book. Their hopes for a better future depend in good part on policy makers creating space for their ideas and actions.

Unlike PRSPs, SAPRI/CASA supported people's mobilization and efforts to explain the impact of economic policies on their lives.

To date, that space has not been created. While political democracy has been promoted, albeit selectively, from the North, real democratic choice for both civil society and governments in the arena of economic policy has been severely limited by the IFIs and their Northern Board members. Governments have been urged to improve their governance, but not so that they will better respond to the interests of their own people when the most important economic decisions that affect the latter are being formulated. Meanwhile, the Washington-defined concept of 'country ownership' of economic programmes has meant little more than government acceptance of IFI-promoted policies rather than a national consensus developed around a home-grown policy programme. And the increasingly common processes of consultation with civil society organizations on development programming, whether on the part of the IFIs or governments, rarely cover these policies in any comprehensive way, and almost always lack follow-up mechanisms of accountability to those consulted.

The SAPRI/CASA experience demonstrated that mechanisms for meaningful popular participation in economic decision making can be established. In countries on four continents, civil society organizations representing a wide range of population groups and economic and social sectors came together to produce collective analyses of adjustment programmes that point the way to new directions in economic policy. Through negotiated terms of engagement, a level playing field was created in each country so that citizens had the freedom, the resources and the power to develop their own processes of outreach and cooperation, to select priority policy issues for analysis, and to build local analytical capacity where needed. These decentralized processes were matched in their effectiveness by the formation of well-organized civil society and, in the case of the SAPRI countries, tripartite committees that can provide the fora for the development and implementation of new economic options.

SAPRI/CASA demonstrated that mechanisms for meaningful popular participation in economic decision making can be established.

Despite IFI claims to the contrary, such options, old and new, continue to exist, much as they have for the countries of the North, as witnessed by the diverse policy choices taken during the process of economic development in Europe, the United States, Japan and other East Asian nations over the past two centuries. The lack of diversity in the economic policies implemented across much of the South during the past generation is a direct result of IFI conditionality, not of an absence of policy alternatives. The consistent nature of the policy programme imposed on borrowing countries has also engendered a similarity of problematic results at both the sectoral and macroeconomic levels.

In the field investigations, it is striking that the SAPRIN civil society networks consistently focused their attention on the policies that had a direct impact on the domestic productive capacity of their respective countries. While fiscal and social policy were by no means ignored and the efficacy of the privatization of essential services was challenged by the analysis, the major emphasis was on the need for policy shifts in key economic sectors, and on the enterprises in which most of the working poor are engaged, in order to better meet local needs and provide decent jobs and income. In the public fora, gainful employment and the creation of healthy and productive local economies – through changes in prevailing trade, monetary, sectoral, labour and fiscal policies – were emphasized over the Bank's far narrower approach to poverty reduction, which precludes alternatives to these basic adjustment measures. The state's role was seen by civil society as being critically important, not only in providing essential services and in protecting the environment, labour rights and vulnerable population groups, but also in levelling the economic playing field so that local enterprises can compete in the national as well as the global marketplace.

Gainful employment and the creation of productive local economies through changes in prevailing economic policies were emphasized over the Bank's approach to poverty reduction.

The SAPRI/CASA findings strongly suggest the need for governments to be free to engage in industrial and agricultural planning processes and to elicit, as part of those processes, the organized input of civil society and other key economic and social actors who understand the local political economy and hence the probable impact of particular economic policies. In this context, local job-creating enterprises could be upgraded to achieve enhanced competitiveness before being exposed to (and, if not so equipped, destroyed by) foreign competitors with numerous economic and financial advantages. Trade policy could be designed to produce vibrant domestic economies that are geared in the first instance to meeting local needs, including local food security, while utilizing to the extent possible locally produced goods and services. The long-established 'right to development', typically exercised through the support and selective protection of small and medium-sized manufacturing firms and small-scale agricultural units producing in key subsectors, cannot be overemphasized, particularly in the light of the economic histories and current domestic policies of most Northern countries. Similarly, there is a need to redirect financial resources, through regulatory and institutional mechanisms, from speculative activities to innovative domestic enterprises, including those run by women, while reducing the spreads between borrowing and savings rates to increase efficiency and the affordability of credit to these end users.

SAPRIN has chosen not to extrapolate further at the global level on economic alternatives from the country findings, preferring to be supportive of national participatory initiatives that locate the task of developing more appropriate economic options with those intimately involved with local and national realities. At the same time, it has continued its efforts to create the space that the emergence of new approaches will require by applying public pressure on the World Bank and its Northern Board members.

Much as the national reports and National Fora had generated extensive media coverage in the SAPRI countries, the release in Europe of the global report upon which this book is based garnered significant public attention in Northern nations that are represented on the Bank's board and that helped finance SAPRI. Press, radio and television coverage and public debates involving SAPRIN members and top government officials highlighted the failures of adjustment programmes and forced the Bank and its president to re-engage SAPRIN after almost a year of ignoring the results of the joint

SAPRI initiative. At two subsequent meetings in Washington requested by Wolfensohn to discuss the report, the Bank president told members of SAPRIN's global steering committee that he was ready to move on the issues raised in the document.

That expressed interest has yet to be translated, however, into effective action or meaningful change within his institution. A Wolfensohn proposal to involve SAPRIN and other civil society organizations in the shaping of economic policy through PRSPs and the Bank's own Country Assistance Strategy (CAS) processes in the SAPRI countries was not operationalized after a series of delays by Bank managers. The most promising opportunity presented itself in Ecuador, where the SAPRIN team recommended the reactivation of the SAPRI tripartite committee as part of a national consultative CAS process so as to support innovation in the new government's economic programme. The Bank's unwillingness to engage in a participatory and public policy-making forum of this type with built-in accountability is a telling commentary on the institution's continued refusal to entertain new departures in national economic policy, even with major political change and shifts in economic thinking taking place across South America.

The Bank president's expressed interest in acting on adjustment issues raised in SAPRI has not been translated into effective action or institutional change.

The Bank's continued commitment to economic orthodoxy and control over national economies has not been limited to Latin America. Despite unprecedented popular backlash against adjustment policies at both the local and global levels, the institution's staff and board recently undertook a rewriting of internal operational guidelines to consolidate a major global expansion of adjustment lending and the continued determination of national economic reform programmes by the Bank and Fund. Similarly, while sensitive trade negotiations in Geneva pit many Southern countries against Northern powers on agricultural issues, the Bank's chief economist urged the former to open (unilaterally) their agricultural markets yet further. To this end, Bank staff have provided technical assistance, informally but clearly tied to lending operations, in the liberalization of Southern trade regimes. Meanwhile, a Bank programme has promoted and supported public–private partnerships in the provision of essential social services, with the effect of privatizing services for high-end users in borrowing countries and often leaving a shortage of resources for affordable and quality service provision for the less affluent.

The Bank's participation in the imposition of damaging economic policies on client countries continues despite its much-publicized foray into relationships with civil society. The institution claims that it seeks constructive engagement with civil society, that it is committed to consultation with populations affected by the projects and policies it supports, and that it is working, with civil society's assistance, to reduce poverty. The outcome of the SAPRI initiative, including the Bank's post-SAPRI performance, contradicts these claims. The findings of the SAPRI investigation not only represent the perspectives of the people themselves in the South; they are also the result of a long and intensive process in which the Bank was directly and intimately involved. The challenge to respond, in a meaningful and concrete manner, to the analysis, demands and voices of the people of the South, whether they are expressed in major engagements like SAPRI and the World Commission on Dams or in ongoing country assessments, is a challenge that the Bank and its president have failed to meet. SAPRI is also a test of Bank member governments, including those that invested or participated in the multi-year investigation, that have chosen so far to ignore the adjustment-related causes of poverty and inequality.

The Bank's participation in the imposition of damaging economic policies continues despite its much-publicized relationships with civil society.

Thousands of organizations and hard-working people invested their time, their insights and their trust in this lengthy process. They have explained how policy interventions from afar have affected the world in which they live and work. They have helped to present the evidence, as reflected in this book, and they have every right to expect a meaningful response and effective action. The fact that SAPRI participants have witnessed, instead, the continuation of Bank-promoted adjustment programmes in their respective countries has underscored the importance of expanding the mobilization, educational efforts, capacity building and advocacy upon which the SAPRIN network was built. This enhanced strength will be necessary, for, if there is to be constructive change and democratic choice in economic policy making, civil society will have to make its way into the centre of the decision-making process.

SAPRIN National Steering Committees

Bangladesh Civil Society Steering Committee
Centre for Policy Dialogue, Professor Rehman Sobhan, Convener
Dhaka University, Professor Wahiduddin Mahmud, Co-Convener
PROSHIKA: A Center for Human Development, Mr Mahbubul Karim
Federation of Bangladesh Chambers of Commerce and Industry (FBCCI), Mr Yussuf Abdullah Harun MP
Bangladesh Rural Advancement Committee (BRAC), Mr Fazle Hasan Abed
Association of Development Agencies in Bangladesh (ADAB), Dr Qazi Faruque Ahmed
Coalition of Environmental NGOs (CEN), Ms Khushi Kabir
Jatiyo Shangshad (National Parliament), Advocate Rahmat Ali, Member of Parliament
Bangladesh Krishak League (Farmers' League)
Bangladesh Trade Union Kendra (Trade Union Centre), Mr Nurul Islam
Bangladesh Jatiyotabadi Sramik Dal (Nationalist Workers' Party), Mr Nazrul Islam Khan
Bangladesh Mohila Parishad (Women's Council), Ms Ayesha Khanam
Bangladesh Road Transport Workers' Federation, Mr Manjurul Ahshan Khan
National Association of Small and Cottage Industries of Bangladesh (NASCIB), Ms Maleka Khan
Karmajibi Nari (Working Women), Ms Shireen Akhter
Bangladesh Khetmajur Union (Agricultural Workers Union), Mr Saiful Huq

Ecuador Civil Society Steering Committee
Instituto de Ecología y Desarrollo de las Comunidades Andinas (Institute for Ecology and Development of
   the Andean Communities, IEDECA), Ivan Cisneros/Alex Zapatta
Federación de Trabajadores Libres de Guayas (Workers Federation of Guayas Province, FETLIG), María
   Chacha
Cámara de la Pequeña Industria de Manabí (Chamber of Small Industry of Manabí Province), Byron Coral
Comité de Desarrrollo de las Comunidades Fronterizas de Esmeraldas (Committee for the Development of
   the Border Communities of Esmeraldas Province), José Vargas
Asociación de Trabajadores Universitarios y Politécnicos del Ecuador (Association of University and
   Technology Institute Workers), Nidia Solís
Red de Mujeres de Azuay (Women's Network of Azuay Province)
Confederación Unica de Afiliados al Seguro Social Campesino (Confederation of Affiliates to the Peasant
   Social Security System, CONFEUNASSC), Rodrigo Collaguazo
Confederación Nacional de Barrios del Ecuador (National Confederation of Low-Income Urban
   Communities of Ecuador), Fernando Rodríguez
Confederación de Nacionalidades Indígenas de la Amazonía (National Confederation of Indigenous Peoples
   of the Amazon), Juan Bosco Kasent
Coordinadora Política de Mujeres Ecuatorianas (Alliance of Ecuadorean Women for Political
   Advancement), Luz Haro/Zonia Palán
Comisión por la Defensa de los Derechos Humanos (Commission for the Defense of Human Rights,
   CDDH), Victor Hugo Jijón
Facultad de Economía de la Universidad de Cuenca (Economics Department of the University of Cuenca),
   Carlos Carrasco

El Salvador Civil Society Steering Committee
Fundación Nacional para el Desarrollo (National Foundation for Development, FUNDE)
Asociación Salvadoreña de Desarrollo Integral (Salvadoran Association for Integrated Development, ASDI)
Fundación Salvadoreña para la Promoción Social y el Desarrollo Económico (Salvadoran Foundation for Social Advancement and Economic Development, FUNSALPRODESE)
Federación de Asociaciones y Sindicatos Independientes de El Salvador (Federation of Independent Trade Unions of El Salvador, FEASIES)
Asociación de Medianos y Pequeños Empresarios Salvadoreños (Association of Small and Medium-Scale Salvadoran Enterprises, AMPES)
Unidad Ecológica Salvadoreña (Salvadoran Ecological Group, UNES)
Red para la Infancia y Adolescencia (Network for Children and Adolescents)
Consejo Nacional de Iglesias (National Council of Churches)
Coordinadora de Organismos de Derechos Humanos de El Salvador (Alliance of Human Rights Organizations of El Salvador)
Foro Agropecuario (Agrarian Forum)
Asociación de Radios y Programas Participativos de El Salvador (Association of Community Radios and Participatory Programming, ARPAS)

Ghana Civil Society Coordinating Council (CivisoC)
Trade Union Congress, Mr Kwasi Adu-Amankwah
Gender Centre, Mrs Dorcas Coker-Appiah
Ghana National Association of Teachers (GNAT), Mr John Nyoagbe
Densu Industries, Mr John Atta-Nyamekye
Ghana National Association of Farmers and Fishermen (GNAFF), Mr G. K. Bedzrah
Save the Children Fund, Mr Greg Ramm
Green Earth Organisation, Mr Balertey Gormey
Centre for the Development of People (CEDEP), Mrs Yaa Peprah Agyeman Amekudzie
Northern Ghana Network for Development, Mr Donald Amuah
Assemblies of God Relief and Development Services, Mr Ernest Asigri
Professional Network (PRONET), Mr Ben Thompson
Ghana Association of Private and Voluntary Organisation and Development (GAPVOD), Mr Kofi Adu
Volta Region Association of Non-Governmental Organisations (VORANGO), Mr Tenasu Kofi Gbedemah
Ghana National Association of Farmers and Fishermen (GNAFF), Mr Kwaw Koomson
Association of Small Scale Industries, Mr Samuel Oppong-Boadi
Civil Servants Association, Mr Kawawa Joris
Islamic Council of Development and Humanitarian Services (ICODEHS), Alhaji Alhassan Abdulai
Ghana Registered Nurses Association (GRNA), Mr Joe Quist
University Teachers Association of Ghana (UTAG), Dr I .K. Acheampong
National Union of Ghana Students (NUGS), Mr Kwesi Amponsah-Tawiah
Integrated Social Development Centre (ISODEC), Mr Charles Abugre
Third World Network–Africa (TWN), Dr Yao Graham

Hungary Civil Society Steering Committee
National Alliance of Agricultural Cooperators and Producers, Dr László Filipsz
National Alliance of Gardeners, Dr Károly Merenyi
Council of Leftist Cooperation, Janos Sipos
Coalition for Health, Zoltanne Karadi
Trade Union of High School Educators, László Kis-Papp
Air Working Group, Erzsébet Beliczay
Antifascist Alliance of Hungarian Gypsies, Albert Horvath
Hungarian Academy of Sciences, Zoltán Santha
Alliance of Hungarian Women, Dr Judit Asbothne Thorma
Alliance of Hungarian Trade Unions, Ferenc Rabi National
Alliance for Associations of Technology and Natural Science, László Szegner
Association of Hungarian Economists, Károly Lorant/János Hoós
National Association of Large Families, Zsuzsanna Morvayne Bajai
National Representation of Pensioners, Ervin Mihalovits
Alliance of Social Associations, Miklos Havas
Society Union, Károly Boór
National Alliance of Hungarian Trade Unions, Erzsébet Hanti
Society 1st of May, Thomas Morva

Mexico Civil Society General Council
Acción Popular de Integración Social (Popular Action for Social Integration, APIS)
Alianza Nacional de Trabajadores Petroleros (National Alliance of Oil Workers)
Asociación Mexicana de Uniones de Crédito del Sector Social (Mexican Association of Social Sector Credit Unions, AMUCSS)
Asociación Nacional de Empresas Comercializadoras del Campo (National Association of Rural Marketing Companies, ANEC)
Asociación Nacional de la Industria de la Transformación (National Association of Transformational Industries, ANIT)
Campaña *El Banco Mundial en la Mira de las Mujeres* (Women's Eyes on the Bank Campaign)
Central Independiente de Obreros Agrícolas y Campesinos (Independent Group of Agricultural Workers and Peasants, CIOAC)
Centro Antonio de Montesinos (Antonio de Montesinos Center, CAM)
Centro de Derechos Humanos Agustín Pro (Center for Human Rights Agustín Pro)
Centro de Estudios para el Cambio en el Campo Mexicano (Center of Study for Change in the Mexican Countryside, CECCAM)
Centro de Investigación y Acción para las Mujeres (Center for Research and Action for Women, CIAM)
Centro Nacional de Comunicación Social (National Center of Public Communications, CENCOS)
Centro de Reflexión y Asesoría Laboral (Center for Labor Support, CEREAL)
Colectivo Mexicano de Atención a la Niñez (Mexican Center for the Care of Children, COMEXANI)
Comité de Defensa del Pueblo de Zaragoza (Committee for the Defense of the People of Zaragoza)
Comisión Mexicana de Defensa y Promoción de los Derechos Humanos (Mexican Commission for the Defense and Advancement of Human Rights, CMDPDDHH)
Comunidades Eclesiales de Base (Christian Base Communities, CEB)
Convergencia de Organismos Civiles por la Democracia (Convergence of Civil Society Organizations for Democracy, CONVERGENCIA)
Coordinación Nacional de Organizaciones Cafetaleras (National Coordinating Group of Coffee-Growing Organizations, CNOC)
Costureras y Costureros 19 de Septiembre (19th of September Sewers Group)
Departamento de Justicia y Paz, Comisión Episcopal de Pastoral Social (Peace and Justice Department of the Episcopal Church's Pastoral Commission)
DECA Equipo Pueblo (People's Team for Economic, Social and Cultural Rights)
Desarrollo Integral Autogestionario (Self-Help Integrated Development)
Enlace, Comunicación y Capacitación (Outreach, Communication and Training)
Enlace Rural y Regional (Rural and Regional Outreach)
Frente Auténtico del Trabajo (Authentic Front for Work, FAT)
Frente Democrático de Chihuahua (Democratic Front of Chihuahua Province, FDC)
Frente por el Derecho a Alimentarse (Front for the Right to Eat, FDA)
Fundación Mexicana de Apoyo Infantil (Mexican Foundation for Children's Support, FAI)
Foro de Apoyo Mutuo (Mutual Support Forum, FAM)
Grupo de Educación Popular entre Mujeres (Popular Education Group among Women, GEM)
Grupo de Estudios Ambientales (Environmental Studies Group, GEA)
Grupo de Información sobre Reproducción Elegida (Information on Reproductive Choice Group, GIRE)
Instituto Mexicano de Educación Comunitaria (Mexican Institute for Community Education, IMDEC)
Maderas del Pueblo del Sureste (Agroforestry for the People of the Southeast)
Milenio Feminista (Feminist Millenium)
Movimiento Amplio de Mujeres de Guanajuato (Women's Movement of Guanajuato Province)
Movimiento Ciudadano por la Democracia (Citizens' Movement for Democracy, MCD)
Mujeres para el Diálogo (Women for Dialogue)
Mujeres Guerrerenses por la Democracia (Guerrero Province Women for Democracy)
Promoción, Servicios de Salud y Educación Popular (Healthcare Advancement, Services and Popular Education, PRODUSSEP)
Proyecto de Investigación Institucional sobre el Campo Mexicano (Institutional Research Project on the Mexican Countryside, PIISECAM–UNAM)
Proyecto de Desarrollo Integral de la Zona Sur Oriente de Iztapalapa (Integrated Development Project of the Southeast Area of Iztapalapa, ZOSOI)
Red Mexicana de Acción frente al Libre Comercio (Mexican Action Network against Free Trade, RMALC)
Servicios de Desarrollo y Paz (Development and Peace Services, SEDEPAC)
Servicios Informativos Procesados (Processed Information Services, SIPRO)
Transparencia (Transparency)

Unión de Comunidades Indígenas de la Zona Norte del Istmo (Union of Indigenous Communities of the Northern Area of the Isthmus, UCIZONI)
Unión de Esfuerzos para el Campo (Joint Efforts for Rural Advancement, UDEC)

Philippines Civil Society Steering Committee
Freedom from Debt Coalition (FDC), Lidy Nacpil
Alliance of Concerned Teachers (ACT), Enrique Torres
Kristiyanong Ugnayan Para sa Sambayanan–Alyansa ng mga Nagiisang Magulang (Christian Fellowship for the People and Alliance of United Parents, KRUS–ANAWIM), Clarissa Gatinen
Sosyalistang Partido ng Paggawa (Socialist Labor Party – SPP), Sonny Melencio
Philippine Network of Rural Development Initiatives (Philnet–RDI), Anabelle Amaga
TriPeaceDev – West Mindanao (Tripeople's – Filipinos, Lumads and Moros – Center for Peace and Development), Rowil Aguillion
Bukluran sa Ikauunlad ng Sosyalistang Isip at Gawa (Association for the Advancement of Socialist Thought and Praxis, BISIG), Raffy Albert
Task Force Detainees of the Philippines (TFDP), Ian Rivera
Philippine Alliance of Human Rights Advocates (PAHRA), Renato Mabunga
Institute for Popular Democracy (IPD), Ernesto Tomas
Womanhealth Philippines, Ana Maria Nemenzo
Culture and Sports Employees Union, Candy F. de Juan
Public Sector Labor Integrative Center (PSLINK), Annie E. Geron
Upland Development Institute – Cordilleras, Manny Cunanan

Uganda Civil Society Steering Committee
World Vision, Moses Dombo
Organisation for Socio-Economic Change and Advancement (OSCA), Joseph Okune
Uganda Women Medical Doctors (UWMD), Dr Zainab Akol
VREDESEILANDEN COPIBO (VECO), Kevin Akoyi Makokha
Uganda National NGO Forum (NGO–F), Warren Nyamugasira
Department for Women's Studies of Makerere University, May Sengendo
National Association of Women's Organisations (NAWOU), James Kiwolu
Uganda Council of Churches/African Women's Economic Policy Network (AWEPON), Hellen Wangusa
National Organisation of Trade Unions (NOTU), Justus Cadribo
Action Aid Uganda (AAU), Jane Ocaya
Uganda Women's Network (UWONET), Sheila Kawamara
National Union of Disabled Persons of Uganda (NUDIPU), James Mwandha
Uganda Small Scale Industries Association (USSIA), James Kawooya/David Bakalamye
Parliament/World Vision, Winnie Babihuga
Foundation of African Development (FAD), Mugumya Bukenya
Disabled Women's Resource Organisation (DWRO), Hajati Nalule
Uganda National Farmers' Association (UNFA), Victoria Ssebagereka
United Nations Development Programme (UNDP), Joseph Opio Odongo
Radio Uganda – Gender Section, Julie Gipwola
OXFAM GB, Kennedy Tumutegerize
The Media – New Vision, Peter Mwesigye
South Western Uganda Agricultural Development Agency (SWUADA), Chris Boonah
Uganda Joint Christian Council (UJCC), Rev. Canon Kaiso
Volunteers Effort for Development Concerns (VEDCO), the late Amos Galiwango
Development Networks of Indigenous Voluntary Associations (DENIVA), Jassy Kwesiga
Uganda Manufacturers' Association (UMA), Edith Mukasa
SMACA/Makerere University Department of Forestry, Prof. Byaruhanga Karungi

Zimbabwe Civil Society Steering Committee
Zimbabwe Congress of Trade Unions (ZCTU)
Poverty Reduction Forum
Institute of Development Studies, University of Zimbabwe
Zimbabwe Council of Churches
Zimbabwe Coalition on Debt and Development
Ecumenical Support Services
Africa Community Publishing and Development Trust

Zimbabwe Youth in Business
Zimbabwe Industrial Relations Association
Confederation of Zimbabwe Industries (CZI)
Zimbabwe Farmers Union (ZFU)
Southern Africa Micro-finance Capacity Building Facility
Women Action Group
Zimbabwe National Chamber of Commerce
Zimbabwe Women Resource Centre Network
Zimbabwe Women's Bureau
Development in Practice
Silveira House
Self Help Development Foundation
Glen Forest Training Centre
Women in Law and Development in Africa (WILDAF)
Housing People of Zimbabwe
Consumer Council of Zimbabwe
Gender & Economic Reforms in Africa – Zimbabwe Chapter
Association of Women's Clubs
Help Age Zimbabwe
National Association of the Disabled
Development Innovations and Networks (IRED)
Zimbabwe Broadcasting Cooperation Radio 4
Inter Press Service (IPS)
United Nations Children's Fund – Harare
Norwegian Peoples Aid
Friedrich Ebert Stiftung Foundation
Redd Barna – Zimbabwe
Oxfam America
Oxfam UKI

Bibliography of SAPRI/CASA National Reports

Bangladesh

Bhattacharya, Debapriya and Titumir, Rashed A.M. *Bangladesh's Experience with Structural Adjustment; Learning from a Participatory Exercise.*
http://www.saprin.org/bangladesh/research/BDS.pdf

Ali Rashid, Mohammed. *Impact of Trade Policy Reforms on Industrial Capacity and Employment in Bangladesh.* http://www.saprin.org/bangladesh/research/ban_trade.pdf

Choudhury, Toufic Ahmad and Raihan, Ananya. *Implications of Financial Sector Reforms in Bangladesh.* http://www.saprin.org/bangladesh/research/ban_finance.pdf

Zohir, Sajjad. *Impact of Reforms in Agricultural Input Markets on Crop Sector Profitability in Bangladesh.* http://www.saprin.org/bangladesh/research/ban_agri_input.pdf

Murshid, K. A. S. *Implications of Agricultural Policy Reforms on Rural Food Security and Poverty in Bangladesh.* http://www.saprin.org/bangladesh/research/ban_agri_policy.pdf

Rahman, Rushidan Islam. *The Consequences of Structural Adjustment Policies on the Poor in Bangladesh.* http://www.saprin.org/bangladesh/research/ban_poverty.pdf

Hundker, Nasreen. *The Impact of Structural Adjustment Policies on Women in Bangladesh.*
http://www.saprin.org/bangladesh/research/ban_gender.pdf

Toufique, Kazi Ali. *The Impact of Structural Adjustment Policies on the Environment in Bangladesh.*
http://www.saprin.org/bangladesh/research/ban_environment.pdf

Ahmad, Muzaffer. *Governance, Structural Adjustment and the State of Corruption in Bangladesh.*
http://www.saprin.org/bangladesh/research/ban_corruption.pdf

Atiur Rahman, Mirza Md. Shafiqur Rahman, Adul Quashem, Zulfiqar Ali and Arifur Rahman. *The Impact of Structural Adjustment Policies: An Assessment Using Participatory Techniques.* http://www.saprin.org/bangladesh/research/ban_par.htm

SAPRIN. *Bangladesh Opening National SAPRI Forum.*
http://www.saprin.org/bangladesh/bangladesh_opening_national_sapr.htm

Ecuador

SAPRI/Ecuador National Tripartite Committee. *Country Report: Ecuador/Informe de País: Ecuador*. http://www.saprin.org/ecuador/research/ecu_final_ctry_rpt.pdf / http://www.saprin.org/ecuador/research/ecu_info_pais.pdf

Ordóñez Cordero, Simón (research coordinator, Centro de Estudios Latinoamericanos – CELA). *Los Impactos del Ajuste Estructural en los Sectores Populares del Ecuador 1982-1999: Una Lectura Distinta Desde la Percepción y Experiencia de los Actores*. http://www.saprin.org/ecuador/research/ecu_cela_rpt.pdf (Summary translation by Juan Fernando Terán. *The Social and Economic Impacts of Structural Adjustment Policies in Ecuador 1982-1999: Executive Summary*. http://www.saprin.org/ecuador/research/ecu_sapri_rpt.pdf)

Santos, Enrique (research coordinator, University of Cuenca). *Impacto Social de la Política de Subsidios Básicos (1982-1999): Informe Final*. http://www.saprin.org/ecuador/research/ecu_cuenca_rpt.html (Summary translation by Juan Fernando Terán. *The Social Impact of Basic Social Subsidies in Ecuador 1982–1999: Executive Summary*. http://www.saprin.org/ecuador/research/ecu_soc_sub.pdf)

SAPRIN. *Ecuador Opening National SAPRI Forum*. http://www.saprin.org/ecuador/ecuador_opening_national_sapr.htm

El Salvador

Rubio, Roberto (ed.). *El Impacto de los Programas de Ajuste Estructural y Estabilización Económica en El Salvador*. http://www.saprin.org/elsalvador/research/els_cover_index.html (English summary by SAPRIN. *The Impact of Economic Stabilization and Structural Adjustment Programs in El Salvador: Executive Summary*. http://www.saprin.org/elsalvador/research/els_exec_summ.pdf)

Dada Hutt, Oscar. 'Liberalización del Sistema Financiero en El Salvador', in Rubio, Roberto (ed.). *El Impacto de los Programas de Ajuste Estructural y Estabilización Económica en El Salvador*. http://www.saprin.org/elsalvador/research/els_chap2.pdf (English summary by Raúl Moreno. *The Liberalization of the Financial System in El Salvador: Summary*. http://www.saprin.org/elsalvador/research/els_sum_financial_sys.pdf)

Montecinos, Mario. 'La Flexibilización del Mercado Laboral en El Salvador', in Rubio, Roberto (ed.). *El Impacto de los Programas de Ajuste Estructural y Estabilización Económica en El Salvador*. http://www.saprin.org/elsalvador/research/els_chap4.pdf

Ochoa, María Eugenia. 'Privatización del Servicio de Distribución de Energía Eléctrica en El Salvador', in Rubio, Roberto (ed.). *El Impacto de los Programas de Ajuste Estructural y Estabilización Económica en El Salvador*. http://www.saprin.org/elsalvador/research/els_chap3.pdf (English summary by Raúl Moreno. *Privatization of Electricity Distribution in El Salvador: Summary*. http://www.saprin.org/elsalvador/research/els_sum_privatization.pdf)

SAPRIN. *El Salvador Opening National SAPRI Forum*. http://www.saprin.org/elsalvador/elsalvador_opening_national_sapr1.htm

Ghana

Britwum, Akua, Kwesi Jonah and Ferdinand D. Tay, for the Tripartite National Steering Committee. *Ghana Country Report*.
http://www.saprin.org/ghana/research/gha_country_rpt.pdf

Dinye, Romanus D. and Nyaba, Clement F. A. *Trade Policy and Domestic Manufacturing in Ghana*. http://www.saprin.org/ghana/research/gha_trade.pdf

Akabzaa, Thomas, and Darimani, Alhaji Abdulai. *Impact of Mining Sector Investment in Ghana: A Study of the Tarkwa Mining Region*. http://www.saprin.org/ghana/research/gha_mining.pdf

Avle, S. K. and Ekey, Francis. *The Impact of SAP on Availability of and Access to Health Care in Ghana*. http://www.saprin.org/ghana/research/gha_health.pdf

Agyeman, D. K., William Boateng and Akinyoade Akinyinka. *The Impact of SAP on Access to and Quality of Tertiary Education in Ghana*.
http://www.saprin.org/ghana/research/gha_education.pdf

SAPRIN. *Ghana Opening National SAPRI Forum*.
http://www.saprin.org/ghana/ghana_forum1.htm

Hungary

Hoós, János, Károly Lóránt and Thomas Morva (eds.). *Socio-Economic Impact of Structural Adjustment in Hungary*. http://www.saprin.org/hungary/research/hun_summary.pdf

Fodor, Lászlá with Károly Boór, Csaba Gombár, Éva Voszka and Gábor Obláth. 'Economic Liberalisation and Deregulation in Hungary', in Hoós, János, Károly Lóránt and Thomas Morva (eds.). *Socio-Economic Impact of Structural Adjustment in Hungary*.
http://www.saprin.org/hungary/research/hun_summary.pdf

Lóránt, Károly with Sándor Bessenyei, Erzsébet Hanti, Zoltán Kárpáti and Márton Vági. 'Privatisation and Its Impact on Society', in Hoós, János, Károly Lóránt and Thomas Morva (eds.). *Socio-Economic Impact of Structural Adjustment in Hungary*.
http://www.saprin.org/hungary/research/hun_summary.pdf

Hoós, János with Rezsö Gál, József Kozma, Károly Mayer and László Szakadát. 'The Reform of the Public Utility Sector and Its Impact on the Economy, Environment, Consumers and Local Government', in Hoós, János, Károly Lóránt and Thomas Morva (eds.). *Socio-Economic Impact of Structural Adjustment in Hungary*.
http://www.saprin.org/hungary/research/hun_summary.pdf

Ferge, Zsuzsa with Tamás Morva, István Sziklai, Noémi Wells and István György Tóth. 'The Reform of Public Sector Involvement in Social Provisions', in Hoós, János, Károly Lóránt and Thomas Morva (eds.). *Socio-Economic Impact of Structural Adjustment in Hungary*.
http://www.saprin.org/hungary/research/hun_summary.pdf

SAPRIN. *Hungarian Opening National SAPRI Forum*.
http://www.saprin.org/hungary/hungary_opening_national_sap.htm

Mexico

Comité Coordinador de CASA/México (ed.). *¡Cuánta Bondad! Veinte Años de Ajuste Estructural en México.* http://www.saprin.org/mexico/research/indice.htm (English summary by Coordinating Committee of CASA/Mexico. *Adjustment and Poverty: Twenty Years of Crisis in Mexico.* http://www.saprin.org/mexico/research/mex_summary.pdf)

Román Morales, Luis Ignacio. *¿Qué es el Ajuste Estructural? Racionalidad e irracionalidad de las políticas económicas de libre mercado.* México: ITESO y Proyecto CONACYT-SIMORELOS, 1999. http://www.saprin.org/mexico/research/mex_0_indice.htm

Pérez Rocha Loyo, Manuel. *MPyMES, Trabajo, y Condiciones de Vida Frente al Ajuste Estructural en México.* http://www.saprin.org/mexico/research/capituloIII/III-1.pdf

Cortez Ruíz, Carlos. *El Ajuste Estructural y sus Efectos sobre la Reproducción Social en el Campo Mexicano en el Período 1982–2000.*
http://www.saprin.org/mexico/research/capituloIII/III-2.pdf

SAPRIN. *Mexico Opening National CASA Forum.*
http://www.saprin.org/mexico/mexico_forum1.htm

Philippines

Lopez, Marie. *The Impact of Trade Liberalization on Labor in the Philippines: A Summary Report.*
http://www.saprin.org/philippines/research/phi_trade_sum.pdf

Tambuyog Development Center, Center for Empowerment and Resource Development, the Philippine Network of Rural Development Initiatives and Pablo Medina. *The Impact of Structural Adjustment Programs on Food Security in the Philippines: A Summary Report.*
http://www.saprin.org/philippines/research/phi_food_security_sum.pdf

J.J. Josef, Jean Enriquez, Rowil Aguillon, Ian Rivera and Jenny Llaguno. *The Impact of Investment Liberalization and the Mining Act of 1995 on Indigenous Peoples, Upland Communities and the Rural Poor, and on the Environment: A Summary Report.*
http://www.saprin.org/philippines/research/phi_mining_sum.pdf

Simbulan, Nimia P., Carol Almeda and Merwin Salazar. *The Impact of Budget-Related Structural Adjustment on Education and Health-Care Services in the Philippines: A Summary Report.*
http://www.saprin.org/philippines/research/phi_services_sum.pdf

SAPRIN. *Philippines Opening National CASA Forum.*
http://www.saprin.org/philippines/philippines_forum1.htm

Uganda

Akoyi Makokha, Kevin, for the SAPRI/Uganda National Steering Committee. *Uganda Country Report: A Synthesis of Four SAPRI Studies.*
http://www.saprin.org/uganda/research/uga_country_rpt.pdf

Ddumba-Ssentamu, J. and Mugume, Adam. *The Privatization Process and Its Impact on Society in Uganda.* http://www.saprin.org/uganda/research/uga_privitazation.pdf

Bazaara, Nyangabyaki. *Impact of Liberalisation on Agriculture and Food Security in Uganda.*
http://www.saprin.org/uganda/research/uga_liberalization.pdf

MSE Consultants Ltd. *The Impact of Public Expenditure Management Under SAPS on Basic Social Services in Uganda: Health and Education.*
http://www.saprin.org/uganda/research/uga_public_expend.pdf

Muwanga, Nansozi K. *The Differences in Perceptions of Poverty in Uganda.*
http://www.saprin.org/uganda/research/uga_poverty.pdf

SAPRIN. *Ugandan Opening National SAPRI Forum.*
http://www.saprin.org/uganda/uganda_forum1.htm

Zimbabwe

Tekere, Moses. *Trade Liberalisation Under Structural Economic Adjustment – Impact on Social Welfare in Zimbabwe.* http://www.saprin.org/zimbabwe/research/zim_trade_lib.pdf

Moyo, Theresa. *Financial Sector Liberalization and the Poor in Zimbabwe: A Critical Appraisal.*
http://www.saprin.org/zimbabwe/research/zim_fin_sect.pdf

Chiripanhura, B. M., and Makwavarara, T. *The Labour Market and Economic Development in Zimbabwe: 1980–2000.* http://www.saprin.org/zimbabwe/research/zim_labour_market.pdf

Makamure, John, James Jowa and Hilda Muzuva. *Liberalisation of Agricultural Markets in Zimbabwe.* http://www.saprin.org/zimbabwe/research/zim_agriculture.pdf

Dhliwayo, Rogers. *The Impact of Public Expenditure Management Under ESAP on Basic Social Services in Zimbabwe: Health and Education.*
http://www.saprin.org/zimbabwe/research/zim_public_exp.pdf

Arnold Sibanda, Arnold. *The Role of the State with respect to Agriculture, Trade Liberalisation, Financial Reform and Labour Markets.*

Nyathi, Talent and Makoni, K. *ESAP and Lives of Ordinary Citizens Today: Views of Ordinary Citizens Around Zimbabwe on Effects of Economic Structural Adjustment Programmes (ESAP).*

SAPRIN. *Zimbabwe Opening National SAPRI Forum.*
http://www.saprin.org/zimbabwe/zimbabwe_forum1.htm

Index

50 Years Is Enough campaign 4
Abosso Goldfields Ltd 156, 162
Accra 13, 60
Africa 8, 89-90
African Women's Economic Policy Network
    (AWEPON) 8, 18
agriculture, agro-industry 50, 66; bananas 148;
    beans 141, 210; cocoa 159; coffee 137, 141, 144,
    210; cotton 136, 141, 209; credit access 75, 77,
    79, 133, 136, 138-40, 143, 145-6, 150-1, 207-9;
    employment in 65-6, 95, 97, 100, 160, 164, 171,
    209; export-oriented 67, 94-5, 132-45, 207, 209-
    10, 219; extension services 138, 143, 146, 148,
    150-1, 208, 219; farmers' associations 14-15, 17-
    20; and financial sector liberalization 75, 77, 79;
    gender divisions in 146-7; Green Revolution and
    142; horticultural products 136, 141, 148; invest-
    ment in 137, 139, 143; livestock 136-8, 141-2;
    maize 136, 141, 210; and mining 160, 164, 171;
    monocropping 148, 219; poultry 137; privatiza-
    tion and 133-4,139, 148; protection of 3; reform
    of 2, 132-52, 203-4, 207-11, 219; rice 132, 137,
    139, 142, 145, 210; shifting 165, 171; small 3, 18,
    94-5, 132-52, 204, 207-11, 219, 223; SAP effects
    on 12, 23, 34, 94-5, 132-52; subsidies 23, 133-4,
    136-7, 139-40, 150, 208; subsistence 152; tobacco
    141; and trade liberalization 132-52, 203-4, 207-
    11; wheat 210; workers' associations 14-15; see
    also fisheries, food security, forestry
aid/agencies 1, 3, 99, 131
Alliance of Social Associations (ASA, Hungary) 17
alternatives to structural ajustment 30, 71, 85-6,
    108, 131, 151-2, 172-3, 201-2, 263, 221-3
Argentina 8, 12
Asia 2, 8, 52, 63, 65, 182, 222; East 222; South 40,
    51; South-east 51
Asociación Latinamerica de organizaciones de
    promocion (ALOP) 8
Associated Goldfields 156
Australia 157, 162

Bangkok 13
Bangladesh 8, 14-15, 24-7, 31, 36-8, 40-1, 43, 49,
    51-3, 55-63, 65-6, 68, 72-3, 76-7, 79, 81-3, 110-
    11, 113, 115-16, 122-3, 125, 127, 132, 134-5,
    138-40, 142, 145, 148-50, 205-6, 212; agricul-
    tural sector adjustment in 132, 134-5, 138-40,
    142, 145, 148-50; balance of payments 53; civil
    society in 24-7, 115; Coalition of Environmental
    NGOs 15; employment in 60-1, 63, 65-6, 68,
    111, 116, 122-3, 125, 205-6, 212; Federation of
    Bangladesh Chambers of Commerce and Industry
    14-15; financial sector liberalization in 72-3, 76-7,
    79, 81-3, 205-6; food security in 140, 142;
    imports in 52, 205; industry in 51-3, 55-63, 65-6,
    68, 110-11, 113, 115-16, 122-3, 125, 127, 205-6;
    National Association of Small and Cottage
    Industries 14; Opening National Forum in 57,
    115-16, 123; privatization in 73, 110-11, 113,
    115-16, 122-3, 125, 127, 133-4, 139, 212;
    research process (SAPRIN–World Bank) in 25-7,
    31; Road Transport Workers' Federation 15; state
    role in 72-3; terms of trade 53; and trade liberal-
    ization 36-8, 40-1, 43, 49, 51-3, 55-63, 65-6, 68,
    135,139, 148, 205-6; see also BRAC,
    PROSHIKA
Bangladesh Rural Advancement Committee
    (BRAC) 14
Barnex (Prestea) Ltd 162
Bastión Popular 98
Belgium 10
BGL 162
Bonn 30
Brazil 8
Brussels 33
Budapest 28
Bugkalot people 162
Bushenyi district 147

Canada 47, 157, 166
capital flight 74, 220
Central America 8
centralization/decentralization 12, 21, 178, 184-5,
    194, 214, 216, 222
Chiapas province 20, 100
childcare 20, 163, 216
children 16, 20, 97-100, 108, 125-6, 140-1, 146,
    163-4, 172, 185, 188, 194-5, 199, 212, 215;
    see also education
Chile 117
China 51
churches 16-18, 21
Citizens' Assessments of Structural Adjustment
    (CASA) 8, 10, 13, 20-1, 30, 33, 36, 54, 57, 65,
    69, 88, 100, 132, 149, 153, 175, 177, 203-4, 207,
    209, 211-13, 215-21
civil society, access to official documentation 8,
    11-12; and agricultural sector adjustment 135,
    143, 146; in Bangladesh 24-7, 115; and budget
    formulation 202; and debt repayment 215; in

Lightning Source UK Ltd.
Milton Keynes UK

175065UK00001B/9/A